UNDERSTANDING ISLAMIC BANKING

Also by Joseph DiVanna:

Redefining Financial Services: The New Renaissance in Value Propositions (Palgrave Macmillan, 2002)

Thinking Beyond Technology: Creating New Value in Business (Palgrave Macmillan, 2003)

Synconomy: Adding Value in a World of Continuously Connected Business (Palgrave Macmillan, 2003)

The Future of Retail Banking: Delivering Value to Global Customers (Palgrave Macmillan, 2004)

Strategic Thinking in Tactical Times (Palgrave Macmillan, 2004)

People – The New Asset on the Balance Sheet (Palgrave Macmillan, 2005) (with Jay Rogers)

Joseph A. DiVanna

Understanding Islamic Banking

The Value Proposition That Transcends Cultures

Diversity in Global Banking Series

Published in the United Kingdom
By Leonardo and Francis Press, Ltd
Parker House
48 Regent Street
Cambridge, CB2 1FD
Tel: +44(0)1223.704670
www.leonardoandfrancis.com

First published 2006
Reprinted 2007
Reprinted 2008

Printed in the United Kingdom by
University Press, Cambridge

Typesetting and editing by
Aardvark Editorial Limited, Norfolk

Cover design by Joseph A. DiVanna

ISBN-13: 978–1–905687–00–8
ISBN-10: 1–905687–00–1

A catalogue record for this book is available from the British Library

A catalog record for this book is available from the Library of Congress

To my dear friends throughout the Middle East, Africa, and Europe, my sons Frank and Leo, and my wife Isabel, without whose help writing would be impossible.

To my friend and mentor Barbara Herman, who passed away much too young in 2006 – she will be missed by many.

This book is also dedicated to the people who tragically lost their lives in Amman, Jordan in November 2005, just a short time after my visit. It was my original plan to write this book at some time in the future. However, the warm friendship and unparalleled hospitality of the people of Jordan during my visit inspired me to write this book sooner rather than later.

CONTENTS

LIST OF FIGURES

LIST OF TABLES

ABOUT THE AUTHOR

Joseph A. DiVanna is a banking strategist, business author, global speaker, and currently the director of Cambridge-based financial services think tank Maris Strategies Limited. Joe's research seeks to understand the fundamentals of twenty-first-century business in their historical roots and present characteristics to shed light on their possible future developments. His articles have appeared in journals such as IBM's *Building an Edge* and *Financial World Magazine*, and in the corporate newsletters of banks, technology companies, and multinational businesses.

A prolific writer, his first six books include topics such as financial services, strategy, technology, human capital, and the emerging global synergistic economy ("synconomy"). Featured in *The Economist*, where he was labeled a "polymath", Joe tested his methodology for rapid strategy creation by sequestering 30 experts in a room for 24 hours, which resulted in the book *Strategic Thinking in Tactical Times* (Palgrave Macmillan, 2004).

A frequent public speaker, Joe's lectures on topics such as innovation, leadership, strategy, socioeconomic behavior, value management, and return on process have been heard in the US, Europe, Asia, the Middle East, and Africa. As a keynote speaker and chairman of conferences such as Banking Technology Africa, Middle East Financial Technology Exhibition and Conference (MEFTEC), and the Arabian Society for Human Resource Management (ASHRM), his views on global business have been instrumental in shaping the strategies and operations of organizations worldwide.

Joe's great interest in Middle Eastern banking and finance provides insight and thought leadership to financial institutions throughout the region. As a management consultant, he has worked with many Fortune 500 companies, such as Axalto, BT Global, CR2, Credit Suisse, Hewlett-Packard, HSBC, IBM, J. P. Morgan, Lexmark, Masterfoods, Microsoft, Misys, TNS Sofres, Troika Dialogue, UBS, and VISA International, and numerous financial institutions, to face the challenges of the new economic and business environment.

PREFACE

European corporations and American businesses frequently ask me three central questions when they want to expand their business into Islamic marketplaces: what is the best way to understand Islamic society? What are the key services needed for banking customers and businesses to transact business within their local Islamic society? How should services be structured for Islamic businesses as they become more interconnected with their non-Muslim counterparts? The underlying premise of their questions is simple: what do Muslims value in products, services, and financial intermediaries? For many years, my response was to go to the local area and spend time with people in their environment – the proverbial "walking a mile in their sandals". However, today my advice is less physically arduous and more mentally challenging: read the Holy *Qur'an*. As a non-Muslim, I have found that the Holy *Qur'an* answers a number of questions on the value people place on the actions of others within society, how people behave within the constructs of the Islamic financial system. Just as you cannot understand how to operate complicated machinery without a manual, you cannot begin to appreciate Islamic culture without an understanding of, in a very Western expression, "what makes Muslims tick".

Geopolitical events since 1980 have steadily fostered an interest in Islamic banking and commerce by Western corporations and financial institutions. Faced with limited growth in mature consumer markets, global institutions have now turned their attention to the rapidly emerging economic zones for new opportunities to provide financial services. Recent global economic activities have suddenly led financial services companies operating in Western economies to realize that one-quarter of the world's population is Muslim, representing a vast underserved market. Almost one billion people spread across the world have a direct matching demographic profile: a religious conviction that demands they behave in financial matters within a defined set of guidelines. Within this broadly defined Islamic demographic profile are all the subcategories of customers, from rich to poor. The subcategories of Muslims can be directly correlated to elements of value generated by financial institutions. It is within this context that institutions offering global financial services can no longer ignore Islamic banking. To most Westerners, Islamic banking is cloaked in religious mystery, with practices and policies that seem foreign and arcane. Ironically, the fundamental constructs of the Islamic banking model, especially in areas such as the treatment of usury, are remarkably similar to the approach used by banks in Christendom during the Middle Ages. Unfortunately, few people take the time to understand the shared philosophical and economic heritage between Islam and Christianity.

This book examines the essential value proposition of Islamic banking and the intrinsic transactions used to facilitate commerce in today's global marketplace by placing into context the interactions of financial transactions between Muslims themselves and between Muslims and non-Muslims. The primary intent of this book is to explore the various interpretations of *Sharia* law and offer insight on what may be the next generation of Islamic banking practices. This book is not intended to be an authoritative source on *Sharia* law or the principles of Islamic values; there are far more enlightened sources that should be consulted on this matter, many of which are quoted and referenced during the course of our exploration of Islamic banking. What we intend is simply to match *Sharia* principles and current practices of Islamic banking with new practices to be developed so that Islamic banks can remain competitive in the new banking environment.

Any examination of Islamic banking would be incomplete without exploring both sides of the issues found as Islamic finance intersects with global commercial interests. Because *Sharia* principles are interpretive, offering a wide variation in application of principles to practices, we must examine both ends of the philosophical spectrum. This examination is not intended as a political debate but as a mechanism to understand the fundamental principles that drive the value proposition of Islamic banking for Muslim and non-Muslim customers. In looking at economic *fatwas* and other less tolerant interpretations of *Sharia* principles, we must assess their impact on the brand identity for Islamic banking, in much the same way as failures and scandals marred the image of savings and loans in the US during the 1970s and 80s. Functionally, the vast majority of savings and loans provided a valuable service to the community as an alternative source of banking, and the professionals who worked in these institutions were honest, hard-working people with integrity and a sense of public trust. However, the industry was devastated with guilt by association; as savings and loans faltered, customers scrambled for better institutions. In the case of Islamic banking, the extremes of economic *fatwas* are magnified by the media, and their impact on the overall value proposition must be assessed.

From my encounters with Muslims in all parts of the world, I have come to understand that Islam is a religion that extols morals, ethics, and fairness, coupled with a sense of tolerance, acceptance, and peaceful coexistence for those who come to appreciate its values and give the believers of Islam the respect they are due. As one who is a novice at reading the Holy *Qur'an* as a means to comprehend Islamic thinking, I have come to a better understanding of Muslims and the principal message of peace, brotherhood, and sense of community, under a framework of ideals which offer a path to a behavior which sets Muslims apart from other people. Through a greater awareness of the main tenets of Islam, I, like many other readers, became increasingly aware of two diverging sociological phenomena: the rise of individuals using Islamic values to promote specific agendas, and a growing misunderstanding of Islamic values by non-Muslims. As a beginner reader of Islamic texts and merely the recipient of hospitality from people of Islamic nations, my interpretations, understanding, and assessment of Islamic values may indeed be naive or in some cases simply wrong. In the latter case, if my understandings of the Holy *Qur'an*'s messages are a misinterpretation, I beg forgiveness, especially from all my Muslim friends who have given so much of their time in an effort to educate me.

ACKNOWLEDGEMENTS

Like all writers, I notice that the list of people to acknowledge grows with each passing year. It is gratifying to see that after many years interacting with financial institutions, government agencies and businesses in Asia, Africa, Europe, and the Middle East, subjects like Islamic banking are finally studied on a par with conventional Western economic banking and finance. I make no claim to be an expert on *Sharia* principles or the contents of the Holy *Qur'an* and the *Sunnah*. My understanding of Islamic values comes from three separate sources: my interactions with Islamic organizations based in various parts of the world, Muslims who I consider dear friends and who have taught me some fundamentals, and research performed by Maris Strategies Ltd, commissioned by banks, financial institutions, and technology corporations, on Islamic banking and the economic behaviors of people in the region.

I would be remiss not to acknowledge a few of the many people who helped to form my perspectives on the subject and who have extended unrivaled hospitality to me during my many travels to distant lands. My early misconceptions of Islam were quickly corrected by discussions with Saleh M. Al-Jewair and Mohammed A. Al-Khalfan from Saudi Aramco, who patiently corrected many of my misunderstandings about Islamic society. Their willingness to have frank discussions with me during my short visits prompted me to begin the research for this book and sparked my curiosity enough to set me on a course to read the Holy *Qur'an* for insight into the principles that guide the lives of over one billion people.

A personal thank you is due to the Arabian Society of Human Resource Management (ASHRM) for giving me an opportunity to express my views on the human resource challenges in the Middle East.

I wish to extend a personal thank you to M. Omar Hefni, Dr. Ananth Rao, and Dr. Boualem Chennouti at Dubai University College for their hospitality and for allowing me to share my views on global issues with their students.

Special thanks to Dr. Idries M. Al-Jarrah at the Department of Finance, Faculty of Business Administration, University of Jordan, Amman for giving me the opportunity to present my concepts on banking and finance to students.

During my many trips to the Middle East, several people were instrumental in directing the course of my research. Thank you especially to Dr. AAhad M. Osman-Gani of the Nanyang Business School, who is a fount of knowledge on the issues of human capital and the challenges facing human resource managers in the Islamic world.

Another individual who shaped the course of my research was Nadia H. Al-Saeed, at the Ministry of Information and Communications Technology, in the Hashemite Kingdom of Jordan. During our discussion on the Middle East as an economic region, her insight into the fact that human capital is the one consistent natural resource led me to realize that my research on Islamic banking should be constructed on the value that financial services organizations bring to the people they serve and the communities in which they operate.

Much of my research for this book is due to the matchmaking efforts of Martin Dolan, CEO of CR2, who has encouraged bankers and financial services professionals throughout the Middle East to contact me to share their knowledge on this subject. A long-time thought partner and friend, Martin's insight on the applied use of technology in the region saved me from making gross assumptions on how successful or unsuccessful a given technology is within a nation state.

Waleed Sadek and Tarek E. Elhousseiny from VISA International in Egypt persuaded me to expand my research into the complexity of banking challenges in the Egyptian marketplace, which has led to the development of my views on how Islamic banking can play a leading role in enriching the lives of its customers.

I want to thank especially Michael Hanlon, David Morgan, and Abdullah Garib of the Islamic Bank of Britain for their time in educating me on their operations.

Another individual whose insight on Islamic banking shaped my thinking is Stephen Timewell of *The Banker* magazine. His vast knowledge on the global economic issues facing Islamic banks and all banks operating in the Middle East and Africa provided me with the necessary context in which best to derive an overall value proposition for Islamic institutions.

My research would not be possible without the kind support of the fellows of King's College, Cambridge who graciously granted me permission to research medieval architecture and methods of construction during the Middle Ages. That research led to a deeper understanding of the economics of building during that time and ultimately to my research on the nature and behavior of institutions engaged in banking, trade, and finance during the past ten centuries.

My research for this book, and indeed all my research, would not be possible without the support of the numerous banks and financial institutions that have engaged me as an adviser or reviewer of their strategic initiatives.

I am very grateful to Dr. Iraj Toutounchian, Professor of Economics, Az-Zahra University in Tehran for taking the time to share his insight on Iranian finance.

I owe an enormous debt to the editorial team at Aardvark, who did what one would have thought to be impossible: transformed my grammatically incorrect sentences and many stylistic mistakes into a coherent book in less than one month.

To Syed Faisal Abbas, Mark Beaumont, and Paul Stott of Media Generation UK – thank you for giving me the opportunity to develop the program and base content of the 2006 MEFTEC.

The geographical richness of this text would not be possible without the efforts of Janice Nagourney and the people of Thought Leaders Internaional in Paris and the UK, who provide me with the privilege of sharing my views with audiences around the world.

Finally, and most importantly, I owe an enormous debt to my wife Isabel, who diligently reads all my text, challenges my views, and bravely tries to keep me on schedule.

Every effort has been made to trace all the copyright holders, however, if any have been inadvertently overlooked, the publishers will be pleased to make the necessary arrangements at the first opportunity.

INTRODUCTION

To begin our journey into a banking, finance and economic system used by approximately one-quarter of the modern world, we should start by considering two simple questions: what is Islamic finance, and how is it different from banking services found in institutions operating in the West, East, and other regions? More specifically, what is the underlying value proposition for Islamic banking in the current socioeconomic context where customers are driving firms to deliver more and more value? Finding a single definition of Islamic banking and finance is difficult to come by, due to numerous interpretations. To most Western bankers and some Muslims, the general definition of what constitutes Islamic banking appears ambiguous, differing slightly in each country, becoming less clear as one get closer to the details of financial instruments and transactions. The lack of clarity is simply because the rules governing transactions are based on *Sharia* principles that are internalized, in that they are interpreted by a local Islamic scholar whose views reflect those of the local community. However, the vast majority of Islamic banks agree on the basic principles, although individual banks may differ in their application of *Sharia* principles. For the most part, the variations in how Islamic banks approach the application of *Sharia* principles can be equated to the laws of the country in which they operate, the objectives of the banks, an individual bank's circumstances and experiences, and the need to interact with other interest-based banks, among others. In the following paragraphs, we will describe the salient features common to all banks.

To non-Muslims, the lack of clarity in a formal definition makes Islamic banking and finance seem overly complex and significantly different to bank operations in conventional institutions. However, financial services professionals often take for granted that if we consider conventional banking at a macroeconomic level, Western banking has the same fundamental characteristics. For example, at the macroeconomic level, banking transactions in the US appear to be performed within a set of commonly accepted rules and principles. At a microeconomic level, one must also recognize that each state has its own banking regulatory structure. Thus, for a bank to operate nationally in the US, it must comply with the regulatory requirements of all 50 states. As such, this book will approach the subject of Islamic banking using two perspectives: macroeconomic and microeconomic. An assessment of the macroeconomic level reviews the similarities of Islamic banking from region to region as a means to recognize Muslim financial principles in a global context. Examining the variations of interpretations at a microeconomic level provides a greater understanding of the challenges that Islamic banks will meet as they compete for local customers. That said, one of the more comprehensive definitions comes from the State Bank of Pakistan:

> Islamic banking has been defined as banking in consonance with the ethos and value system of Islam and governed, in addition to the conventional good governance and risk management rules, by the principles laid down by Islamic *Sharia*. Interest-free banking is a narrow concept denoting a number of banking instruments or operations, which avoid interest. Islamic banking, the more general term, is expected not only to avoid interest-based transactions, prohibited in the Islamic *Sharia*, but also to avoid unethical practices and participate actively in achieving the goals and objectives of an Islamic economy.[1]

The difficultly in defining Islamic economic activity is twofold: firstly, Islamic finance covers a broad spectrum of financial activities, transactions or legal interpretations of unambiguous transactions such as interest-free banking, and secondly, the wide array of activities which are indigenous to financial, business and banking transactions, ranging from mortgage-like products to migrant remittances. What is clear is that Islamic banking has three distinct characteristics: it is interest-free, it is multipurpose and not purely commercial, and it is strongly equity-oriented.[2] Perhaps a more telling aspect of Islamic banking is that banks operating under an Islamic system face fewer solvency and liquidity risks than their conventional counterparts do.[3]

Fundamentally, Islamic *Sharia* principles forbid "interest" but do not prohibit all gains on capital. *Sharia* law simply requires that the performance of capital must be taken into consideration when rewarding capital. Therefore, in financial terms, the use of capital must add value and not be devoid of risk (Holy *Qur'an,* 2:275).[4] Islamic banking is a system of exchange based on the premise of an equitable transfer between two parties, whereby there is equality in sharing risk, and a clear title to the owning and handling of physical goods (assets). In many cases, conventional banks or financial institutions that facilitate the transfer of value between two parties typically play the role of a hands-off intermediary. Islamic banks also act as hands-on intermediaries as they deal and trade in assets purely for the purpose of income generation or profits. Their key difference is that Islamic banks convert money into assets based on their utility.[5] An Islamic bank must handle the risks associated with the transfer of assets, trades and other ancillary transactions, adhering to the best practices of corporate governance and the principles outlined in *Sharia* law. If the profits generated from these transactions are considered compliant and free of interest, they are said to be permissible or *halal*, and the proceeds are in turn passed on to the investors as income. If they do not meet *Sharia* principles, they are considered unsuitable or *haram*, and the *Sharia* advisers to the institution may in many cases assess a penalty to the intermediary to correct the mistake.

For our purposes, the following characterization should provide boundaries to the scope of this book:

> Islamic banking and finance are the activities, transactions and interactions initiated by financial institutions whose intentions, goals, objectives, and operations are based on principles prescribed by the Holy *Qur'an* and the *Sunnah*.

It is important to remember that *Sharia* principles are not simply a prohibition of interest; they are also designed to avoid unethical practices and participate actively in achieving the goals and objectives of an Islamic economy.[6] Islamic institutions provide customers with the means to facilitate the transfer of value between parties by measuring their intentions against the fundamental social values expressed in the Holy *Qur'an* and the *Sunnah*. Therefore, Islamic institutions are set apart from other financial institutions in two ways: they must review their intentions against a moral and ethical lens before they take action, and the products or services they bring to the market must reflect the direct values and beliefs of their customers, ranging from strict fundamentalism to moderate multicultural environments. Simply, Islamic financial institutions assess the needs of the communities they serve in order to create products that reflect the values and beliefs of their customers, unlike non-Muslim institutions that create products with the specific intention to get customers to adapt to a new banking behavior.

The key components of the Islamic financial value proposition are the adherence to a set of fundamental principles and a governing observance to Islamic philosophy as illustrated in Figure 0.1.

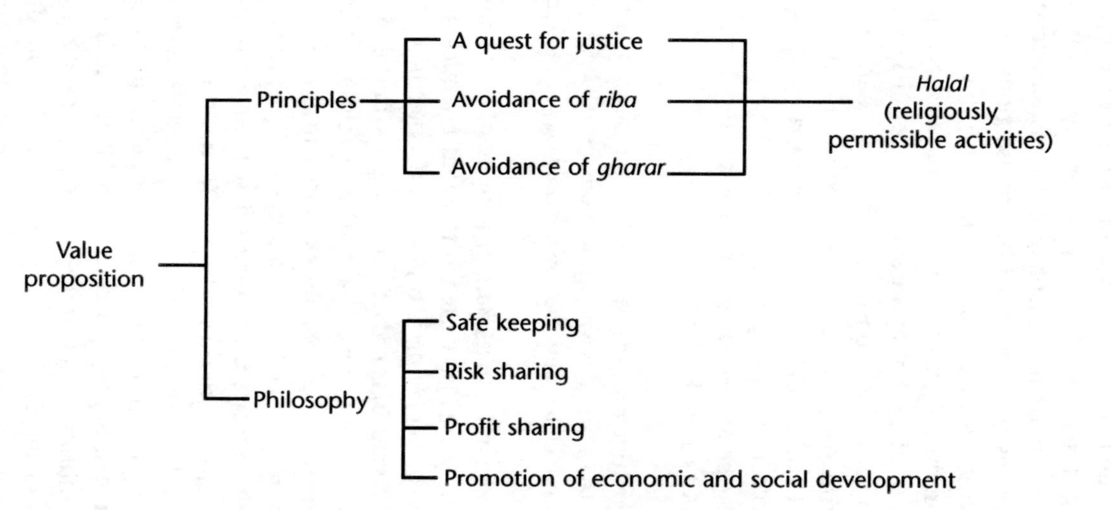

Figure 0.1 Islamic banking value proposition

The Islamic banking value proposition comprises two mutually reinforcing aspects: a set of principles that guides the nature or behavior of financial transactions, and a philosophical sense of equity. If we look at the fundamental tenet of Islamic banking and finance, the value proposition is more than simply equating transactions involving Muslims with interest-free banking. Financial interactions governed by Islamic principles are not limited to transactions that may or may not be simply interest-free or without an unjustified increase, but include a host of transactions that center on a more universal quest for justice or a sense of fair and equitable exchange.

The two key philosophical ideas which provide the basic ideals for an exchange between parties – that of risk sharing and a sense of service to the greater community – are not exclusive to financial institutions. Individuals should practice these ideals in their daily lives. The idea of risk sharing is built on the concept that the lender must share in the borrower's risk. Fundamentally, the broad interpretation of *Sharia* principles is that predetermined interest rates assure a return to the lender and may fall unduly on the borrower. They do not anticipate events that may not be within the scope of the borrower's control; in other words, a fixed interest loan does not recognize the will of Allah. Therefore, lending with fixed interest is considered exploitative, socially unproductive, and economically wasteful. Under *Sharia* law, the preferred method of financing is an equitable arrangement of shared profit and loss. In addition, the second philosophical pillar is the promotion of economic activity and a general sense of improvement to society in the course of specific business practices and through almsgiving (*zakat*).

Although the general framework of the Islamic value proposition seems self-evident, because principles and philosophical ideals are open to interpretation, Muslims engaged in financial transactions must in good conscience consult individuals who have a more profound knowledge of *Sharia* law, as Warde points out:

> No definition of Islamic finance is entirely satisfactory. To every general criterion a financial institution owned by Muslims, catering to Muslims, supervised by a *Sharia* Board, belonging to the International Association of Islamic Banks (IAIB) etc., one can find some significant exception.[7]

When a *Sharia* board governs the actions of a bank or financial institution, they are considered Islamic. The board is simply a committee of religious advisers whose opinion is sought to gain clarity on a variety of issues centered on the behavior and conduct of a plethora of financial transactions. *Sharia* boards are regularly consulted when an institution develops a new product or considers entering into transactions where the nature of the exchange is not clearly understood. In addition, *Sharia* boards carry out religious audits of the bank's activities.

It must be remembered that Islamic finance involves more than simple banking-like transactions. Over the past few decades, Islamic society has seen the emergence of Islamic mutual funds, insurance companies, securities firms, a rapidly growing number of non-Muslim financial institutions offering Islamic products, and, more recently, an emerging number of other, non-traditional, financial service providers entering the Islamic marketplace.

With the rising number of financial institutions, products and services vying to provide a wider range of services to facilitate Islamic society, the true differentiator between Islamic finance and transactions that do not comply with *Sharia* principles is that the latter usually seek to maximize profits. The key concept to remember is that Islamic finance holds itself up to a religiously inspired set of values that acts in much the same way as the basic functions of conventional (non-Muslim) regulatory frameworks.

For Western bankers and non-Muslims, the inevitable question is: how can a financial system operate without interest rates, treat lenders and borrowers equitably, and work toward the overall improvement of society? The answer is not simply that over time Islamic institutions have developed complex profit-and-loss-sharing mechanisms, or the use of interest-like alternatives, such as instituting offsetting service charges or merely acting as buying agents from which assets are leased and then transferred at the end of the term. Islamic banking is interpretive, adaptive, and, above all, dynamic, in that the elucidation of *Sharia* law reflects the local culture and social fabric of the communities it serves, as we will see throughout this book.

Chapter 1 reviews the value proposition of Islamic banking in a historical context. In the past few years, numerous books have been written, each laboring to define, describe and clarify what Islamic finance is. Chapter 1 does not intend to add to the overabundance of material on this subject; it merely presents a short history of Islamic finance as a foundation on which to set contemporary issues into a context of how today's Islamic banking products fit into a value proposition to global Muslim customers. In addition, the basic underpinning of Islamic financial thought is examined to ascertain the applicability of current and future Islamic products to non-Muslims.

Chapter 2 places the fundamental principles of Islamic banking and finance in a macroeconomic context by exploring the primary issues such as usury, joint ventures, profit sharing and risk, as a baseline for understanding how *Sharia* principles are applied to financial transactions. As part of the macro-level analysis, other aspects of Islamic finance will be examined, such as the basic constructs of non-interest mortgages, debt instruments, and the issues of how Muslims are penalized under the tax codes within various nation states.

Chapter 3 investigates the variations of Islamic financial thought by reviewing the interpretations of *Sharia* principles in various global locations. The intention of this chapter is not to be an exhaustive source of local idiosyncrasies, but rather to illustrate the complexity of providing services across regions, as Islamic banks expand into new markets. The organizations and institutions discussed demonstrate the variety and diversity of Muslim culture and the ways in which local services must be provided.

Chapter 4, emphasizes the rudiments of the Islamic value proposition by analyzing the variations of Islamic banking under the constructs of any corporate value proposition. Within this analysis, opportunities for Islamic banking that are different to their Western counterparts are identified, whereby banks are able to add value beyond their customer bases to the greater communities they serve and, indeed, their national economies.

Chapter 5 explores several theoretical future possibilities for Islamic banking as a component of an interoperating global monetary system. Concepts such as Islamic monetary union, the rising use of electronic money, and the development of *Sharia* standards for financial institutions operating globally as Islamic banks each have broad implications for Islamic banking in the future.

Throughout the book, we shall see how Islamic banks have a clearly defined value proposition that converts directly to a set of unique opportunities. We shall assess how the opportunities for existing Islamic banks to compete and perhaps surpass the services of conventional banks are limited by the world's most precious commodity – time. To compete in global markets, Islamic banking must innovate, embrace technology and, above all, reduce its operating costs to demonstrate to Muslims and non-Muslims around the world that a moral economy coupled with ethical investing is not simply a better way to live; rather, it can set the standard for banking operations regardless of faith.

Notes

1 What is Islamic Banking? State Bank of Pakistan, December 2005, available at http://www.sbp.org.pk/ibd/faqs.asp.

2 Mohamed Ariff, Islamic Banking, *Asian-Pacific Economic Literature*, **2**(2) (September 1988), pp. 46–62.

3 Iqba, Zubair and Mirakhor, Abbas *Islamic Banking*, International Monetary Fund, Occasional Paper 49, Washington DC: International Monetary Fund, 1987.

4 Arberry, Arthur *The Koran Interpreted*, London: Oxford University Press, 1964, p. 41.

5 Ayub, Muhammad *Interest, Mark Up and Time Value of Money*, Islamic Banking Department, State Bank of Pakistan, available at http://www.sbp.org.pk/departments/ibd/Interest_Mark_Up.pdf.

6 Frequently Asked Questions, State Bank of Pakistan, October 2005, available at http://www.sbp.org.pk/ibd/faqs.pdf.

7 Warde, Ibrahim *Islamic Finance in The Global Economy*, Edinburgh: Edinburgh University Press, 2000.

1

A SHORT HISTORY OF ISLAMIC FINANCE

Some practices that today we call "financial transactions", such as financing trade, lending money, profit sharing, almsgiving, and other social interactions whereby people exchange items of value, are not as new as many may think. Transactions involving the transfer of tangible goods and services, whether they have been underwritten by a formal recognized monetary currency, a system of barter, or merely an unwritten social contract, have been the foundation of societal cohesion for many centuries. We can argue that the need to transfer items of value between people under a formal or informal system of exchange is one of the basic elements of social interaction that keeps a society together. When people perceive that the transfer of value between parties is not equitable, social structures rapidly decay. Representing the fair and equitable transfer of value, financial transactions are the building blocks of business and, in recent centuries, the lifeblood of international commerce.

For the purposes of our discussion on Islamic banking and finance, let us consider a broad definition of financial transactions. Fundamentally, financial transactions are actions that result in a transference of value between two or more parties. These actions are reflected in a set of conscious or unconscious socially acceptable behaviors constituted by rules and manifested in customs, regulations or laws that reflect the communities in which the transference occurs. The rules act to galvanize society by establishing an agreement of how to pass value between parties in a way that is fair and equitable. Throughout time, societies have established value exchange systems that represent the interests of the people of means within the society. Historically, these systems are constructed to serve their creators, who, in many cases, have been the elite classes of society such as the wealthy or individuals with political power.

Islamic economy is a financial system that operates in observance of Islamic law, commonly referred to as *Sharia* principles. Although contemporary media sources and academic writers describe Islamic banking in many ways, for the context of this book we use the following definition:

> Islamic banking is the group of financial activities based on a set of Islamic rules governing transactions known as *fiqh al-muamalat.*

The basic tenet of the Islamic value proposition is a prohibition on the paying and receiving of interest (*riba*), and a fundamental belief in the sharing of profit and risk (*mudarabah*) in the conduct of business. In summary, Islamic banking fulfils the same basic intention as conventional banking. However, Islamic banking operates in accordance with an overall set of guiding principles based on common Islamic concepts described in the Holy *Qur'an* and the *Sunnah,* such as profit sharing (*mudarabah*), safekeeping (*wadiah*), joint venture (*musharakah*), cost plus (*murabahah*), leasing (*ijarah*), and the prohibition of interest (*riba*).

These concepts, representative of Islamic banking, are not new. For many centuries, Muslim societies living in nations in all parts of the world have strived to develop ways to assimilate their religious values within the economic and banking activities of the nations in which they live. The process of assimilation follows two distinct paths: a liberal or non-interventionist approach, whereby Islamic values are seen as compatible with modern secular institutions and laws within certain limits, or a conservative traditionalist approach, where the expressed goal is to produce a true Islamic society and subsequent monetary system. In today's global economy, the vast majority of Muslims fall within a gradient of tolerance between these two paths.

There are numerous books on the detailed history of Islamic banking; for the purpose of understanding its inherent value to today's global customers, we will only go back through the last four decades. During that time, Muslim bankers and religious leaders worked to fashion financial instruments similar to today's ethical investing as a means to conform to Islamic law. Two key concepts acted as motivating factors to form both the financial products themselves and in many cases the fundamentals of the institutions in which they operated: Islamic revivalism and a practical response to the problems of debt. As argued by Timur Kuran, Islamic revivalism reflects a desire to promote the beliefs of an Islamic identity, which in turn acts as a catalyst to shape the financial products up to and including the present day.[1] The momentum of Islamic revivalism coupled with the rising economies of the Gulf region have led to the emergence of a greater demand for a more ethically based economic system, bound within a regulatory system that is driven by religious principles.

If we consider Islamic banks in their historical context, we can clearly see that they follow a progression similar to that of conventional banks, in that they were established like other banks to provide a service that is valued by the communities they serve. For example, in the sixteenth century, inns in the Netherlands evolved into the facilitators of trade and commerce not by choice, but because merchants realized that they were located at the nexus of the road and canal systems and then found them a convenient place to leave money and goods for safekeeping and exchange. So it is with Islamic banking, with an initial undertaking in the 1950s to establish an Islamic financial institution in Pakistan and then, in the 1960s, the establishment of banks such as the Mit Ghamr Savings Bank in a rural area of the Nile Delta and Perbadanan Wang Simpanan Bakal-Bakal Haji in Malaysia.

According to Wilson, the Pakistani experiment was initiated by local property owners who loaned money to smaller landowners to supply them with the necessary capital for agriculture, which was repaid without interest with an added charge to cover the bank's operating expenses.[2] The clear value proposition of this initial foray into Islamic banking exhibited great success while it simultaneously contributed to its ultimate failure. As Wilson points out, the bank's failure is attributed to two fundamental problems: unrealistic forecasting on the demand for capital, and a lack of autonomy by the bank over its own operation, as property owners played too active a role in lending decisions. In the Pakistani case, the value proposition for Islamic banking was compelling, clearly understood by the landowners who needed capital for their operations.

The Egyptian Mit Ghamr Savings Bank venture into Islamic banking in the 1960s also achieved great initial success, growing from a single rural location to a network of branches having the same clear value proposition, with one variation: borrowers had to have some level of deposits in the bank to get a loan.[3] A change in the nation's political environment severely hindered its operations until 1971, when the bank reemerged as the Cairo-based Nasser Social Bank, providing services to assist social concerns such as small projects and higher education for economically disadvantaged students.

In Malaysia, the value proposition for Islamic banking was brought about by a fundamental need for Muslims to save for expenses during their pilgrimage to Mecca.[4] In order to accumulate monies for their pilgrimage, Muslims in Malaysia typically saved by accumulating livestock, property and other goods until the time they were ready to travel,

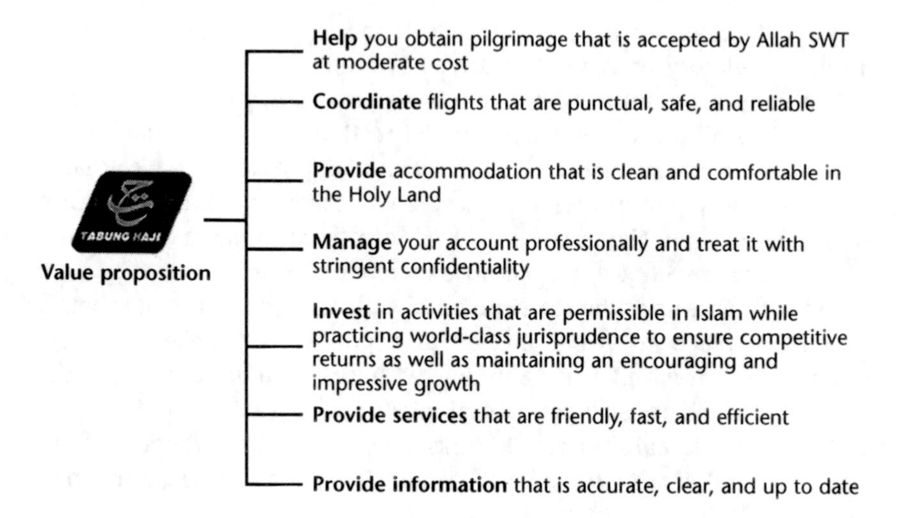

Figure 1.1 Lembaga Tabung Haji's value proposition

when they sold them to raise sufficient funds to make the journey. This practice was damaging to the family finances, the rural economy, and national economic growth.[5] Even after several name changes and merged operations, Lembaga Tabung Haji's value proposition remains the same after 40 years, as illustrated in Figure 1.1.

In the 1970s a number of Islamic institutions formed, such as Dubai Islamic Bank, Islamic Development Bank, Islamic Investment Company, Islamic Banking System International Holding (Luxembourg), Islamic Finance House, Islamic Bank International of Denmark, Dar-al-mal-al-Islami (Geneva), and Kuwait Finance House (to name a few). The list continued to grow slowly throughout the Middle East during the 1980s, with the granting of an Islamic bank license in Saudi Arabia to the 50-year-old Al-Rajhi Company, creating the Al-Rajhi Banking Investment Corporation.[6]

In 1974, long before Islamic banking became an area of study unto itself, the Union of Arab Banks (UAB) identified that one of the weaker aspects of the Islamic banking value proposition was a lack of clear standards.[7] The UAB was founded to foster cooperation between member banks, coordinate activities, and act as a central source for common Arab economic practice. Today, a number of organizations are working to unify Islamic banking under a common set of operating principles, as we will discuss in Chapter 5.

The turning point for Islamic banking was the establishment of the

Islamic Development Bank (IDB) in 1975, which began the 30-year journey whereby Islamic banking became a viable alternative model for financial intermediation.[8] Philosophically, how did Islamic banking come into being?

The Schools of Thought

All Islamic financial institutions have *Sharia* boards to structure investments and financial transactions. *Sharia* boards interpret the Holy *Qur'an* and the *Sunnah* to ensure adherence to Islamic values in the formation of financial services offerings. Although the establishment of *Sharia* law, sometimes called Islamic law, seems relatively straightforward, it is often a source of confusion for non-Muslims. In Chapter 5, we will discuss the efforts to develop global *Sharia* standards for Islamic banking. One area of puzzlement for conventional bankers is why each *Sharia* board (or specifically *Sharia* boards in various geographical regions) seemingly operate from different sets of rules. As stated above, this happens because scholars who make up *Sharia* boards interpret the law in a manner that best reflects the beliefs of the societies in which they operate. In some areas, the interpretation of *Sharia* law is more conservative in approach; in other regions, it can be more liberal, in a sense, *Sharia* law can seem more exclusive or more inclusive of global economic activities.

To understand the diversity of Islamic banking, we must briefly discuss the fundamental constructs of Islamic jurisprudence or *fiqh* that are the rulings of Islamic scholars, which fall into four Sunni schools of thought (*madzhab*):

- *Shafi'i* (typically predominant in parts of Africa, Bahrain, south of the Arabian peninsula, Indonesia and Malaysia)
- *Hanafi* (Turkey, the Balkans, Indian subcontinent, central Asia, west Africa, Egypt and China)
- *Maliki* (Morocco, Algeria, Tunisia, Libya, southern Egypt, Sudan and regions of west and central Africa, and several Gulf states)
- *Hanbali* (principally Saudi Arabia).[9]

In Sunni Islam, the four schools of thought coexist; there is no dissention over these differences, and Muslim students typically develop an understanding of each school. In the application of *Sharia* principles, the four schools of thought can be used interchangeably depending on the circumstances. *Sharia* scholars can use law from one school if it is deemed more appropriate to the situation and another school for another situation. Even though the four schools of thought share many of the same philosophies and rules, there are many instances where what may appear similar in nature is viewed very differently. The divergence is often found in the classification of what is considered forbidden and meritorious.[10]

Muslim jurists/scholars (*imams*) accumulate their respective interpretations of *Sharia* rulings into a codified system called a *madhhab*. In many cases, the *madhhab* of a specific jurist is tabulated by subject so followers looking for interpretations can easily retrieve them. The differences of the *madhahib* stem from rules mentioned or inferred by the Holy *Qur'an* and the *Sunnah*, which fall into two broad categories: clear and unambiguous expressions, or expressions that require interpretation. Unambiguous expressions can easily be understood by laymen and are universally agreed on by scholars, such as the times of prayer, fasting during *Ramadan*, the percentage of almsgiving, and specific prohibitions such as pork and wine, to name but a few. However, when expressions are unclear, they require interpretation from a *Sharia* scholar or *imam*, based on the context in which they are used. The situational interpretation offered by the Islamic scholar in the context of Islamic banking is a unique characteristic of its value proposition simply because of its adaptive nature.

Without digressing too deeply into the details of *Sharia* interpretation, it is to our advantage to take a few moments to understand the fundamentals of Islamic thought on this matter, because of their importance to the overall value proposition that Islamic banking portrays to banking customers. Given that the interpretation by an Islamic scholar is situational, the action may have an entirely different set of consequences. For example, in the Holy *Qur'an*, "Divorced women shall wait by themselves for three periods [*qur*]" [2:228],[11] where the word *qur* has two tangential meanings in reference to a waiting period: menstruation or purity. The Hanafi and Hanbali schools interpret this to mean menstruation, and the Malaki and Shafi'i schools read this to mean the purity between two menstruations.[12] Although the actual means of interpreting the exact reference of time may be the subject of debate, what is generally agreed on is the reason for the waiting period, which is to determine the condition of the woman with reference to pregnancy. Both opinions are supported by evidence and arguments supporting their view cannot simply be dismissed outright.

Another reason for differences is the use of words within a given context, as words can be used figuratively or literally, such as *wudū*, figuratively, ablution before prayer, or literally, cleanliness, purity and the washing of hands.[13] Although there are many other causes of difference between interpretations, the vast majority of *Sharia* law is widely agreed on and the differences are a source of dynamism and flexibility. A qualified *Sharia* scholar will use his best efforts to discover the actual intention of the Holy *Qur'an* and *Sunnah*.[14] His obligation to Allah is to work to the best of his ability. Another *Sharia* scholar, however, may disagree with his specific interpretation, but he can never accuse the disagreeing scholar of a violation of *Sharia*. Perhaps one of the most comprehensive works on this subject is *The Mercy: In the Difference of the Four Sunni Schools of Islamic Law*, which is a reference book designed to acquaint the followers of the four schools of *fiqh* with the rulings of the other schools.[15] The overall process used by *Sharia* scholars for interpretation is called *fiqh*, better known as the science of *Sharia*, that is, discovering the true understanding of what is intended. *Fiqh* is a logical process whereby the actions of Muslims are categorized in five distinct classifications:[16]

- *Fardh* (must be done): actions considered good deeds that must be done such as five daily prayers, and failure to do these are counted as a bad deed or a sin.
- *Mandub* (recommended): actions that are recommended such as extra prayers after the obligatory *salaah*, prayer that is performed in the afternoon right after the sun moves away from its zenith (*zuhr*) and prayer (*maghrib*), which is performed right after the sun sets over the horizon. Doing the *mandub* counts as a good deed and not doing it does not count as a bad deed or a sin.
- *Mubah* (allowed): this category is left undecided and basically each person chooses whether to do it or not, such as eating apples or oranges. Doing or not doing the *mubah* does not count as a good or bad deed. The intention of the person can change *mubah* to *fardh, mandub, makruh*, or *haram*. Other things could also change the status of the *mubah*. For example, any *mubah* becomes *haram* if it is proven harmful, and any necessary thing to fulfil a *fardh* is a *fardh* too.
- *Makruh* (hated): actions that are detested and hated, such as growing very long fingernails or sleeping on the stomach. Not doing the *makruh* counts as a good deed and doing it does not count as a bad deed.
- *Haram* (prohibited): actions that are prohibited for the Muslim, such as stealing and lying. Doing the *haram* counts as a bad deed and not doing it counts as a good deed.

Fiqh is collected in a number of books studied by students and used by Islamic scholars to interpret actions according to rules found in a specific school of thought. The result of the process of understanding by the *Sharia* scholar is to issue a *fatwa* or legal opinion based on the interpretation. With the introduction of the internet, a number of sources for *fatwa* are emerging to provide Muslims with a greater understanding of rulings by Islamic jurists such as Islam and Fatwa Questions in South Africa.[17]

One important variation on the subject of *fatwa* and Islamic jurisprudence that must be mentioned is the Jaferi school in Iran, Iraq and parts of Afghanistan. Associated more closely with Shia Islam, the rulings of early Islamic jurists are followed more closely than their counterparts in other parts of the Islamic world. This is due primarily to the hierarchical nature of Shia Islam. However, we could argue that although the structure may appear to restrict interpretations, it also provides a greater degree of flexibility because each *imam* has considerable latitude to alter a decision in accordance with his opinion.

The schools of thought provide *Sharia* scholars with a framework in which to interpret the principles of Islam to the people within a given community. For Islamic banking, the variations of interpretation may seem confusing to conventional bankers. However, the diversity of interpretation is also a distinct competitive advantage to the Islamic value proposition as it makes Islamic banking inherently adaptive in nature. *Sharia* scholar al-Qasim ibn Muhammad is quoted as saying, "The difference of opinion among the Companions of Muhammad is a mercy",[18] which is a testament to the flexibility of the *Sharia* system. How is the *Sharia* system similar to Christian values, and did they ever coexist peacefully?

The Similarities to Medieval Christian Banking

In today's contemporary debate between the academics who study financial services and banking industry professionals, one question which often arises is: how can an economic system thrive without the charging of interest? The concept of an interest-free economic system should not be alien to conventional bankers in Europe and other large economies because at one time in history, the same basic principle guided the Christian economies of the Middle Ages. In fact, Udovitch argues that: "A strict and pervasive religiously inspired prohibition against usurious transactions was a powerful cultural feature shared by the medieval Islamic world in the Christian West."[19] Without emulating the great debate, it is important to review the overall value proposition of medieval banking to contrast the difference between Islamic banking of today with conventional banking. Two central questions rise from this line of examination:

- Have Christian societies simply lost their sense of values as their economic systems matured and later on became consumed by interest-based greed?
- Once Islamic banking becomes mainstream and places itself firmly on the path to maturity, will it also experience decay in values over a 500-year period?

To answer these two questions properly would require much more space than the few pages allotted in this book. The intent of our brief historical look at the subject is twofold: to place the medieval root of the debate on interest within the context of today's value proposition, and to spark debate on this topic beyond academic circles into the industry itself.

As we have shown, there are numerous variations on how Islamic banking is brought to market, according to various schools of Islamic thought. The variations center on the interpretations of *Sharia* principles that are universal in nature throughout Islam. During the Middle Ages, Christian ecclesiastics were fiercely against usury, arguing that it was against the natural order of things – "a sin of cosmic proportions" – which was a direct reflection of the Aristotelian view on lending, whereby the natural law was of a "just equality": whatever was lent was returned, nothing more, nothing less.[20] By the thirteenth century, St. Augustine defined usury as practiced by anyone who expected to receive back more than the amount lent, which was not confined merely to money but also included agrarian commodities. The Church established cannon law, prohibiting borrowing money where the lender would receive more that the original amount. Critics of various implementations of today's Islamic banking compare the formulaic methods of calculating the time value of money with a method of circumventing cannon law used by European bankers during the Middle Ages known as *contractum trinius*.[21] The structure of *contractum trinius*, illustrated in Figure 1.2, is simple and efficient, and it shows how it could be adapted to various transaction types.

What brought about the *contractum trinius*? In the medieval period, individuals who needed to borrow money were typically traders, sometimes farmers. A medieval investor was someone who provided the needed capital or materials within a fixed amount of time (usually one year). Time was cyclical (each season followed the next until the year

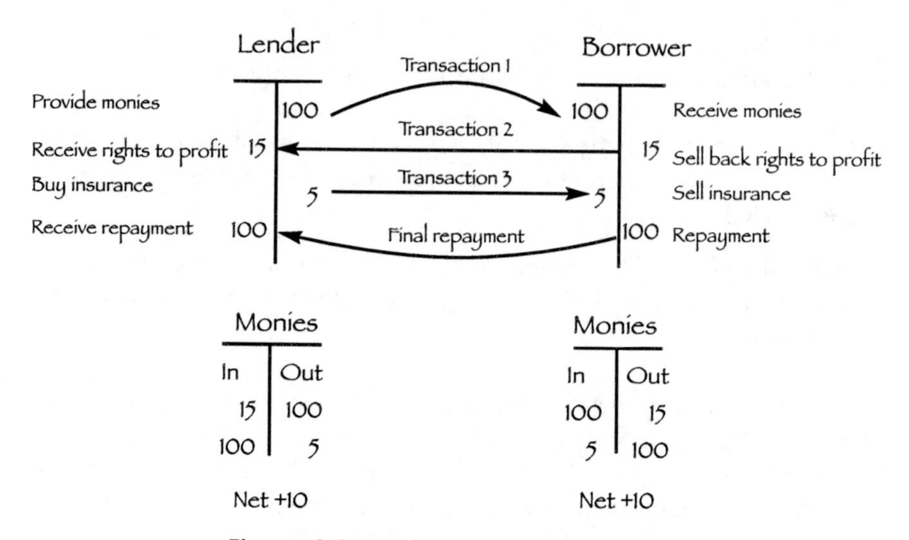

Figure 1.2 Medieval *contractum trinius*

came full circle). The vast majority of medieval people did not associate time with the idea of a linear progression. As the demand for capital increased during the later Middle Ages, bankers' creativity resulted in *contractum trinius,* a simple three-step process to appear interest-free:

- *Transaction 1:* the investor would provide capital, a commodity or an asset for a period of time, typically a year, to the recipient
- *Transaction 2:* the investor would sell back the right to any profit made over a prearranged percentage of the investment, for a predetermined fee
- *Transaction 3:* the investor would then purchase insurance on the loan from the recipient, to hedge against the recipient's ability to repay the investment.

The insurance was a hedge against the recipient's inability to repay the investment. The series of transactions provided the same mechanical effects of an interest loan. Nevertheless, when viewed holistically, the process does not reinforce the medieval ethics of natural equality. It also exclusively protects the investor, unbalancing the risk relationship between profit and loss in the overall transaction.

In the modern conventional banking context, a lender (a bank, for example) loans money and expects to receive interest in return. In many

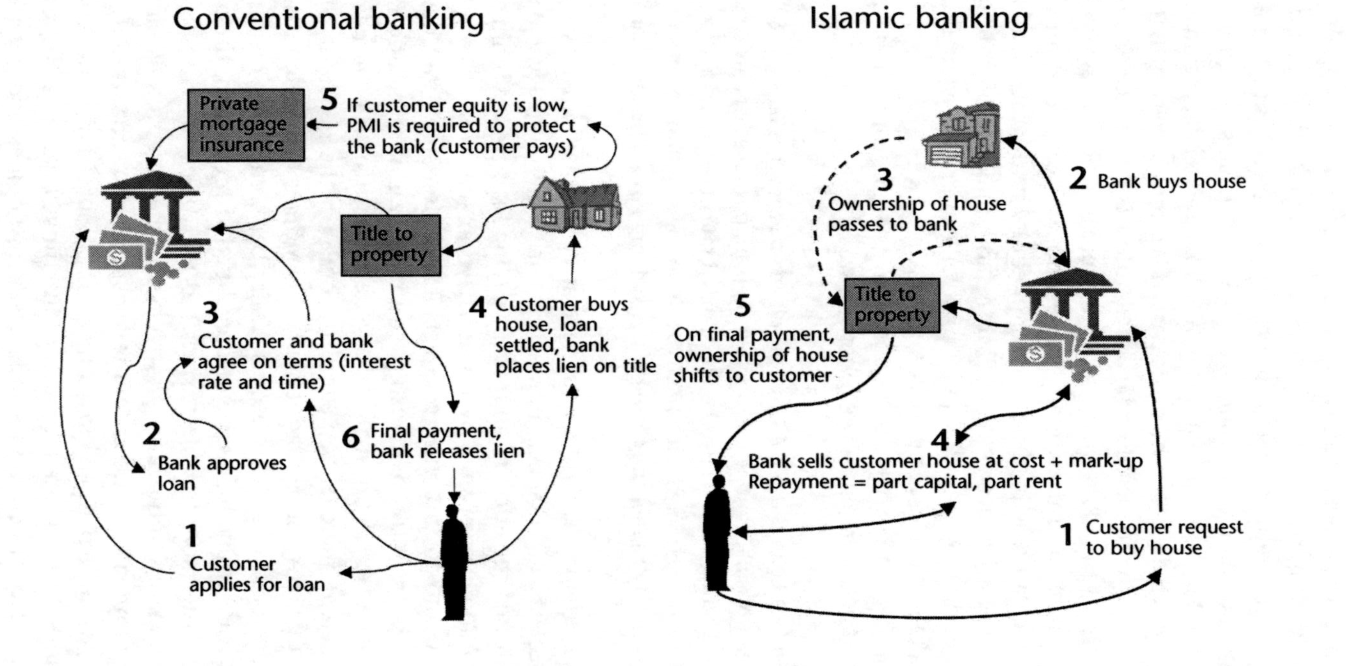

Figure 1.3 Contemporary variations of *contractum trinius*

cases, when a customer's ability to repay is in question or the bank assesses the lending risk as above moderate, the lender may require additional fees (for example a higher interest rate on credit card or personal loans, or private mortgage insurance – PMI). PMI acts the same as its medieval counterpart – as an insurance for the lender against non-repayment (see Figure 1.3). The tragic part in Western society is that many lenders assess PMI on people who have little cash to place as a down payment, effectively adding extra cost on people who can afford it the least. To add insult to injury, many lenders do not advise customers that once they reach a predefined percentage of equity under their loan agreement, they no longer need to pay PMI. A large majority of uninformed customers continue to pay PMI premiums long after the required period and lenders rarely advise them to stop paying.

Tarek El Diwany explains the modern Islamic equivalent of the medieval *contractum trinius* in the following way:

> An Interest Free Loan is *halal,* A Gift is *halal,* and a Promise is *halal,* individually these are permissible contracts, but when they are put together this equates to an Interest Bearing Loan. This is because a fixed rate of return is predetermined by banks, such as HSBC. If I lend you a 100 on the condition that you return 150, this is clearly *haram,* and these banks are doing just as the Christians did.[22]

A *contractum trinius* was just one of several clever manipulations of the technical aspects of financial transactions in which medieval bankers merely replicated the effect of an interest-paying loan by combining three legal transactions permissible by cannon law: an investment contract, a sale of profit, and an insurance contract. The earliest significant development in cooperative or partnership contracts was first mentioned by Muslim law and very occasionally in a Venetian source called *rogadia* ("by prayer"), whereby merchants pledged to transport the goods of another without charge.[23] As Lopez points out, the *rogadia* was widely used by Jews, Muslims, and Christians because usury between fellow members of their faiths was forbidden. As the medieval period progressed, the *rogadia* evolved into the more flexible partnership the *compagnia* (companions, literally the "sharers of the same bread"), where the investor's liability was joint and unlimited. The success of the *compagnia* also earmarked its eventual decline, as more partnerships came into widespread use and a few bad debts encountered by a small number of interlinked partnerships resulted in a cascade of contract failures, often leaving families and even entire towns in a state of economic collapse.

Another example of interest-like transactions can be found in letters of exchange, where one party receives an advance in a local currency and promises repayment at another time in another place with another currency. What could be construed as interest was easily masked in rates of exchange and fees. These mechanisms were in effect a dry exchange (*ricorsa*) and were extremely useful for companies that had a continuous flow of payments to and from the same locations.[24] Here again, we can see that the need to facilitate commerce caused medieval bankers to be creative in their approach not merely to circumvent interest, but also to provide financial instruments that were inherently valued by business.

It is important to remember that the intention of these medieval contracts was not the generation of interest. Rather, there was a fundamental shift in the value proposition these transactions offered to a society that was changing from financing agrarian needs to providing capital for merchants and trade. Simply, the medieval need for investment was shifting from loans for consumption to loans for production;[25] and here resided the continued ingenuity of the medieval merchants and bankers. Medieval merchants and bankers did not lose or become uninterested in following their morals and ethics; on the contrary, they were extremely concerned with how to facilitate the changing needs of society to make people's lives better. Trade and commerce brought levels of profit and wealth unattainable under the agrarian-centric model of commerce during the pre-Renaissance. Braudel points out that even well into the eighteenth century, England's Richard Baxter was proselytizing capitalism by encouraging people to use their riches for public good and to be of use to their communities, which is reminiscent of the Greco/Roman/Islamic/medieval ethics of fair and just economic activity.[26]

The progression of medieval contracts, which originated using the same set of fundamental beliefs as Muslim finance, is essential to appreciate in the context of where the value proposition for Islamic banking stands today and what path it may take in the future. *Sharia* scholars will continue to review the modern adaptations and use of more sophisticated techniques in facilitating interest-free commerce with an ever-watchful eye toward the future. As we can see, the evolution to today's conventional interest-driven banking industry did not happen over one single event, rather it was a slow gradual process made manifest within Christian economies to facilitate the monetary needs of a world becoming less agrarian and more commerce-centric, as depicted in Figure 1.4.

The three central issues that transformed society's views on usury can be directly linked to the overall value proposition of the process of capital provision. First of all, the nature of the Western world's understanding of time was changing from a cyclical mindset to the recognition of a linear

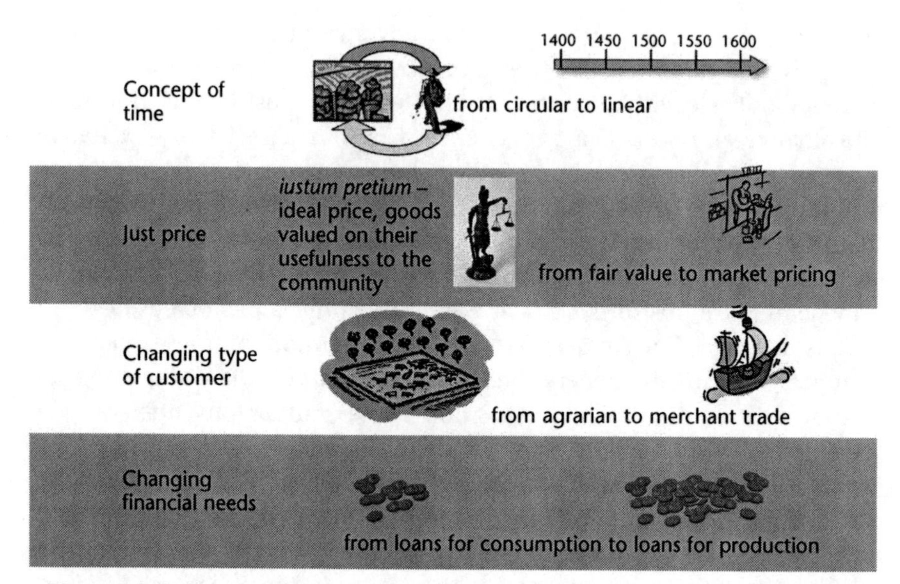

Figure 1.4 Key factors that altered the medieval Christian investment

progression. This had a direct implication on the value of goods, commodities, and money as, from that point onward, the value of each was seen as relative. A second factor, that of just price, was also changing as society's attitude shifted from being based on the idea of fair price or ideal price (*iustum pretium*), based on a good's usefulness to the community, to being founded on market-driven forces of supply and demand. Simply, the Christian Church found that over time it was impossible to fight the combined forces of everyday life; as scholars debated, people still needed to eat, farmers to plant and harvest, and businesses to engage in commerce and trade.[27]

Another factor one must consider is the centralized nature of the Christian Church that acted to concentrate matters of legal infraction due to its hierarchical structure. This is very different from Islam's decentralization of *Sharia* principles, whereby local scholars interpret the law that technically reflects the local community. What other differences are there between the two fundamental elements of Christian (medieval) and Islamic finance, and how can this help us understand the present and the future of Islamic banking?

The Variations and Divergence from a Common Root

At the dawn of the Middle Ages, Christians, Jews and Muslims had one overarching thing in common: a condemnation of usury. Although the people of these three great religions identified usury as something that was universally unjust to their people, their beliefs were not universal in the application of usury. The principles of usury prohibition applied to people within the religious sect; as was seen in the case of Jewish money-lenders, they considered usury among Jews forbidden, but saw no problem lending money to Christians under usurious circumstances. The conditions of socioeconomic change that transformed medieval society are important to understand from the perspective of value proposition in today's Islamic banking, because many of the social attitudes, monetary controls, and use of money parallel the events that shaped the Christian economy during the Renaissance. It would be premature and perhaps naive to postulate that we are at the beginning of an Islamic Renaissance or a fundamental reevaluation of the world's monetary systems, but the concept of a unified transnational Islamic monetary system is more than just an academic exercise.

Throughout the European Middle Ages, there was a continual change in the nature of economic conditions which, when coupled with the rapidly accelerating need for capital by business during the fourteenth century, established a chain of events that would decouple Christian society from its belief against usury. It is important to note that the divergence in belief toward usury as something inherently wrong did not change within the teaching of the Church until the twentieth century; however, the application of the doctrine from the Church was made according to the economic circumstances of a given century.[28] Simply, the Church has been consistent to this day in identifying that excessive or exploitive practices are outside its moral and ethical teaching, but the position of the Church in regards to its role in the economic activities of the society has waned. The contravention of the fundamental Christian principle against the charging of interest did not happen overnight. It was a process that began in the late fifteenth century and continued as a matter of controversial debate within Christian society until usury was brought to a conclusion in the 1917 Code of Canon Law, Canon 1543:

> If a commodity which is consumed by its first use be lent on the stipulation that it becomes the property of the borrower, who is bound to return to the lender not the thing itself, but its equivalent only, the lender may not receive any

payment by reason of the loan itself. In the giving or lending of such a commodity, however, it is not in itself unlawful to make an arrangement for the recovery of interest at the rate allowed by the civil law, unless that rate is clearly excessive.[29]

Understanding the process of gradual acceptance of usury by Christian society is important to realize the implications of this acceptance to the Islamic banking value proposition for two reasons: firstly, because it helps us to realize the dynamics of economic activity relative to the present and future value proposition of Islamic banking. Secondly, because it helps us to assess the impact of the current long-term goals of standardized practices to regulate Islamic banking in a global environment.

Usury has always been a topic of great deliberation, a subject that has filled and will continue to fill countless volumes of debate by theologians and scholars from many of the world's religions. For our purpose, this brief review of history is to develop an understanding of the process in which usury became more and more accepted within Christian society. To maintain a sense of brevity on the subject of usury and the process of disassociation from a centrally controlled set of moral behaviors, we must brutally summarize a historical timeline and select historical markers to refocus our thinking back to the implications for the value proposition for Islamic banking.

Early Medieval

In 1140, the Concord of Discordant Canons (*Concordia discordantium canonum*), stipulated that to demand or receive or even to lend expecting to receive something greater than the original capital is to be guilty of usury. Another important aspect was the identification that usury was not confined to money only, but that the concept could and should be applied to other material things. The Church also decreed that anyone who receives usury is guilty of plundering, being considered the same as a thief. The philosophical ideas behind the condemnation of usury is that to make a profit on money lent is to make a profit on time, and time does not belong to men; it belongs to God. Therefore, those who committed usury were, in short, stealing from God.

The final revelation was that the prohibition against usury applies to laymen as well as clerics, and in the case where a member of the clergy was implicated, punishments should be administered with greater severity. In 1139, the Second Lateran Council condemned the practice of usury, branding it despicable and blameworthy by divine and human laws. The Council also denoted that the ferocious greed of usurers would prevent them from gaining eternal salvation, therefore they would be deprived of a Christian burial unless they repented.

We see that in the early medieval period, the discourse on usury centered on the exploitation of the less fortunate who were often considered the victims of usury. The intention was not to regulate commerce and the need for capital, as it only began to rise at that period, when merchant trade increasingly became a larger part of the medieval economy. The second aspect in the attitude toward usury is the identification of a social enemy, the Jewish moneylender. Failing to curb the economic behavior of people, the Church took a bold step to penalize the supply of capital at the Third Lateran Council in 1179, which declared all usury (regardless of interest rate) forbidden. This declaration provided an easy reason for Christians to be absolved of repaying debts to the Jews.

By 1314, the Council of Vienne considered those who promoted usury to be enemies of the faith, as the law stated: "If indeed someone has fallen into the error of presuming to affirm pertinaciously that the practice of usury is not sinful, we decree that he is to be punished as a heretic."[30] The overall intention of the doctrine against usury was to identify that the prevalent high interest rates were considered exploitative, to note that loans were typically sought out by the destitute, and to reaffirm that one should extend kindness toward the poor.

What is important for us to remember in the light of today's value proposition for Islamic banking is that the fundamental tenets expressed in the medieval Christian doctrine are very similar to those of Islamic principles. This similarity is important when taken in the macroeconomic context of today's rapidly globalizing economy, because as we see in the medieval period, the redefinition of the characteristics of value were eroded in small incremental steps over a long period of time. The convening of liturgical councils to intercede in the affairs of society were not proactive mechanisms to teach a moral behavior; rather they were reactive measures to curb behavior that was already on the rise throughout medieval society.

Late Medieval

During the fifteenth century, the rise of capital suppliers (Jewish moneylenders or pawn banks) and Lombards (traveling bankers) became a virtual monopoly as a source of funds for merchants, farmers, and the poor.

Pawnbrokers charged rates as high as 60 percent, and the Lombards 43.5 percent to as high as 80 percent.[31] The high rates coupled with an overall hatred of the lenders motivated cities like Florence to enact regulations that capped interest at 20 percent in an attempt to alleviate the problem.

In 1462, the Franciscan order established the *montes pietatis* or charitable pawnbrokers, lending money based on collateral only to the very needy. The success of the Franciscans enabled the widespread dissemination throughout Italy in a few short years. Although lending money on a strictly non-profit basis was successful at first, the demand for capital was so high and the cost of administration growing to such a point that the Franciscans were forced to exact some type of additional fee. Factions within the Church, who labeled this activity usury, elevated the issue of usury until it was brought to a resolution by the Fifth Lateran Council and Pope Leo X, on 4 May 1515. Pope Leo X declared the institution meritorious and any public expression of *anti-mons pietatis* sentiments incurred excommunication.[32] The fee to cover the running expenses of the offices was typically capped at 6 percent or less.

The *montes pietatis* is important to our examination of the value proposition of Islamic banking because it brings into view the treatment of an administrative fee for the expense of facilitating transactions of a lending nature. Although the overall operating principles of the *montes pietatis* (to relieve the suffering of the poor by circumventing the business of money lending) were maintained, the institution would not have been viable in the long term without the intervention of the central religious authority. This is an important factor for Islamic banks today, in that providing capital and taking deposits requires an ever-watchful eye on the overall health of the institution.

At this point in our historical examination of the different attitudes toward usury within Christian society, it is also important to note three macroeconomic factors that altered the social perception of usury. First, the changing relationship between people and money itself began to reshape the medieval concept of the fair use of money. Second, the change in the fast moving economy as the new world (the Americas) created an unending demand for capital of all forms. Third, the change in the economic understanding of risk as a mechanism to put money to fair use.

As Braudel pointed out, the fundamentals of medieval thinking on usury were inherited from Greek philosophers and Roman law and centered on the concept that the repayment of a loan should be equal to what was lent, and repayment over time with an additional cost or value associated with time was wrong because time belongs to God alone.[33]

Usury in this context refers to any loan (*mutuum*), which results in a profit; however, the *mutuum date inde nil sperantes* was a loan not considered as usury because the lender expected nothing but repayment of the original sum for a specified period of time. The debate of St. Thomas Aquinas on the Aristotelian concept that money exists by convention not nature and inherently has no value in itself was the source of concern over the morality of usury and lending. Because money was a representative measure of the value of other things, it would be contrary to nature that money would be vendible because the ownership of money and its use are the same. In St. Aquinas's view, usury separated the used money from ownership money, thereby enabling the usurer to sell the same thing twice. The same argument can be made today, as conventional banks lend more money than is on deposit at any given time.

The changing nature of commerce and trade during the Middle Ages together with the moral and philosophical debates within the Church laid the foundation for the formation of new business relationships. Merchant sea trade demanded greater amounts of investment capital and introduced new risks for investors. The increased risk brought on by the uncertainty of sea travel helped provide the necessary moral balance to lending, in that the lender's capital was at risk on a par with the merchant. The shared risk/shared reward scheme reinforced the Aristotelian view of natural balance. The new levels of commerce spawned numerous forms of partnerships and new types of contract. One example can be found in Germany, where an insured investment meant that the lender could charge a fair price in view of sustaining potential losses. Therefore, shared risk is no longer a requirement.

The emerging contractual relationships in late medieval times worked in tandem with three distinctly different entities: a partnership recognized as legitimate and free of usury, an insurance contract whereby the capital provider did not pay an insurance premium, opting to accept a smaller percentage of the total profits in order to preserve capital, and a contract which guaranteed the investor a fixed 5 percent return on the profits.

Several other factors that shaped the medieval mindset included the realization that the value of money was affected by supply and demand, whereby over time what was lent might be returned at full face value but was worth less than when it was lent. This line of thinking shifted the debate from simple usury to one of risk, fair use, and the generation of profits. In addition, throughout the Renaissance and into the seventeenth century, there was a consistent gradual decline of the influence of the Church in economic affairs.

Modern Times

The Church took little official interest in matters of usury after the seventeenth century. The encyclical of 1745 by Pope Benedict XIV stated that the nature of the sin called usury had its proper place and origin in a loan contract (*mutuum*), whereby one returned to another only as much as he had received. The act that constituted a sin rested on the fact that sometimes a creditor desired more than had been given. One hundred and fifty years later, in 1917, the Code of Canon Law number 1543 described the act of usury as not in itself illicit to contract for legal interest, unless interest rates were found to be manifestly excessive. Over time, the Christian definition has struggled to make a clear distinction between the cost of capital and interest.

In Islamic finance, the prohibition on interest does not imply that capital is costless; Islam recognizes that capital is an aspect of production. However, it is *haram* to make a prior or predetermined claim on the productive surplus in the form of interest. Under *Sharia* principles, the owner of capital can legitimately share the profits made by the entrepreneur because it is the ratio of profit sharing not the rate of return itself that is predetermined.[34]

As we have seen, many of today's arguments on usury, profits, fees, and what constitutes *haram* and *halal* were indeed much debated in Christian society during the Middle Ages and the Renaissance. For the value proposition of Islamic banking today, many of the opinions expressed during the medieval period have manifested themselves in parallel to the different variations of interpretation in *Sharia* principle by a variety of scholars in different parts of the world. This variation in interpretation is considered by some a weakness in the current value proposition, whereas by others it is seen as diversity which also constitutes its inherent strength. In the next chapter, we will explore the global variations on interpretation, not to identify inconsistencies in the interpretation of *Sharia* principles, but rather to understand how these variations enable the value proposition of Islamic banking to adapt to many socioeconomic circumstances in today's global economy.

Notes

1 Kuran, Timur, The Genesis of Islamic Economics: A Chapter in the Politics of Muslim Identity, *Social Research*, **64**(2) (Summer 1997), available at http://www.mtholyoke.edu/acad/intrel/kuran.htm.

2 Wilson, Rodney *Banking and Finance in Arab Middle East*, London: Macmillan – now Palgrave Macmillan, 1983.

3 Ahmed, A., Contemporary Experiences of Islamic Banks, *Journal of Objective Studies,* 1992.

4 Islamic banking in Malaysia, Wikipedia, December, 2005, available at http://en.wikipedia.org/wiki/Islamic_banking_in_Malaysia.

5 Lembaga Tabung Haji, Background of TH, December, 2005, available at http://www.tabunghaji.gov.my/th/bi/bi-latarbelakang_th.asp?lthmenu=0.

6 Islami Bank of Bangladesh Limited *Concept and Ideology: Evolution of Islamic Banking,* December, 2005, available at http://www.islamibankbd.com/page/ih_1.htm.

7 Union of Arab Banks, Beirut, Lebanon, October, 2005, available at http://www.uabonline.org/UABWeb/profile/profile_1.htm.

8 Molyneux, Phillip and Iqbal, Munawar *Banking and Financial Systems in the Arab World,* Basingstoke: Palgrave Macmillan, 2005, p. 148.

9 The Four Schools, The Internet Encyclopedia, December, 2005, available at http://www.internet-encyclopedia.org.

10 *Sharia,* The Encyclopedia of the Orient, November, 2005, available at http://i-cias.com/e.o/Sharia.htm.

11 Arberry, Arthur *The Koran Interpreted,* Oxford: Oxford University Press, 1964, p. 32.

12 Some Questions About Divorce, http://mac.abc.se/home/onesr/h/56.html.

13 Kandhlawi, Shaykh al-Hadith Muhammad Zakariyya, translated by Mawlana Muhammad Kadwa, *The Differences of the Imams,* Santa Barbara: White Thread Press, 2004, p. 23.

14 *The Four Schools of Thought in Islam (Madzhab),* VictoryScent, November, 2005, available at http://www.victoryscent.co.uk/4madhabs_1.htm.

15 As-Safadi, Al-Qadi Muhammad ibn Abd Ar-Rahman *The Mercy: In the Difference of the Four Sunni Schools of Islamic Law,* London: Dar Al Taqwa, 2004.

16 Islamic Dictionary, Muttaqun Online, Winter Park: Muttaqun Foundation, December, 2005, available at http://muttaqun.com/dictionary3.html.

17 Islam and Fatwa Questions, Mayfair, South Africa, November, 2005, available at http://www.fatwa.org.za/.

18 Ucko, Hans *Communicating Identities and Valuing Differences in a Changing Europe, World Council of Churches,* WACC – European Region, Strasbourg, March 10–11, 2005, p. 14, available at www.wacc.org.uk/wacc/content/download/1644/9364/file/identity.pdf.

19 Udovitch, Abraham *Bankers without Banks: Commerce, Banking and Society in the Islamic World of the Middle Ages, The Dawn of Modern Banking,* Los Angeles: Center for Medieval and Renaissance Studies, University of California, 1979, p. 256.

20 Kaye, Joel *Economy and Nature in the Fourteenth Century,* Cambridge: Cambridge University Press, 2000, p. 81.

21 Islamic Banking, Middle East Open Encyclopedia, Iraq Museum International, December 2005, available at http://www.baghdadmuseum.org.

22 el Diwany, Tarek, Step by Step You Shall Follow Them, Education Exchange and Dinar Exchange Meeting, 30 April 2004, available at http://www.dinar-exchange.co.uk/index.php?page=April_2004.

23 Lopez, Robert *The Commercial Revolution of the Middle Ages, 950–1350*, Cambridge: Cambridge University Press, 1995, p. 73.

24 Lopez, Robert *The Commercial Revolution of the Middle Ages, 950–1350*, Cambridge: Cambridge University Press, 1995, p. 104.

25 Hunt, Edwin and Murry, James *A History of Business in Medieval Europe 1200–1550,* Cambridge: Cambridge University Press, 1999, pp. 70–4.

26 Braudel, Fernand *The Wheels of Commerce,* Vol. 2, London: William Collins Sons, 1982, p. 567.

27 Braudel, Fernand *The Wheels of Commerce,* Vol. 2, London: William Collins Sons, 1982, p. 565.

28 Coulter, Gary *The Church and Usury: Error, Change or Development?,* research paper, Emmitsburg, Mount Saint Mary's Seminary, 1999, p. 47.

29 Boyle, Leo *Is Usury a Sin?, Catholic FAQs: Morality,* Kansas City, Missouri: Society of Saint Pius X, August 5, 2005, available at http://www.sspx.org/Catholic_FAQs/catholic_faqs__morality.htm#usuryasin.

30 Coulter, Gary *The Church and Usury: Error, Change or Development?,* research paper, Emmitsburg, Mount Saint Mary's Seminary, 1999, p. 10.

31 *Montes pietatis,* The Catholic Encyclopedia, Vol. X, online edition, 2003, available at http://www.newadvent.org/cathen/10534d.htm.

32 *Montes pietatis,* The New Catholic Dictionary 1910, online, 2005, available at http://www.catholic-forum.com/saints/ncd05567.htm.

33 Braudel, Fernand *The Wheels of Commerce,* Vol. 2, London: William Collins Sons, 1982, p. 562.

34 Ariff, Mohamed, Islamic Banking, *Asian-Pacific Economic Literature,* **2**(2) (September 1988), pp. 46–62.

2

GLOBAL BANKING AND ISLAMIC VALUES

For the past few decades, the banking and financial services needs of Islamic customers have been ignored on a global scale. During that time, in loosely connected regional pockets, Islamic banking took root and grew, recently achieving an annual growth rate of 15 percent. Islamic banking is steadfastly emerging as an economic system with supporting banking and financial infrastructures that are accompanied by promising standards and other disciplines that set it on a par with what is today labeled "conventional banking". Today, Islamic banking is functioning in some capacity in over 75 countries, ranging from a total conversion of the economic system known as "Islamization" in countries such as Iran, Pakistan and Sudan (that occurred in the early 1980s) to hybrid systems that are evolving to interoperate between conventional and Islamic banking, as in Bahrain, Dubai, Qatar, and Malaysia. El-Gamal argues that for Islamic banking systems to be viable in the long term, they must first act dualistically: initiating transactions with other Islamic banks in an Islamic way, and interacting with institutions that are interest-based, such as the hybrid banking system in Malaysia.[1]

In a global context, many banking services, such as the flow of capital between nations in the form of loans, mortgages and credit cards, must be rethought from the Islamic perspective. Capital flow, for example, should be placed into a more appropriate scheme of foreign direct investment (FDI) and the establishment of transnational equity markets, whereby foreign investors can directly participate in long- and short-term financing opportunities. The key to this shift in thinking is that transnational capital is no longer loaned with an expected return; investment capital is simply an investment that constitutes a share in ownership and a share in risk. According to Dr. Muhammad Nejatullah Siddiqi, foreign capital combines in partnership with local capital to form two kinds of foreign capital: *murabahah*-based long-term partnerships with predetermined schedules of withdrawals, and short-term capital based on *ijarah*, *salam* or *istisna* invested as common stock and other financial instruments.[2] In Siddiqi's view, market controls must be in place to minimize the destabilizing effects of withdrawals of foreign capital, which can easily be brought about by negative investor sentiment and the media.

The Spectrum of Applied Islamic Banking

Overall, the financial instruments that have been developed under the broad definition of Islamic financial products have become more innovative in design and more contemporary in their application of *Sharia* principles to the problems of modern banking and people's lifestyles. Islamic financial systems are most adaptive when they work in tandem with conventional banking systems, as exemplified in the cases of Malaysia, Bahrain and several countries in the Gulf region. Standardization and transparency are seen by global customers as current shortfalls in the Islamic value proposition. To address the issue of standardization, organizations such as the Bahrain-based Liquidity Management Centre (LMC) and the International Islamic Financial Market (IIFM) have been established to act as global coordinators in the operations of Islamic banks. Subsequently, to give confidence to foreign markets on the issue of transparency within Islamic banking and finance, the Bahrain Monetary Agency has produced an industry-specific comprehensive reporting framework. The Malaysian approach to the integration of Islamic banking is to operate both Islamic and conventional banking systems as competitors in an environment of co-opetition. Under this framework, both systems interoperate within an evolving regulatory system, with Islamic banking predicted to rise from 8 percent to 20 percent by 2010. The key factors that affect the Islamic banking value proposition are that the Bahrain and Malaysian systems are adaptive and inclusive.

Several countries have defined national objectives to migrate to a total Islamic-based economy. The banking systems in these countries are said to be undergoing complete or partial Islamization. In 1984, Iran converted its economy to a banking system free of usury. Although similar in the fundamental principles of Islamic banking, in other Muslim countries there are number of conceptual differences between the Iranian implementation of Islamic banking and versions found in other Islamic-based national economies. In Pakistan, the Modaraba Association of Pakistan was incorporated in April 1994 to: "promote the Islamic way of business and in particular, encourage public awareness of the role of *mudarabah* in the provisions of Islamic modes of financing."[3] The overall value proposition in Pakistan is rising due to the deliberate steps taken to bolster Islamic banking with support from government initiatives. Similarly, in Sudan, Islamic banking operates at a national level using financial instruments based on *murabahah, musharakah* and *mudarabah,* the latter two types becoming more prevalent. Unlike Pakistan, the Islamic-based financial system in Sudan has significant challenges that are not specifically part of the overall Islamic value proposition.

As banks in North America, Europe and Asia struggle to expand their value propositions to be desirable to greater numbers of people, Islamic banks are challenged to contain their value propositions. Seemingly counterintuitive, restraining the value proposition of Islamic banks is a growing concern because of three key issues: the sudden plethora of products and services, a limited number of available resources, and a defined marketplace (Muslims and perhaps a small percentage of non-Muslims). In addition, Islamic banks must be cautious in their expansion of products so as not to appear to customers to be trying to be all things to all people. An inherent part of the value proposition is a sense of community that may become blurred in a cacophony of brands, products, and services.

One factor that hampers the Islamic value proposition on a global level is the lack of sufficient infrastructure for banking, payments, and electronic commerce. This is especially true in the rural areas of emerging nations. Infrastructure in the context of the value proposition in many cases is simply providing access to services with technology and non-technological means. In nations where illiteracy rates are high, providing basic educational services is considered an infrastructure project that extends a bank's resources beyond the confines of a traditional banking relationship with their client. The strength of the value proposition in a global context can be found in the growing amount of capital flowing into Islamic banks worldwide, providing the means for Islamic banks to participate in a wide range of financing opportunities from retail products based on *Sharia* principles to the complicated financing needs found in large-scale project lending.

Perhaps the biggest opportunity for Islamic banks in the development of their value propositions is to provide financial services to specific segments of a nation's population that are not currently served by banking products (the "unbanked"). In conjunction with this comes the challenge of applying Islamic values to other primary banking services, as demonstrated by Grameen Bank, which applies classical Islamic values using conventional lending practices to provide credit to the poorest of the poor in rural Bangladesh without any collateral.[4] Islamic financial institutions have a first-mover advantage over their foreign competitors due to their knowledge of the local economic conditions, customer behaviors, and overall community needs. Banking services that will redefine the administration of social welfare systems, provide entrepreneurs with access to capital and offer direct links to foreign direct investors do more than generate fee income; they raise the standard of living within the community. As a result, providing banking services that have a direct impact on facilitating the lifestyles of customers such as society's underbanked, small and medium-sized enterprise (SME) micro-financing and remittances under the Islamic value proposition has two immediate effects: it produces new customers (as more people find employment), and increases the amount of discretionary income to existing customers as their wealth expands. In this chapter, we explore the emerging opportunities for Islamic financial institutions to apply their value propositions to a wide range of market scenarios. The companies highlighted in this chapter do not constitute an exhaustive list of examples of what is happening in the world of Islamic finance; rather, they offer a sample of the innovations bringing a higher degree of value to the application of Islamic ideals to the modern economy.

Informal Systems of Exchange

For centuries, informal systems of exchange or systems technically labeled "informal funds transfer" (IFT) have existed to facilitate various aspects of trade and commerce. Throughout the Islamic world, informal systems of exchange are used for transferring funds, both domestically and internationally. One system, which finds its roots in the Arabic term for transfer *(hawala)* or the Hindi word for "trust", exists under different names in various regions of the world such as *hundi* and *padala*.[5] The *hawala* system is an informal channel for transferring funds and sometimes commodities from one location to another using *hawaladars* (agents or brokers) (Figure 2.1). The *hawaladars* operate in every country where there are migrant or emigrant populations and handle a wide variety of transactions. The vast percentage of *hawala* transactions are initiated by emigrant workers living in one country with family members living in another country. Funds are typically sent from the worker to the family. In some instances, the reverse happens, and funds are sent out to someone living abroad as a student or as a new immigrant needing funds to start a business.

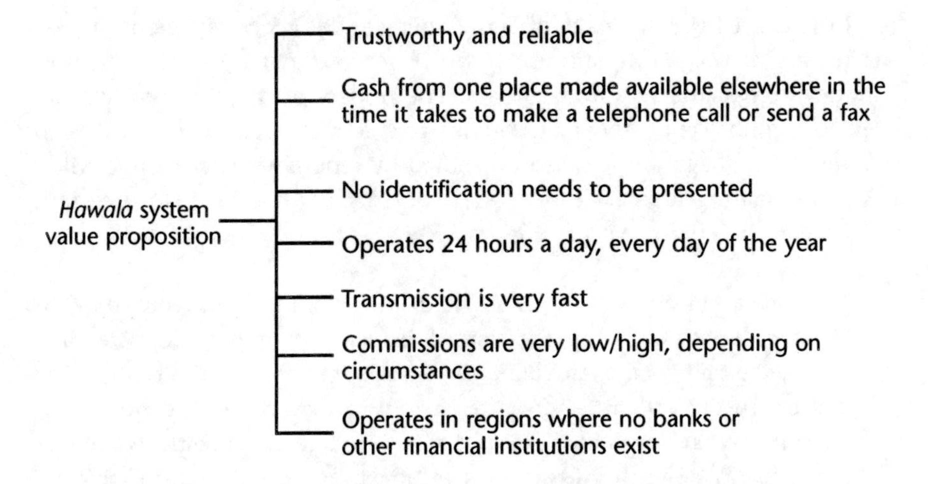

Figure 2.1 *Hawala* system value proposition

As recently as 2001, the volume of transactions and the funds transferred through informal money transfer systems were for the most part ignored by banks and governments because the amounts per transaction were so low that the cost to service this activity was seen as prohibitive. However, in the post September 11, 2001 banking environment, this area of international transfer has come under greater scrutiny and surveillance. Chris Skinner, a financial services analyst with TowerGroup, notes that the US's Patriot Act, passed in October 2001, made it a crime for businesses engaged in remittance services, such as *hawala*, if they failed to register with the US Treasury's Financial Crimes Enforcement Network (FinCEN).[6]

Islamic financial intuitions have been hesitant to engage in the remittance business of emigrants and immigrants because of the longstanding perception that it was cost prohibitive. However, new technology provides the means to supply these services as part of the overall value proposition that banks offer customers. Unfortunately, in many countries, the lack of a robust infrastructure and trained staff have prevented institutions from engaging this market with the same vigor as consumer markets. During the next few years, the environment for *halawa* is going to change as banks and governments begin to tally the total volume of the informal money transfer markets, because they will realize that the sheer volume of transactions is well beyond the original estimates of the overall costs. From the government perspective, remittances represent a large pool of untapped capital that is non-regulated, non-taxed, and untraceable.

In late 2001, in the wake of September 11, the US government alleged that *halawa* was the channel of choice for terrorist networks to move money across international borders. The impact of these allegations has led to a global crackdown on *halawa* transfers in many countries, even though this allegation has been disputed by reputable scholars like Nikos Passas, a visiting scholar at the College of Criminal Justice at Northeastern University in Boston, Massachusetts:

> The evidence in the 9-11 attacks shows that most of the funds received by the hijackers reached the US through formal financial institutions (e.g., wire transfers, credit card use). Even some of the cash that entered the country was declared to the authorities. In other terrorism cases, correspondent banking accounts have also been used. The role of trade in legal commodities is also very important. *Halawa* networks are, thus, by no means the only or main vehicle of illegal funds transfers or financing of terrible acts.[7]

Because of the sudden interest in remittances by international governments and law enforcement agencies, in Pakistan, the *halawa* brokers have witnessed a 75 percent decline in business. However, this downturn in the informal system has had a positive impact on the domestic economy. Oil and gasoline imports are essential to the growth of the nation. The sudden shift away from the informal economy to formal banking channels is generating large amounts of American dollars needed to support foreign exchange, trade, and commerce. Banks in Pakistan estimate that expatriate Pakistanis send US$11 billion a year into the country, while remittances through official banking channels average just US$1 billion a year.[8] This move from the informal system to the formal financial system will act to inject necessary funds into the banking system that will in turn strengthen the overall value of the rupee.

To gain a better understanding of the overall impact of remittances, let us put them into perspective. The estimated global volume of remittances is in excess of US$232 billion in 2005, according to the World Bank. The average daily turnover in traditional foreign exchange markets worldwide is estimated at US$1.9 trillion.[9] VISA International's VisaNet facilitates US$949 billion in annual transaction volume,[10] which by comparison makes the *halawa* market look relatively small. However, given the national economies of many of the recipient countries, the impact on national gross domestic product (GDP) is extraordinarily high.

During the next decade, the interconnected global economy will present four key challenges for most nations: job creation, attracting FDI, access to capital (micro-financing, remittances, and payment systems) for

SMEs, and financial education. These macroeconomic issues are not new for many nations within emerging economies, who have had to persevere through a series of sociopolitical and economic shortfalls over the past four decades. To overcome these challenges, economic growth is predicated on achieving international parity with four key infrastructures: financial, transportation, health, and communications. Critical to the success of any national economic agenda is a financial infrastructure that is the foundation for government, business, and private services to be delivered. Islamic banks play a vital role in the development of these infrastructures, and they must be at the vanguard of establishing the technological platforms for economic success. In order to capitalize on new opportunities, Islamic banks must collaborate with other financial institutions to establish a stable, predictable, and dynamic financial infrastructure through a process of financial services renewal, with initiatives such as central bank strengthening and national banking revitalization.

A National Payment Strategy

So as to compete in the global economy, nation states must develop macroeconomic strategies that foster economic growth and long-term business viability. A national payment strategy provides the underpinning for institutional strengthening and financial sector reform. Within the context of a national payment strategy, migrant remittances are slowly being recognized by governments as a fundamental component of the global economy, because of their direct contribution to accelerate the rate of economic growth by acting as an external income source to people who are typically within the lower 50 percentile of wage earners. This translates into the expansion of productive employment opportunities while increasing the purchasing power and savings rates of individuals within the nation state. As said above, in the large majority of cases, migrant remittances represent a substantial portion of GDP. Overall, the development of a financial infrastructure to facilitate migrant remittances is the first step toward financial reinvigoration and a small measurable step in the larger process of economic growth.

Remittances are an opportunity for Islamic institutions to facilitate the transference of monies sent from one individual household to another. Remittances today constitute the fastest growing and more stable capital flow to developing countries. Due to the weakness of the retail banking sector in many emerging economies, over 70 percent of all remittances are sent by informal means, that is, they are sent via *halawa* intermediaries

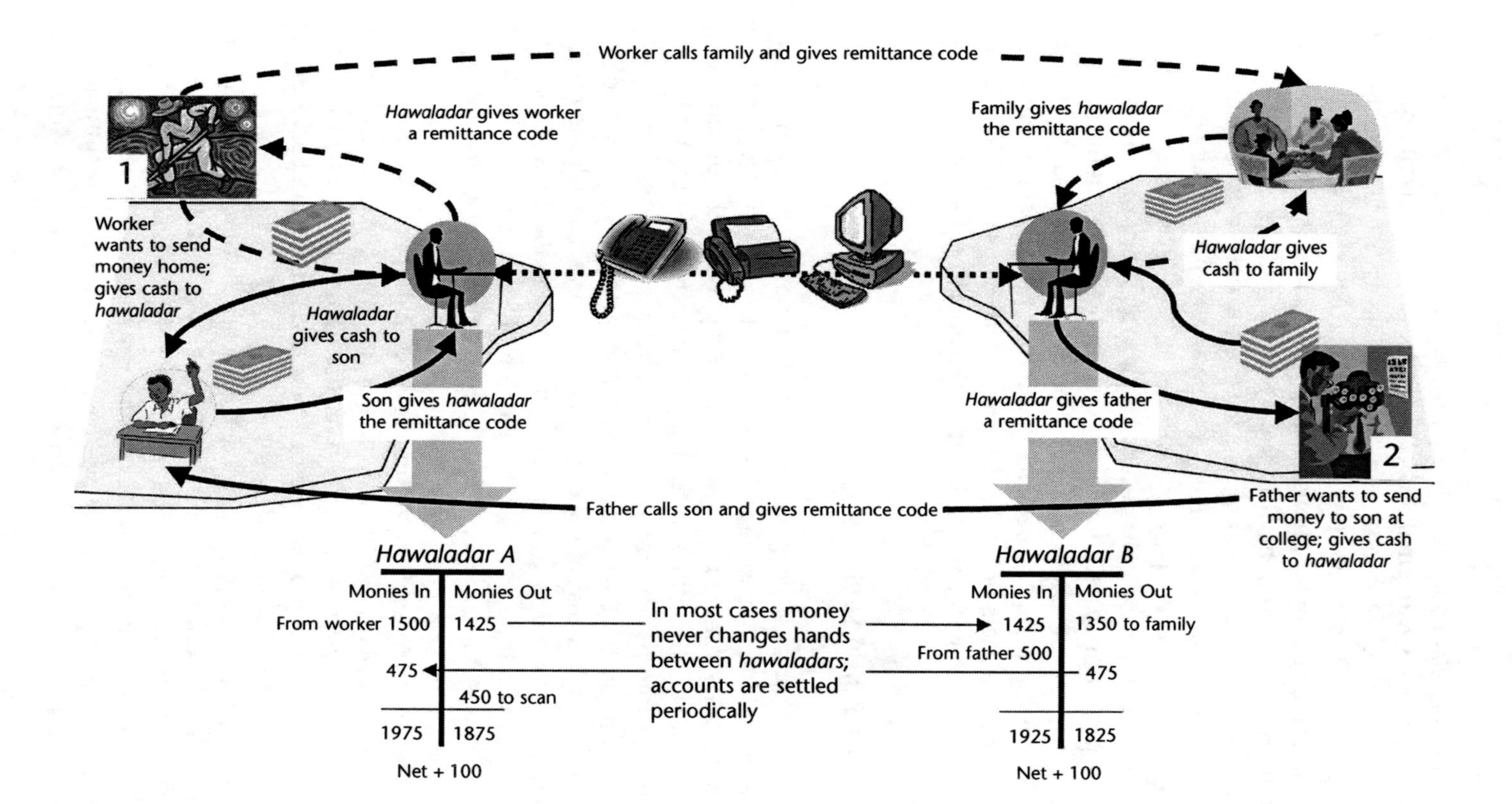

Figure 2.2 The informal remittance process

that are not financial services institutions. There are three problems with this situation:

1. Fees charged by intermediaries can range from 1 percent to sometimes as high as 30 percent, which means that sending money to a home nation represents a loss of money for those who are already relatively poor.
2. They are not traceable, which means that the proceeds of "underground" economy transactions may be passed conveniently and secretly.
3. Every so often, monies are lost and cannot be recovered, leaving those in need of help with nothing.

An initial *halawa* transaction can be a payment from an individual in country A to another customer in country B (Figure 2.2). The financial intermediary, in this case a *halawadar,* from country A receives funds in one currency from a local individual and, in return, gives him/her a code for authentication purposes. Then, the *halawadar* counterpart in country B delivers an equivalent amount in the local currency to a designated beneficiary who needs to disclose the code to receive the funds. The *halawadar* in country A can charge a fee to cover the administrative costs or recover the expense through an exchange rate spread. Once the transaction is complete, the *halawadar* in country A has an obligation to his/her counterpart in country B. The two *halawadars* settle their accounts by various means: financially by reversing the process in a future transaction from country B to country A, or by goods and services.[11]

Regional/Virtual Financial Synergy

The global economy has demonstrated the interdependence of economic activity among countries and amplified the need for national initiatives to be reinforced by international cooperation. In order to sustain growth, create jobs, and increase trade and investment, national strategies must work synergistically with neighboring nations, trading partners, and countries which host migrant workers as they reside, provide labor and pay taxes. Each nation state must devise a national payment strategy that best serves the needs of their people. However, the specialist nature of these strategies tends to identify factors, components, and economic elements that are similar to national objectives. The underlying similarities in how payments are processed, the rules that govern the behavior of payers and payees, bring into focus explicit opportunities for international collaboration. This can be seen when banks pool their resources to establish shared services such as credit card processing, reducing their overall operating cost and improving efficiency without negatively affecting their market differentiation.

To compete in the today's economic climate, nations with emerging economies must identify and exploit opportunities that can be leveraged through cooperation and collaboration. One can speculate that in the near future, we may see the emergence of an international network strictly for Islamic remittances, perhaps The Islamic Money Network. A network of this nature would require that each nation should develop their national payment strategies from a common template, whereby the strategies can be consolidated and cooperative opportunities could be identified and moved into action.

New Opportunities for Islamic Banks

Ancillary services like migrant remittances are important for Islamic banks for three distinct reasons:

1. They represent new sources of revenue or fee income.
2. The remitted funds are typically used to buy, sell, or save – all actions that can easily be channeled to existing banking services.
3. Perhaps more importantly, these funds are primarily used to improve the recipients' standard of living, which conforms with the value proposition of Islamic banking.

A low-cost, fast, reliable, well-managed remittance product is capable of transforming a local economy because of the ways in which remittances affect households, local communities, and national economies. Nations with large migrant workforces can measure the significant impact of their local economies and direct impact on the GDP. This aspect of direct impact on both local and national economies is a unique opportunity for many Islamic banks as they spread their operations into new geographical marketplaces.

Emerging Islamic Financial Products

It might be premature to say that today there is a renaissance in Islamic banking and finance. However, it is undeniable that today more and more people are beginning to take notice of Islamic banking due to a rising inter-Islamic awareness of the current lack of Islamic services globally, and a compelling value proposition based on serving the community. Like all products and services, Islamic banking and finance is continually evolving to meet the needs of the people it serves. Many products are simply a repackaging or rebranding of old products to cater to contemporary social requirements. Dr. Zeti Akhtar Aziz, governor of the Central Bank of Malaysia, puts the next set of challenges for Islamic banks into perspective:

> As we enter into an increasingly challenging environment, the ability of the Islamic financial institutions to compete by creating innovative and differentiated products, and by adopting strategic positioning to increase unique and tangible value to their customers will be the key to determining performance and relevance. It is imperative that players in the Islamic financial industry reposition themselves to create a unique and sustainable competitive position in responding to the changing environment.[12]

As the fee structure of Islamic banking comes under greater scrutiny by customers, the need for innovation will be paramount for Islamic banks. The impact of innovation on the value proposition for Islamic banking is important not only in the sense that new products will need to crafted to hide or justify higher operating costs; innovation will be needed to reduce operating costs, make reporting more transparent, and enable customers to perform more self-service transactions under a set of automated *Sharia*-compliant products.

Rice and Mahmoud rightly point out that the dramatic growth of Islamic banks over the past three decades has been accompanied by few innovations in banking products and services to customers.[13] Growth has been primarily the product of simply offering services to a market starved of basic services that comply with Islamic principles. Innovation must center on developing a meaningful value-added dialogue with customers so as to inform, educate, and advise on the relativity of their actions to their financial goals and monetary objectives within a framework of *Sharia* compliance. According to Rice and Mahmoud, the focus of innovation to be a differentiating factor in the bank's value proposition must be in developing the customer experience in a way that encourages emotional attachments to the bank's brand, services, and people.[14] This raises the competitive bar for most Islamic institutions because it demands higher attention to detail in the quality of services, which in turn requires significant investment in upgrading the organization's human capital. In the conventional banking market, especially in the US and Europe, product innovation has become synonymous with technology. For Islamic banks, innovation must happen through leveraging the power of technology. Islamic banking and finance has experienced rapid growth in assets; however, the integration of Islamic financial markets is becoming the Achilles heel for Islamic banking. As competition with foreign banks in domestic markets can be moderately controlled, in the international marketplace, a robust financial infrastructure capable of supporting an ever-increasing number of new products and services is vital for long-term financial growth.

If Infrastructure is the Answer, What is the Question?

To be successful in the global economy, a nation must be able to integrate the international financial system with the domestic financial system and incorporate the components of the banking industry, insurance, and the money and capital markets. Currently, the growth and sophistication of Islamic banking is at the vanguard of progress toward a fully integrated, robust, and predictable financial infrastructure in many nations, particularly the Middle East, Africa, the Indian subcontinent, Asia and Southeast Asia. This rapid growth introduces new challenges for the banking industry in those regions, as the pace of growth in the retail Islamic banking markets is accelerating faster than the underlying financial infrastructures and moderately faster than the complementary financial services products, such as insurance and capital markets. While Islamic banking has been the catalyst for significant growth in Islamic financial products and the increased general awareness of the needs of Muslims for financial products that are more in line with their values and beliefs, clearly more effort is needed to collaborate on the development of financial infrastructure through public and private partnerships.

The key to competition in the global marketplace for Islamic institutions is to have a wide range of Islamic-based financial instruments tailored to the various financial needs of Muslims in many nations. To provide these services economically, securely, and with a high degree of fidelity, the pace of technological infrastructure must be accelerated. Perhaps one of the most refreshing approaches to the argument of the appeal of asset-based financing versus interest-based financing comes from John Tomlinson, an Oxford-based economist, who argues that the development of equity markets currently served by debt are a continued misrepresentation by banks. In Tomlinson's view, in the long term, the world economic system will have to shift from being interest-based to being asset-based. Further to this argument, Kahf et al. claim that Islamic banking offers non-Muslims an alternative choice in banking and will continue to grow as a competitive factor in global financial markets, as it extends into multicultural environments in search of Muslim customers.[15] The vast majority of bankers are skeptical of any shift away from an interest-based economy, and ask the question: if a shift happens, when will it happen? Perhaps a more interesting question is not when there will be a sudden shift, but will we be able to understand the characteristics of a dynamic shift toward an equity-based economy if it happens in small incremental actions? Is it possible that a shift that may take 50 years to complete is already underway?

In the US and Europe during the 1990s, small numbers of investors began demanding a choice of investment funds based on ethical investing. Over the past 20 years, the trend that started with "green" or ecological issues has continued and has given birth to numerous investment products, based on an increasing number of ethically based issues beyond an ecological agenda, such as gambling, pornography, alcohol or tobacco, child labor, arms sales, sustainable development, and attention to human rights. This growing concern for ethical issues by investors has led to the establishment of the FTSEGood Index for companies that meet a strict criterion of environmental, human rights, social, and stakeholder issues.[16] In Europe, approximately 150 ethically based investment funds have grown from US$390 million in 1998, to over US$8.4 billion in 2005. Similarly, in the UK alone, ethical investments are on the rise, with a growing number of investment objectives, as illustrated by a few examples in Table 2.1.

As ethics-based investment rises and achieves a continued pattern of growth, a clever marketing campaign designed to educate investors on the fundamentals of the Islamic value proposition targeting non-Muslim investors may not be far off. It is understood that a shift from the conventional debt-based system is not likely to occur quickly, because interest is embedded in almost every aspect of our everyday financial life. However, there are two things that Islamic banks should factor into their strategic plans: firstly, the future is not as far away as it appears (think of banking 20 years ago, no internet, no mobile phones, no rapidly installable ready-to-buy core banking systems). Secondly, Islamic

Table 2.1 Sample of UK ethical investment funds and fund objects

Ethical Funds in the UK[17]	Investment objectives
Aberdeen Ethical World (Global) OEIC Fund	Aims to achieve long-term capital growth through international quality investments based on ethical ("socially responsible") criteria
Allchurches Amity (UK) Fund	Invests in a diverse selection of ethical businesses
Morley Fund Management	Socially responsible investment engagement strategy across all Morley funds
The AXA Ethical Fund	Aims to achieve capital growth over the medium to long term, investing in companies whose products, services, or methods of operation are considered not to be detrimental to the global community
Banner Real Life Unit Trust	Aims to provide long-term capital growth and a reasonable level of income from a diversified portfolio of securities
The CAF Socially Responsible Fund	Long-term investment fund for charities seeking income + capital growth. Investment is international, in companies whose growth is linked to their positive social and environmental impact
CIS Sustainable Leaders Trust	Invests in good quality, responsible, mainly UK, companies, positively involved in improving the environment, quality of life and enhancing human health and safety
Clerical Medical Ethical (UK/European) Fund	Aims to achieve long-term capital growth by investing primarily in shares of UK and/or European companies which meet a range of ethical criteria
The Credit Suisse Fellowship (UK) Fund	Aims to achieve long-term capital growth by investing in companies, which meet defined ethical criteria, predominately in the UK (international when appropriate)

Source: Envocare

banks must realize that if there is a change on the horizon, banks with a strategy of first to market need to have an easily understood value proposition, coupled with a brand identity and a broad range of financial services.

Knowledge–creativity–innovation

If the current use of *Sharia* principles employed by Islamic banks allows them to be profitable and regularly achieve respectable growth figures, then the argument for expanding the network of Islamic banking to the wider community is a compelling one. For Islamic banking to attract more investors and customers, an institution must have diversity in the type and the maturity of *Sharia*-based financial instruments. The vast majority of Islamic banks today are small compared to their conventional counterparts, and the fact that they must provide a comprehensive range of Islamic financial products and services presents a formidable challenge due to constraints on capital, talent, and technology. Islamic banks need innovative approaches that are the result of bringing together their inherent knowledge of their customers, cultures, and markets, together with their ability to apply technology creatively to the delivery of banking services and the optimization of business processes within the institution.

During the past few years, Dow Jones has created 44 Islamic market indexes that track *Sharia*-compliant stocks in many global markets. To establish an Islamic market index, Dow Jones uses a methodology that first rejects companies that are incompatible with *Sharia* principles; next, a company may be excluded if it is deemed to have material ownership in or revenues from prohibited business activities. Finally, companies are subjected to three financial filters in which they must score ratios of less than 33 percent on each filter to qualify: total debt divided by trailing 12-month average market capitalization, the sum of the company's cash and

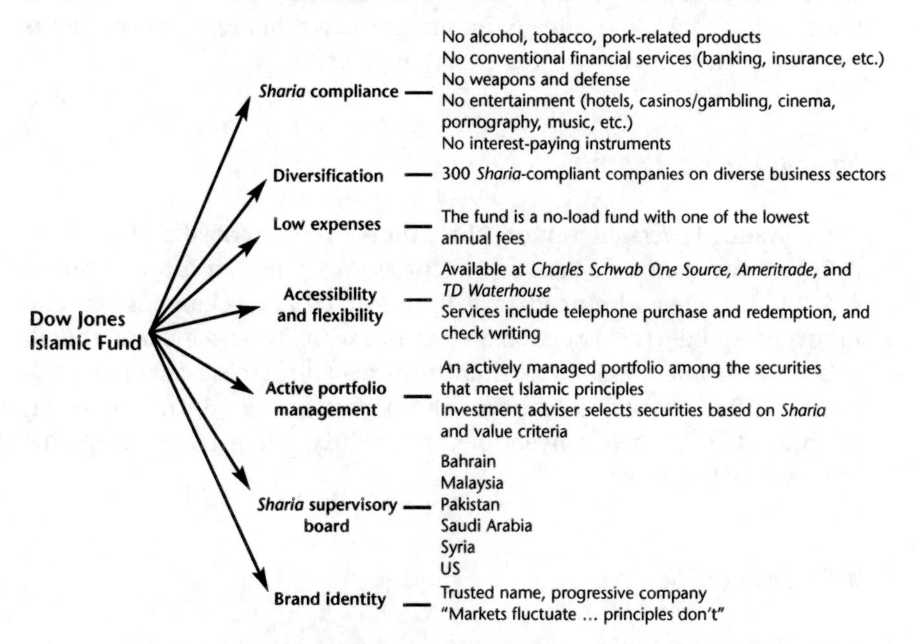

Figure 2.3 Dow Jones Islamic Fund's value proposition
Source: Adapted from Dow Jones Islamic Fund website

interest-bearing securities divided by the trailing 12-month average market capitalization, and accounts receivable divided by the trailing 12-month average market capitalization.[18] On a macro-market level, innovations such as the Dow Jones Islamic Fund (DJIF) are a prime example of blending knowledge and creativity not just to bring a product to market, but also to create an entirely new market.[19] The source of DJIF's success is a clear value proposition that can easily apply to both Muslims and non-Muslims, as illustrated in Figure 2.3.

Muslim banking customers have become more performance-oriented, demanding competitive *Sharia*-compliant financial products that are also competitively priced using efficient and convenient channels. Investors (Muslim and non-Muslim) are taking a more active role in directing their investments, and they are increasingly discerning and demanding a broader range of products and services. In the emerging global financial services market, innovation is the key market differentiator. Innovation for Islamic banks must occur on two distinctly different fronts: the applied use of technology for the delivery and performance of financial products, and the application of knowledge to the unique problems that Muslim customers face in all parts of the world. The new face of innovation takes many forms, occurring in so many Islamic financial services companies that they are too numerous to list here. However, there are a few that have a distinct value proposition which other Islamic institutions can learn, which is why we mention them here.

Bahrain Monetary Agency

The continued oversubscription (three times oversubscribed on January 2, 2006) of the Bahrain Monetary Agency's Al-Salam Government Sukuk (USD) is a strong indicator that financial markets are looking for new and innovative products.[20] Issued in accordance with *Sharia* standards, the Al-Salam Government Sukuk provides investors with a clear value proposition, offering a means to contrast the performance of *Sharia*-compliant instruments with their conventional banking counterparts by comparing the yield of 4.6 percent.[21]

iHilal Financial Services

Product innovations are not always purely technological in nature. Educating a customer to make an informed decision is a process that requires

Table 2.2 iHilal's Islamic investment criteria

Qualitative screen	Quantitative screen	Trading practices

Industry screen:
• Is the company in an industry prohibited in Islam? Examples of industries that are *haram* (or are necessarily involved in *haram* activities) include:
  • alcohol production
  • *riba*-based financial institutions
  • gambling
  • entertainment
Business practices:
• Is the company exploitative in its relationship with customers and suppliers or unethical in its trade practices?
	Debt/asset ratio:
	• Has the company borrowed funds on interest (whether fixed or floating)?
	• It is clear that there should ideally be no interest-based debt, but based on the Islamic legal principle "*li al-akthar hukm al-kul*" (to the majority goes the verdict of the whole) and subsequent scholarly opinions, a company is not a permissible investment if debt financing is more than 33% of its capital
	Interest-related income:
	• Does the company generate any interest or interest-related income?
	• This includes those companies who do not make earning interest their business, but place their surplus funds in investments that yield interest income
	• Ideally, no income should appear from interest-related sources
	• According to some scholars, however, up to 10% of a company's total income can be derived from interest sources
	Monetary assets:
	• Are substantial portions of the company's assets monetary?
	• Watch out for items such as accounts receivables and liquid assets such as bank accounts and marketable securities
	• Various minimums have been set for the ratio of illiquid assets (assets that are not in the form of money) necessary to make an investment permissible
	• Some set this minimum at 51% (again, according to the principle of "to the majority goes the verdict of the whole")
	• A few cite 33% as an acceptable ratio of illiquid assets to total assets
		• Investable funds must be free of interest-based debt
		• The investor cannot borrow on interest to finance his investments, and therefore cannot trade on margin, i.e., borrow to purchase shares
		• Conventional funds such as hedge funds, arbitrage funds, and leveraged buy-out (LBO) funds all borrow heavily in order to finance their investment practices, and they are therefore prohibited for Islamic investors
		Prohibition of speculation:
		• Unlike conventional investors, Muslims are prohibited from basing their investment decisions on short-term speculation
		• As a Muslim, the logic of sound analysis is paramount before making an investment decision
		• Trading is important and should be well timed to take advantage of market prices, but these considerations should go hand in hand with the fundamental value of the companies in which you invest

data, information, knowledge, and wisdom. To determine whether an investment is *halal* or *haram*, iHilal has developed a bi-level criterion for Islamic investments based on a qualitative and a quantitative screen, as illustrated in Table 2.2.

In the case of iHilal's Islamic investment criteria, investors are provided with three independent lenses through which to review an investment decision and learn how to interpret and exploit the results. The investment screening process enhances the element of trust and fiduciary responsibility in iHilal's customer value proposition. The formulaic approach to educating investors to *Sharia* compliance provides investors with confidence that the highest quality companies with a strong potential to deliver long-term value pass the test. Looking at the broad range of iHilal current and potential products in Figure 2.4, one can get a glimpse of what the future has in store for Islamic banking.

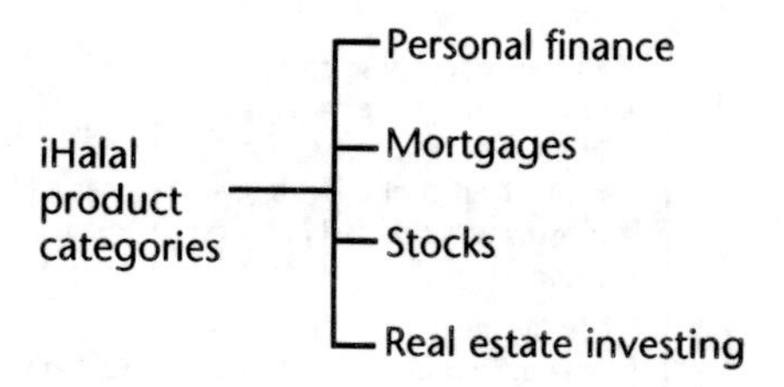

Figure 2.4 iHilal's product offerings[22]

Islamic Mortgages

The traditional concept of Islamic mortgage (based on *murabahah*) is simple: a customer finds a property that he or she would like to purchase. The bank assesses the customer's ability to pay just like a conventional mortgage. Next, the bank purchases the property and subsequently leases the property back to the customer over an agreed term. The customer in return makes monthly payments that consist of two distinct uses of funds: a rent payment for using a house they do not own, and a contribution toward the agreed purchase price of the property. For the duration of the agreement, the bank physically owns the property. When the term of the agreement has come and the customer has completed the final payment, the title to the property passes to the customer. The key point is that during the agreement, the customer is not paying interest. Within the interpretation of *Sharia* law, the price of the rent constitutes fair payment for use of the property rather than a charge for borrowing money.

While all this seems simple, Wilson contends that a growing number of Islamic mortgages are being based on *murabahah*, which is unsuitable for longer term financing because the major risk to the bank is associated with the sale, while the long-term debt burden sits with the home purchaser. Therefore, the risk involved in mortgage financing is not symmetrical, and it is certainly not equally shared.[23]

The problem of Islamic mortgages not charging interest, but rent, is obviously on the existence of fluctuating interest rates on traditional mortgages and inflation in all economies. Seen by some as "a rose with another name", this type of mortgage is, as all elements of Islamic banking, an offering based on an interpretation of Islamic law, and interpretations vary.

From this general understanding of Islamic mortgages, two central questions emerge. Why are Western banks now interested in providing this type of service? Will straightforward mortgages of this type appeal to the financing needs of non-Muslims?

Most societies have a contingent of Muslims living and working within their borders. In the twentieth century, the majority of banks (much to their own detriment) ignored the Muslim population's needs for banking services. Not placing a value on providing services to Muslims was not a result of racism or xenophobia; traditional Western banks did not see a clear way to offset the cost of providing banking products that were uniquely structured for compliance to Islamic law. The answer as to why Western banks are now interested in providing this type of service is simple: suddenly, in the twenty-first century, financial institutions that have been struggling to approach new markets have realized that over 1 billion Muslims do constitute a significant market. This, coupled with the fact that in order to achieve top-line growth objectives, banks must expand into new markets, has made offering *Sharia*-compliant mortgages an issue on the agenda, even if not, as yet, a top priority. The Muslim population in most countries represent a seemingly foreign market right in their own backyard. Providing services to this new market is less costly than attempting to establish branch operations in a foreign geography.

Will straightforward mortgages of this type appeal to the financing needs of non-Muslims? Like any other product, service, or commodity, if the value proposition for Islamic mortgages is strong, then people will buy it. Brand, price, convenience, and above all flexibility are all hallmarks of any value proposition and must be set at levels that compete head to head with non-Islamic financial products. To attract non-Muslims, the value proposition must be greater that a faith-based incentive. Mounting evidence suggests that the appeal to non-Muslims has been underestimated, as recently learned by HSBC Group when it found that over 50 percent of customers for its competitively priced Islamic mortgage product in Malaysia are non-Muslims.[24]

To understand how Islamic mortgages work inside and outside Islam, let us examine a few examples of market offerings.

Islamic Mortgages in the UK

According to the Halifax, the average house price in the UK in 2002 was £120,000, while annual income was just over £27,000. This disparity makes house financing necessary, especially in parts of England where the disparity is much higher than the four times average (being as high as house prices representing 15 times the annual salary in London and surrounding areas).

Until recently, the only bank in the UK to offer Islamic mortgages (the *murabahah* type) was the United Bank of Kuwait, now known as the Al-Ahli United Bank. The *murabahah* mortgage requires 20 percent payment upfront; having found a house, the family contacts the bank, who will then purchase the house and resell it at a higher price, which is determined by the original price of the property. A time schedule for repayment is agreed upon, and the monthly repayment that remains fixed for the life of the mortgage. The person can pay off the whole amount at any point. This option favors those with a certain sum saved toward the initial payment, and can be extended over 15 years. However, many Muslims and specialists in Islamic banking saw the *murabahah* scheme as one of hidden interest and therefore a sin within Islamic law. A second type of mortgage offered was the *ijarah*, whereby the buyer pays a smaller percentage of the total, and the amount to be paid every month is agreed on a yearly basis. The outstanding amount can also be paid off at any time. The difference between this type of mortgage and its counterpart is that in the *ijarah* mortgage, the lender becomes the owner and the buyer will become a leaser from the owner. The amount paid is taken against the total amount lent and contributes toward the purchase of the property. Again, ethical issues arose when people realized that the depreciation of the value of homes was a problem in some parts of England, and also that the ideas of "leasing" and "owning" are substantially different.

A third model of home financing was created in the UK, called "the diminishing partnership model". Originated in Canada and tested for many years by the Islamic Co-operative Housing Corporation Limited of Canada, the model was brought to the UK by Ansar Finance in Manchester through Ansar Housing. This company offers mortgages by extending a prequalification period in which each client purchases shares in the house financing organization in order to gain the right to apply for house financing at a later time. Funds raised by the organization are then used to finance other clients who have completed their prequalification periods. All investors become partners in the enterprise of buying each house (normally, two by two, so partner A and partner B would own the house). Prequalification shares are redeemed against the total cost of the house. While a person or family lives in the house, rent is paid, and distributed among the shareholders (including the family itself). Eventually, over years, the family or person buys all the other individuals' shares and becomes the owner of the house. In the end, a final payment is required to correct any unfairness in market fluctuation and ensure a just deal for all partners.

In 2003, HSBC became the first large multinational group to offer Islamic mortgages outside Islam to cater for Muslims living and working in the UK. With an estimated US$7.5 billion in gross advances to Islamic mortgages until 2006, HSBC is looking to facilitate the lifestyles of the Muslim community as well as tap into a market which, until very recently, was seen as completely closed to Western banks.[25] HSBC Islamic mortgages work by having the bank purchase a house and then lease it back to the individuals interested; repayment is not constituted as rent, but it is taken against the total debt over a period of 25 years (similar to a regular mortgage).[26] Since its creation, HSBC's *halal* mortgage has become a point of controversy among Muslims in the UK, who fear there may be hidden charges and interest and/or feel that if the mortgage deal is indeed as advertised, then it is unfair to non-Muslims, unless the same deal is offered to them.[27]

Philosophically arguable, the principle behind Islamic mortgages outside Islam is simple: people need to buy homes. Buying upfront is only for the very wealthy, so an alternative way that is not considered immoral had to be created. The company Mortgages.co.uk was one of the pioneers in offering mortgages that were not against *Sharia* principles. It specified that it offered two types of mortgage (both of which could be seen and quoted online): the *murabahah* and the *ijarah* mortgage.[28]

Mortgage brokers like Mortgages.co.uk and IslamicMortgages.co.uk offer direct connections to mortgage lenders in the UK including the

United National Bank (*ijarah* only), Al-Buraq-Lloyds TSB (diminishing *musharakah* and *ijarah*) and West Bromwich Building Society (through Ahli United) and, of course, Ahli United (*ijarah*) and HSBC Amanah (*ijarah*).[29] Another UK player, Halalmortgages.com was recently acquired by HalalFinancialServices.com, and it is an online *halal* mortgage provider dedicated to providing viable *Sharia* legitimate choices to UK Muslims who aspire to own their own homes or refinance existing conventional mortgages. It was the first website in the UK solely devoted to *halal* mortgages, presenting useful information and tools. Its role is to match clients with lenders, and ensure that they have access to the best possible *halal* mortgage deals. With the growing number of lending banks complying with *Sharia* principles, Halalmortgages offers a fair service, being associated with Ahli Bank, the United National Bank, and HSBC's Amanah Home Finance. Barclays, Standard Chartered, and Citibank are currently examining the feasibility of adding Islamic mortgages to their banking products. Citibank Malaysia is hoping to be the second in offering *halal* mortgages (both *murabahah* and *ijarah*) in that country, after HSBC successfully launched the product there in 2004. In Malaysia, the value proposition for Islamic mortgages was so compelling that over 50 percent of new mortgage deals are non-Muslim.[30]

Mortgages in Islamic Areas

The existence of mortgages in Islamic countries is new, as are credit cards. Many banks offer them, such as the Arab Bank plc, Dubai Islamic Bank, and the National Bank of Kuwait, which does charge interest. Banks face the issues of interest (*riba*) and *Sharia* regulations, but, as is common in Islamic banking, they prioritize serving the community by facilitating people's lives. In the United Arab Emirates (UAE), Amlak Finance is a known mortgage broker that offers *ijarah* mortgages, whereby buyers can borrow up to 90 percent of the cost of the house over a maximum of 25 years. It specifies that the maximum monthly repayment is 55 percent of a person's salary. Tamweel Home Finance, another mortgage broker, works with Dubai Islamic Bank and Istithmar to provide good mortgage deals, allowing borrowers a maximum of 70 percent of the value of their prospective house. Likewise, in 2004, Mashreqbank launched a number of new mortgage options, basing its marketing strategy on the success of the bank's home loan program, instituted years before. New products include remortgages for foreigners living in the UAE, and a market valuation service in partnership with the UK's Cluttons. Mashreqbank was one of the first to offer mortgage products in the UAE market, which is forecast to be worth US$200 billion by 2010 in the UAE alone.

After the introduction of the mortgage finance law in Egypt in 2001, Egypt's first private mortgage company, Egypt Housing Finance Corporation (EHFC), was created in the same year, jointly owned by the Egyptian American Bank (EAB), the International Financial Corporation, HDFC Investments Ltd (a subsidiary of Housing Development Finance Corporation Limited, India, and the Bank of Alexandria. EAB launched its first credit card in 2000, and saw the introduction of mortgages to its range of products and service offerings as an important step toward providing loans to the population.[31] In the Egyptian economy, where unemployment rates are high and poverty levels are increasing, mortgage solutions are seen as the only way to ensure that future generations will have a place to live, so a fundamental change in the mindset against borrowing money has to take place.

In Malaysia, the mortgage market is being highly coveted by Lloyds TSB and HSBC Amanah. One of HSBC's new products in Malaysia is the Takaful Mortgage Plus, a mortgage insurance whereby the borrower is insured against death or total permanent disability as well as being offered cash back in the end of the payment period. HSBC Amanah offers types of mortgages based on how much the individual wants to borrow, and repayment is flexible; interest is charged. Very few broker houses offer *halal* mortgages in the Malaysian market, but Lloyds is looking into having *halal* mortgages to appeal to the Muslim population in the country.

In Sudan, where Islamic fundamentalism forces banks to take *Sharia* principles in a more literal sense, mortgages are still a problem. Likewise in Indonesia, there has been resistance from the population, who see mortgages as riddled with hidden interest disguised as fees.

Bahrain's Bank of Bahrain and Kuwait (BBK) has recently launched a new mortgage loan for commercial and residential purposes. Similar to Western mortgages, BBK offers joint ownership mortgages, insurance, deferred payment and competitive interest rates. Mortgage loans are available to people of all nationalities resident in the area. As far as *halal* mortgages are concerned, Lloyds TSB has worked with Taib Bank to provide *Sharia*-compliant mortgages in the UK. The multinational bank is also looking to expand further into the Gulf area. In Saudi Arabia, big player HSBC Amanah is also looking to establish itself as a provider of *halal* mortgages.

The US is seeing an increased interest in *halal* products but growth is not expected to be as significant as in the UK. In Illinois, Devon Bank started selling its Islamic banking products (used to make purchases easier and less controversial to Muslims living in the region) to Freddie Mac, one of the nation's largest investors in mortgages and Islamic home financing products, in 2001. Freddie Mac has used *murabahah* mortgages for many years with a good acceptance rate. With 2.5 million Muslim households, the US is a fertile ground for Islamic banking products. In fact, since 2001, many new *halal* mortgages appeared in the US market as Islam followers immigrated into the US for many reasons whilst trying to keep their faith and morals intact.[32]

Islamic Credit and Debit Cards

Since the 1970s, when American Express launched the first credit card in the market, populations worldwide have been using plastic money to purchase goods and, in many cases, to get a loan not limited by time but by credit availability. In the past three decades, the world has found credit cards to be a very convenient method of payment, as they have reduced the need for cash and other identification (in the case of checks), also making international purchases and bookkeeping easier. The acceptance of credit cards as an electronic representation of money is analogous to the transition from gold and silver to paper documents that recorded and represented the transference of money or value during the Middle Ages. As Europeans engaged with Arab communities, they discovered that Arab commerce had advanced in certain areas beyond the means of what was then conventional commerce, as Arabs were using mechanisms similar to bills of exchange (*sutfaya*) and devised forward contracts (*mohatra*).[33]

Credit cards normally work in the following way: a merchant subscribes to a bank so as to have the system to accept credit cards. Customers pay by card, and part of their payment is transmitted to the bank as a charge (amounts vary between 1 percent and 7 percent). This, in turn, makes merchants' profit a percentage smaller, and they compensate by adjusting the price of their products, by simply absorbing the expense as a cost of doing business, or by justifying the expense by realizing the reduction in the cost of handling cash. Customers are normally happy to purchase goods using credit cards because they are a convenient preapproved loan. Credit card customers typically have three inherent behaviors: they pay off the balance at the end of the month; carry the debt into the next month and subsequently pay down the debt over the course of one to three months; or carry the debt, only making the minimum payments for months. In extreme cases, where a credit card user is immature in their knowledge of how to use credit cards as a financial tool, a cardholder will accumulate an amount of debt far greater than their ability to repay the original debt plus the growing amount of interest.

In straightforward terms, customers use credit cards for two distinctly different reasons: as a substitute for cash, or as a ready loan enabling them to purchase something, based on anticipating future funds to repay the loan. To provide these two services, credit card issuers and banks extend credit to customers, charge interest on balances, and in some cases charge an annual fee or other fees to cover their administrative costs. Muslim customers did not receive credit cards well in the past few decades. The primary reason could not be more obvious: *Sharia* principles forbid the charging of interest, and so credit card loans and balances are seen as inherently against *Sharia* principles. For Islamic banks, the implementation of credit cards under conventional standards posed another problem because instead of sharing risk, card issuers pass the burden of the liability of the transaction onto the merchant. Risk management adds yet another cost because on top of all the conventional costs of operating a credit card portfolio – such as credit scoring – transactions must be considered compliant to *Sharia* principles (an added layer of cost not incurred by conventional banks).

The legitimacy of using credit cards is a source of great debate among Islamic bankers, *Sharia* scholars, academics, and Muslim customers. The central question has been: is using a credit card prohibited (*haram*)? Islamic bankers are concerned about the implications of credit cards as a component in their overall value proposition, because credit cards themselves are a direct interface between Islamic finance and the global economy.

Sharia principles allow the use of credit cards, if the credit agreement permits the repayment without interest and cash withdrawals are free of any interest charge. Ancillary charges such as late fees may prohibit the use of the card if the charges are calculated on an interest basis. However, a flat fee basis for administrative processing charges may be considered permissible (*halal*). If the late fee is calculated on a percentage basis, it is a good indicator that the transaction is *riba*. Cards such as those issued by Diner's Club, to whom you must pay off the balance at the end of each month, might have a great appeal to Muslims. Shariffa Carlo Al-Andalusia, a preeminent *Sharia* scholar, has argued that using conventional credit cards in this way is still considered *haram* simply because the cardholder has signed an agreement whereby they would technically pay *riba* should the balance not be paid in full at the end of the repayment period. Under this scenario, a cardholder cannot know what the future will hold and whether circumstances would eventually result in the condition becoming true and *riba* being due.[34]

However, interest is only half the equation, as some *Sharia* scholars have said that a bank should not authorize transactions that originate in places or for purchases that would be *haram* such as nightclubs, liquor stores or gambling casinos. Again, regulations in Islam are more influential on people's lives than in Western society, and so credit cards have not been as well accepted from the start.

The Dilemma of the Global Economy

Although credit cards in Islamic banking have traditionally been seen as *haram*, the perception of what constitutes a credit card has changed in the past three years. Credit cards are now seen as a convenient way to make purchases internationally and on the internet, as well as a good way to reduce the circulating cash in the economy and by definition reduce the "underground economy". Further advantages and enhancements of credit cards, such as frequent flier miles, charitable donations, consumer and purchase protection are viewed by some scholars sometimes negatively and at other times positively. For the traveling Muslim, many services, such as US car rentals, do not allow other methods of payment, so sometimes credit cards are the only means available. At the nexus between Islamic finance and the global economy is the Muslim customer, who is burdened under the current financial environment with having to make moral and ethical choices on a daily basis, just to live in a multicultural world.

Today, many Islamic banks offer variations of credit cards that in turn correspond to the attitude and tolerance of interpretation by their *Sharia* scholars. Interest-free credit card pioneers Shamil Bank, ABC Islamic Bank, and the Dubai Islamic Bank have interpreted *Sharia* principles in a way that offers credit cards under the concept of providing customers with a financial guarantee based on their history, which is allowed under Islamic law.[35] Likewise, one of the earliest examples of an Islamic credit card was created by the AmBank in Malaysia in 2001, named Al-Taslif Credit Card, with installment repayments over a period. Interest rates are 15 percent per annum, but no interest is charged if the customer does not keep a balance. If the agreed repayment based on percentage is made, no interest is charged either. This card also allows charitable donations, as the purchaser collects points with every purchase on the credit card and points are used to offset the annual fee. Once the annual fee is paid, all points go to charity.

In 2002, Bank Islam Malaysia launched the Bank Islam Card, paying specific attention to omit the word "credit" in the card's name. As the first EMV-compliant card in Malaysia, Bank Islam marketed the card based on its value proposition as being fully *halal*, free of *riba* and *gharar* (uncertainty), disclosing the bank's maximum profit to customers upfront. The bank sought to attract 55,000 cardholders in its first year of offering, adding to the 3.6 million credit card holders in the country.[36] In order to ensure compliance with *Sharia*, the bank advised that it would decline payment to non-approved vendors and for immoral purchases, including bars, nightclubs, alcohol merchants, escort and massage services, gambling, and related activities.

Bahrain's first credit card, Shamil Bank's Al-Rubban MasterCard, was launched in 2002, avoiding *riba* but advertising the credit card as based on a financial guarantee. The cost elements in ensuring the guarantee are not, as the bank advised in its own interpretation of *Sharia* principles, against the law. The collateral is the credit card holder's salary deposit, which must be paid into the bank. Also in Bahrain, in 2002, the ABC Islamic Bank launched the Al-Buraq credit card, originally issued only to the bank's employees, and then made available to the public.[37]

In Saudi Arabia, the Al-Rahji Banking & Investment Corporation (ARABIC) was also a pioneer in offering *Sharia*-approved Visa and MasterCard. Dubai Islamic Bank, the first Islamic bank in the world, also offers a Visa charge card with up to 40 days interest-free credit and a guarantee of *Sharia* approval.[38] The National Bank of Sharjiah in the UAE also launched a Visa International credit card in 2004, requiring payment of a minimum of 10 percent of the balance. The gold and classic Visa cards offered by the National Bank of Sharjah present the same enhancements as other credit cards, such as emergency hotline, protection and insurance, and participation in promotional activities.

The Kuwait Finance House is one of the banks whose strategy to implement credit cards has been seen as most interesting. The Al-Tayseer ("ease the way") credit card uses the facility of taking payment for a fixed percentage of the remaining balance plus a flat fee (taken off the balance) for types of card varying between classic and gold card. The typical rate is 30 percent. Visa International and MasterCard have collaborated with the bank to offer a comprehensive credit card that is both Visa and MasterCard at one time, with a single joint credit limit, a single PIN, and a single joint monthly statement.[39] The "dual card, one account" system brings the advantages of offering customers the ability to make the most of offers to both Visa and MasterCard customers. To ensure that the minimum 30 percent is paid monthly, customers must either have their monthly income paid into the bank, or make a monthly fixed deposit. This credit scheme is based on a revolving credit system, as no interest is charged. The compliance to *Sharia* law is heavily advertised on the website, as is the idea of the Al-Tayseer card being the first "revolving credit card" in the Islamic market.

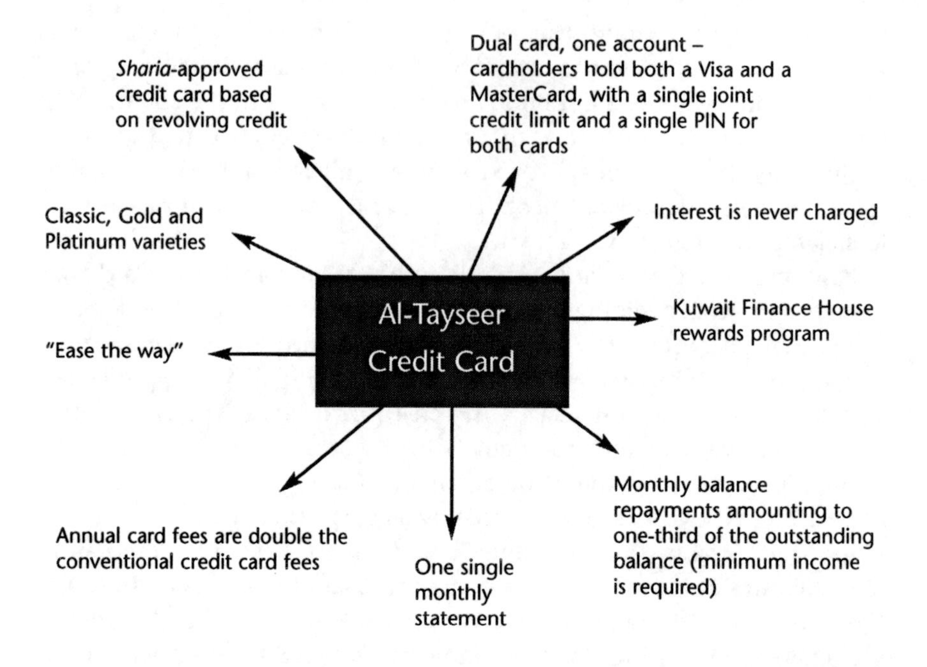

Figure 2.5 Kuwait Finance House Al-Tayseer credit card

In 2004, Standard Chartered Bank in Malaysia decided to overcome the low penetration of credit cards in the Malaysian market by focusing on the demographic group aged between 18 and 25. Standard Chartered is one of the top three issuers in the country, with 400,000 cards, and it is investing heavily in acquiring as customers young Malaysians between 18 and 25, who comprise 10 percent of the Malaysian population (50 percent of the Malaysian population being under 25 years of age).[40] Standard Chartered believes that its strategy will increase its market share by 12 percent by the end of 2005.

The key to Islamic credit cards, once the *Sharia* issues are resolved, is targeting the optimum demographic within society, much the same as a conventional bank. Throughout the Islamic financial community, one can observe companies such as Malaysia's MBF Cards, which launched its first Visa credit card "Gaia". Gaia Visa offers a package targeted at those who are concerned about ecological issues and personal health.[41] Anticipating an increase in the number of women entering the workforce, MBF Cards also launched the Lady Card and Lady Gold MasterCard, designed specifically to benefit women by providing insurance coverage for critical illnesses, a free women's health check-up program, discounts for shopping, beauty and fitness programs, cancer detection, shopping, travel, and children's education.[42]

In England, the Islamic Bank of Britain, which officially started business in 2005, plans to make one of its first market offerings a credit card, but this is not yet available on the market.

In 2004 and 2005 alone, the number of card offerings with *Sharia* law compliance increased dramatically. The Emirates Islamic Bank now offers three types of Visa card with different quarterly fees (blue, gold, and platinum) and an assurance of compliance to Islamic law. Likewise, the Finance House in the UAE has also launched a MasterCard product that will be free for life and offers cash back on certain approved purchases, plus a credit limit up to three times an individual's salary and up to 60 days interest-free credit. The card offers existing customers 1 percent of the total amount spent on the new cards they help to introduce. In Qatar, American Express is launching the first chip card which enables customers to store information such as favorite websites and address book on their credit card. After many years of rejecting the card payment system, Egypt's Calyon Bank's Rotary Visa credit card brings a particular affinity, in that 0.5 percent of amounts paid will be donated to Egypt's Rotary charitable activities and projects. The card features the latest smart card technology.

Surprisingly, for a group of nations that still has problems accepting credit cards at all, one of the most important issues in the local press relating to Islamic credit cards is the EMV compliance issue. Not only does the press – and the banks – emphasize the security factors associated with the use of chip and PIN, but they also show that security alone is not the problem for Muslim customers. The fact that their purchases define their credit rating on a personal level, as many goods and services are simply not allowed and transactions will even be declined by the bank, makes it extremely important that a Muslim's credit card is not stolen and used for immoral purposes.

Visa announced that between March 2003 and March 2004, an average of 730,000 purchases were made by Visa in the GCC (Gulf Cooperation Council) area. This represented 30 percent growth over the previous 12-month period. Saudi Arabia was one of the countries which saw the highest growth rate of Visa usage. In Turkey, consumer credit card spending reached US$25 billions in 2004, with credit card spending being 109 percent higher than a year before. In Lebanon, the number of credit cards grew 33 percent between 1998 and 2005. In the UAE, the credit card market is reported to be growing at a 25 percent annual rate, with 1.5 million credit cards in use in a population of 4.5 million. These figures obviously represent a growing trend and the success of credit cards in Islamic areas.

Revenues, Fees, and Offsetting Cost

To Western bankers, the aforementioned scenario of cards operating without interest does not appear to be profitable. Membership fees provide a source of revenue but fall short of covering operating overheads. The enhanced debit card approach provides an easy way to comply with *Sharia* principles, but leaves few opportunities to generate significant income for the card issuer. However, cards that act like a debit card or prepaid card cater to specific elements of the Islamic banking value proposition, as demonstrated by National Commercial Bank (NCB) of Saudi Arabia's Advance Card, which substitutes a prepaid line for a line of credit, thereby avoiding interest altogether.[43] As a fully *Sharia*-compliant card, NCB's Advance Card provides the consumer with all the same features as credit cards such as purchase protection and travel accident insurance but with no interest charged or extra fees. An additional aspect of this card that mirrors consumer behavior in the West is its appeal to women, young people, self-employed and small establishment employees, who sometimes do not meet the strict requirements of conventional credit card issuers.

Islamic banks will continue to experiment, adapt, and construct new card-based products to comply with *Sharia* principles under Asian or Gulf interpretations. The second area of concern over credit cards is how they are used to facilitate purchases and whether the goods purchased are prohibited, making the transaction *haram*. Prof. Dr. Mohd Ma'sum Billah observers that: "It is sad to see that many marketing strategies for Islamic credit cards talked about product features rather than selling the ethical values and concept underneath to the consumers."[44] The key point is that what determines the legitimacy of the use of a credit card is in the hands of the user, who decides whether to violate the conditions, thus making its use *haram*, or chooses to keep credit card use *halal*.

Fatwas in the Twenty-first Century

One of the more exciting aspects of Islamic finance in the twenty-first century is the use of mass communications technology to propagate the Islamic value proposition. *Fatwas* are legal rulings from *Sharia* scholars based upon the *Qur'an* and the *Sunnah*, passed by a scholar in response to a question. *Fatwas* are one element of the Islamic banking value proposition that does not have a Western counterpart. *Fatwas* establish the basis of Islamic financial behavior, similar in one way to Western regulatory and legal frameworks, dissimilar in that they are proactive whereas Western society is more reactive. The proactive nature of *fatwas* is based on seeking the answer before the transaction.

The advent of the internet has created a new ready source of scholarship for the Muslim ummah (the world community of Islam) in the form of online *fatwas*. In Bunt's view, the internet provides new ways for Muslims to approach traditional bodies of knowledge, and organizations that supply Islamic resources have the potential to reinforce or challenge the conventional pattern of understanding.[45] The more interesting aspect of online *fatwas* in a banking context is that posting the scholarship and ruling of the bank's *Sharia* committee may be an effective marketing tool. A comprehensive body of knowledge on how an institution's products comply with *Sharia* principles is an integral part of the bank's brand identity, similar to products in the US during the 1970s that received the "Good Housekeeping" seal of approval. As centers of Islamic jurispru-

Table 2.3 IslamOnline's database of *fatwa* rulings

• Selling alcohol in a non-Muslim country • Working for a real estate company • Guide for righteous merchants • Interest on one's account • IFA's resolution on allocating investment return • Working for a post office dealing with interest • Disability insurance • A translator helping others to get interest loans • Insuring houses and shops in India • Insuring mosques in the West • Buying and selling undeveloped residential plots • Can a car loan be Islamically justified for necessary needs? • A Muslim is faithful with all people • Investing endowment money to help orphans • What to do with bank interest?	• Running an internet café • A wife supporting her straitened husband • Being a credit card sales executive for a bank • Loans in non-Muslim countries • Purchasing houses with usurious loans in the West • Social welfare in a non-Muslim country • Offering financial consultation • Using special insurance companies to secure a pension • Personal property and its protection in Islam • Taking a student loan in the eyes of *Sharia* • Buying shares of privatized firms • Posthumous promotion • IT job for a bank • How does *Sharia* view insurance? • Working for commercial insurance companies

dence begin to review *Sharia* principles in totality across the world, one can speculate that in the future, Islamic banking authorities might establish levels of certification or affinity. Certification can be structured within degrees of compliance against the evolving international or regional *Sharia* standards. Affinity might be constructed around specific scholars and schools of thought. Short of acting as a source of authenticity, any mechanism that is established raises the level of customer confidence in the institution's fidelity as a financial intermediary.

Fatwas are not limited to financial matters or banking; they are issued across the entirety of Muslim social behavior, as illustrated in Table 2.3 of *fatwa* rulings at IslamOnline.net.[46]

Online *fatwas* and access to Islamic scholars are growing at an unprecedented rate as a result of the low cost of entry provided by the internet. The diversity of viewpoints resident on the internet on one hand demonstrates the wide appeal of Islam as an aggregator of Islamic thought, while on the other hand, the wide spectrum of perspectives also acts to confuse customers. Therefore, one of the key issues for Islamic banks is to use online *fatwas* and other scholarly rulings as an element in their strategy, mechanisms to educate their customers, and reinforce brand identity. There are numerous examples of methods, mechanisms, features and functions that an Islamic bank may use to apply technology-enabled *fatwas* to their value proposition to customers. For example, an organization such as IslamOnline.com offers simple online access to *fatwas*.[47] Fatwa-Online publishes FatwaBase, a searchable eBook, along with audio tapes.[48] A more formal systemized approach can be found at Ask-Imam.com (Figure 2.6), where an answer (or ruling) is subsequently approved by another Islamic scholar and both the answer and the approval are presented online.

Fatwa rulings can be an important part of a bank's value proposition as they enable customers to see how the institution is complying to *Sharia* principles. Websites such as Muslim-Investor.com have detailed biographies of Islamic scholars who answer questions online detailing their qualifications and publications.[49]

Although the diversity of ruling can be considered the strength of the Islamic value proposition for banks, the lack of standardization can also confuse customers who may not be as knowledgeable in matters of *Sharia* principles. We can argue that *fatwas* could be categorized into topics and degrees of severity, codified and analysed to assess the similarity and differences across a wide scholarly base. The resulting amalgam of *Sharia* thought could be then synthesized into a set of broad guidelines that establish the boundaries of financial behavior and the fundamentals of basic financial knowledge for customers. Inside the boundaries of global

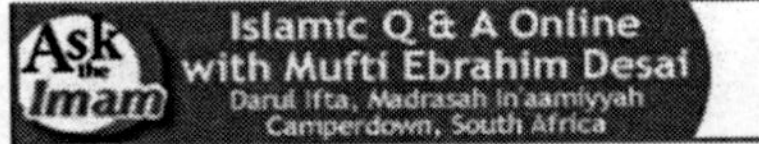

Islamic Q & A Online
with Mufti Ebrahim Desai
Darul Ifta, Madrasah In'aamiyyah
Camperdown, South Africa

بسم الله الرحمن الرحيم

Ask-Imam.com > Money Matters > Question 14471 from United States

Previous

Is a 401k plan haram?

I am working in USA and our employer offers retirement plan in which a set amount of money is taken away from my pay each check before taxes.This gives the following benefits to me: 1)since my taxable income becomes less,I save a significant amount of taxes to govt 2)employer contributes a certain percentage(depends on what I deposit from my pay check) to this account,which is a financial benefit to me from my employer 3)when I am eligible to receive this money back at the time of my retirement,I pay less taxes as I am retired then the problem is that this money is managed by specific firms who invest it in mutual funds and stocks which include banks and other interest-giving companies.We do have option of selecting the "groups of companies" to invest but we do not have a control on selection of companies individually.The "groups of companies" usually include at least some like banks,etc and it is usually quite difficult to know the exact business of the companies .The other option is to keep money in cash but I get interest on cash. It is not mandatory to take retirement plan please advice

Answer 14471 2005-08-31

The money you contribute as well as the amount your employer contributed to this fund is Halaal for you.

However, the returns derived from the investments you mention are at least doubtful and partially Haraam. Hence, the best is to abstain from such investments. Alternatively, you should search for an investment portfolio that is Shari'ah compliant even if the portfolio is managed by non-Muslims.

and Allah Ta'ala Knows Best

Mufti Muhammad Kadwa
FATWA DEPT.

CHECKED AND APPROVED: Mufti Ebrahim Desai

random
View random fatwa
email
Tell a friend
print
Printable Copy
search
Search Q & A's
view
View Q & A's
ask
Ask a Question

Figure 2.6 Ask-Imam.com – online *fatwas*

Sharia thinking is the framework for individual interpretations by Islamic scholars. One of the pioneers in aggregating global *fatwa* knowledge is the European Council for Fatwa Research, formed to attempt to achieve the following aims and objectives:

- Achieving proximity in bringing together the scholars who live in Europe, and attempting to unify the jurisprudence views between them in regard with the main *fiqh* issues.
- Issuing collective *fatwas* that meet the needs of Muslims in Europe, solve their problems and regulate their interactions with European communities all within the regulation and objectives of *Sharia*.
- Publishing legal studies and research, which resolve the arising issues in Europe in a manner which realizes the objectives of *Sharia* and the interest of the people.
- Guiding Muslims in Europe generally and those working for Islam particularly, through spreading the proper Islamic concepts and decisive legal *fatwas*.[50]

Developing standards and the application of *Sharia*-based practices on a global scale is the subject of Chapter 5, which examines the various organizations collaborating and competing to be recognized as a prime source of *Sharia* knowledge. The diversity of interpretations in *Sharia* principles is a characteristic of how the value proposition of Islamic banking is readily adaptable to the needs of the vast numbers of communities served by Islamic banks. The variations in *Sharia* interpretation are a reflection of the customs, cultural idiosyncrasies and social monetary behavior, such as a saving society versus a consumption society, in a local geography. The adaptive nature of how *Sharia* principles are applied to banking products and services in all parts of the world act as a foundation for Islamic banks to learn from, as they innovate new products and services, to which we now turn.

Notes

1 El-Gamal, Mahmoud A. *Can Islamic Banking Survive? A Micro-evolutionary Perspective*, Madison: University of Wisconson, 1997, p. 14, available at http://vlib.unitarklj1.edu.my/pdf/islambank4.pdf.

2 Siddiqi, Dr. Muhammad Nejatullah, Islamic Finance & Beyond: Premises and Promises of Islamic Economics, Harvard University Forum on Islamic Finance, Islamic Finance: Challenges and Global Opportunities, Cambridge, MA, October 1 and 2, 1999, conference paper.

3 Modaraba Association of Pakistan, October, 2005, available at http://www.modarabas.com/html/objectives.htm.

4 Grameen Bank, available at http://www.grameen-info.org/bank/index.html.

5 *Informal Funds Transfer Systems in the APEC Region: Initial Findings and a Framework for Further Analysis*, APEC ARS Working Group Report, September 5, 2003, p. 3.

6 Skinner, Chris, Faith in Banking, *Finextra*, August 2, 2005, available at http://www.finextra.com/fullfeature.asp?id=645.

7 Passas, Nikos *Halawa and Other Informal Value Transfer Systems: How to Regulate Them?*, United States Department of State: International Information Program, available at http://usinfo.state.gov/eap/Archive_Index/Halawa_and_Other_Informal_Value_Transfer_Systems_How_to_Regulate_Them.html.

8 Mangi, Naween, and O'Connell, Patricia (ed), Pakistan Cripples the Money Movers, *BusinessWeek Online*, January 31, 2002, available at http://www.businessweek.com/bwdaily/dnflash/jan2002/nf20020131_6995.htm.

9 Triennial Central Bank Survey, Bank for International Settlements, March 2005, available at http://www.bis.org/publ/rpfx05t.pdf.

10 Visa U.S.A., Welcome and Catuity Unveil Network-Independent Rewards Technology, VISA International, CARTES, PARIS, November 5, 2002, available at http://usa.visa.com/about_visa/newsroom/press_releases/nr138.html.

11 El-Qorchi, Mohammed *Halawa, Finance & Development*, International Monetary Fund, December 2002, **39**(4), available at http://www.imf.org/external/pubs/ft/fandd/2002/12/elqorchi.htm.

12 Aziz, Zeti Akhtar, Governor's Speech at the Launching of Hong Leong Islamic Bank Berhad – Fostering Leadership Role in Islamic Finance, Kuala Lumpur, 19 July 2005, available at http://www.bnm.gov.my/index.php?ch=9&pg=15&ac=180.

13 Rice, Gillian and Mahmoud, Essam *Integrating Quality Management, Creativity and Innovation in Islamic Banks*, American Finance House: Lariba 8th Annual International Conference, Pasadena, California, June 16, 2001, p. 8.

14 Rice, Gillian and Mahmoud, Essam *Integrating Quality Management, Creativity and Innovation in Islamic Banks*, American Finance House: Lariba 8th Annual International Conference, Pasadena, California, June 16, 2001, p. 9.

15 Kahf, Monzer, Ahmad, Ausaf, and Homud, Sami, Islamic Banking and Development – an Alternative Banking Concept?, 1998, available at http://monzer.kahf.com/papers/english/Isbnkand%20dev%20alternative%20banking%20concept.pdf.

16 FTSEGood Index Criteria available at http://www.ftse.com/Indices/FTSE4Good_Index_Series/Downloads/inclusion_criteria.pdf.

17 Envocare, Ethical Fund Managers *Banks and Building Societies*, December 5, 2005 available at http://www.envocare.co.uk/ethical_fund_managers.htm.

18 Dow Jones Indexes, Methodology Overview, November 2005, available at http://djindexes.com/mdsidx/index.cfm?event=showIslamicMethod.

19 Dow Jones Islamic Fund, December 2005, available at http://www.investaaa.com/.

20 Sukuk Al-Salam bonds fully subscribed, press release, Bahrain Monetary Agency, January 2, 2006, available at http://www.bma.gov.bh/cmsrule/index.jsp?action=article&ID=1691.

21 Government Securities, Bahrain Monetary Agency, November 2005 available at http://www.bma.gov.bh/cmsrule/index.jsp?action=article&ID=931.

22 Hilal Corporate Profile, Hilal Financial Services, November, 2005, available at http://www.ihilal.com/iHilalCorporateProfile.pdf.

23 Wilson, Rodney *Standardising Islamic Financial Products*, International Organisation of Securities Commissions, IOSCO Task Force on Islamic Capital Market Meeting, February 16, 2003, available at http://www.sc.com.my/eng/html/iaffairs/ioscoislamicpdf/Standardising.pdf.

24 Islamic Banks: A Novelty No Longer, International Finance, *BusinessWeek Online*, August 8, 2005, available at http://www.businessweek.com/magazine/content/05_32/b3946141_mz035.htm.

25 High Street bank offers Islamic mortgage, BBC News, 1 July, 2003, available at http://news.bbc.co.uk/1/hi/business/3035292.stm.

26 HSBC Offers Islamic Mortgage, Current Accounts, IslamOnline, July 8, 2003, available at http://www.islamonline.net/English/News/2003-07/08/article05.shtml.

27 Fanning, David, Changing times for Islamic mortgages?, *Financial Services Review*, Association of Chartered Certified Accountants, Issue 68, October 2003, available at http://www.accaglobal.com/publications/fsr/68/1016745.

28 Islamic Mortgages, Financial Services Net Ltd, available at http://www.mortgages.co.uk/islamic-mortgage.html.

29 Who Provides What?, IslamicMortgages.co.uk, November, 2005, available at http://www.islamicmortgages.co.uk/whoprovideswhat.html.

30 Banking on Faith, AsiaInc, August 2005, available at http://www.asia-inc.com/August05/Fea_banking_aug.htm.

31 Launching of Egypt's First Private Mortgage Co., German-Arab Chamber of Industry and Commerce, November, 2005, available at http://www.ahkmena.com/Details.aspx?News=825.

32 Sachs, Susan, Pursuing an American Dream While Following the Quran, *New York Times Online*, July 5, 2001, available at http://www.islamfortoday.com/americandream.htm.

33 Dibooglu, Selahattin, On Commerce, Institutions and Underdevelopment: A Comparative Perspective, *Knowledge, Technology and Policy*, Winter 2003, **15**(4), p. 12.

34 Can a credit card ever be Halal?, *Banker Middle East*, **33**, March 2003, available at http://www.bankerme.com/bme/2003/mar/islamic_banking.asp.

35 The best of both worlds, *Banker Middle East*, **40**, October 2003, available at http://www.bankerme.com/bme/2003/oct/islamic_banking.asp.

36 Mahmood, Kazi, Malaysian Bank Launches First Islamic Credit Card in Asia, IslamOnline.net, July 25, 2002, available at http://www.islamonline.net/English/News/2002-07/25/article06.shtml.

37 Can a credit card ever be Halal?, *Banker Middle East*, **33**, March 2003, available at http://www.bankerme.com/bme/2003/mar/islamic_banking.asp.

38 Jackson, Wendy, Islamic finance: unlocking the potential, *MoneyWorks*, January 2004, http://www.getyourmoneyworking.com/2004/JAN/03/Learn_About/Islamic_Finance/D040103967.html.

39 Al-Tayseer Credit Card, Kuwait Finance House, December, 2005, available at http://www.kfh.com/english/Promotions/M-card-details/Tayseer/p1.htm.

40 Standard Chartered to Grow Credit Card Base, Kuala Lumpur: Titanium Alliance Sdn Bhd, December 31, 2004, available at http://www.aspire.com.my/market/news%200412.htm.

41 Account Update, *The Asian Banker*, August 4, 2003, available at http://ww.theasianbanker.com.

42 MBF bullish on upgraded Lady Card, Kuala Lumpur: Titanium Alliance Sdn Bhd, December 24, 2004, available at http://www.aspire.com.my/market/news%200412.htm.

43 Advance Card, National Commercial Bank, Saudi Arabia, available at http://www.alahli.com.sa/personalbanking/advancecard.asp.

44 Ma'sum Billah, Prof. Dr. Mohd *Islamic Credit Card in Practice, Takaful Islamic Insurance*, International Cooperative Mutual Insurance Federation (ICMIF), http://www.icmif.org/2k4takaful/site/documents/Islamic%20Credit%20Card.doc.

45 Bunt, Gary R. *Islam in the Digital Age: E-Jihad, Online Fatwas and Cyber Islamic Environments*, London: Pluto Press, July 2003.

46 Fatwa Bank: 2005 rulings from online queries, *IslamOnline*, December 2005, available at http://www.islamonline.net.

47 IslamOnline, Aljazeera Publishing, available at http://www.islamonline.com.

48 Fatwa-Online, http://www.fatwa-online.com/downloads/dow004/index.htm.

49 Scholar Answers, *Muslim Investor*, July 2005, available at http://muslim-investor.com/scholar-answers.

50 Altikriti, Anas Osama (translator) *First Collection of Fatwas*, Dublin: European Council for Fatwa Research, 1998, available at http://www.e-cfr.org/PDF/eng/Fatwa/Fatwa_e01.pdf.

3

GLOBAL VARIATIONS

The primary focus of this chapter is to show how Islamic banks – unlike their Western counterparts – are actively engaged in shaping the socioeconomic environments in which they operate. Extending their services beyond basic retail offerings, Islamic banks in various nation states provide services designed not to generate fee income per se, but rather to better the lives of their customers by applying innovation in new ways. From micro-finance programs to migrant remittances, Islamic banks in emerging economies are working to redefine existing relationships between customers, competitors, central banks, and policy makers. Typically lacking the financial capital that Western institutions enjoy, Islamic banks in these regions work harder, longer and with greater perseverance than their conventional banking counterparts. The nature of their economic condition is a seedbed for creativity and innovation as they demonstrate repeatedly that necessity is the mother of invention.

The social factors, unique economic conditions, cultural acceptance of products, and various religious prohibitions that are indigenous to a specific geographic region are more numerous than the current range of banking products and services. Collectively, these factors, conditions, acceptances, and prohibitions reflect the fabric of the community at large. Within the community, there are obvious subgroups with different needs or variations in the degree of need. Each subgroup represents an opportunity for a financial institution to supply an exclusive set of services. However, each highly customized set of services represents an increasingly higher cost to the institution. Therefore, Islamic financial services must have two distinctly different strategies to approach these markets: a quest for similarity, and a mechanism to mass customize products and services.

A Quest for Similarity

All financial institutions strive to optimize their cost of operations. Business line managers, together with their counterparts in the information technology (IT) group, work together to bring new technology aimed at reducing the process of banking or increasing the organization's throughput continually. Naturally, the greater the similarities in business process, products, and services, the lower the cost of service delivery and product development. Therefore, all banks endeavor to reach a one-size-fits-all solution. At a banking conference in Europe in 2005, a young technology specialist employed by a major US bank commented on the fact that banking systems would be a lot easier to develop and maintain if customers were not so demanding. In his words, he summarized an IT misconception about customers: "After all, it's only debit and credits, so why can't all customers simply bank the same way, it would be a lot cheaper for them if they would settle for what packaged software offers." An appropriate reply might be, why do people need so many model/style/color cars, why so many choices? The answer is obvious, because customers are people who are also consumers, who want to feel that what they are buying is unique for them. In banking, the need for services to fit specific lifestyles is increasing as the world becomes more interconnected. That said, there is an underlying level of standard services that is applicable to a vast majority of demographic profiles and socioeconomic subgroups. To compete against larger or global institutions, smaller banks need to develop a collaborative strategy on services that are similar or more standardized to reduce their operating cost. For example, banks within a region can collaborate on non-competitive services such as consolidating card processes, which is a generic service that customers rarely understand or even know exists.

A Mechanism to Mass Customize

To differentiate themselves in the global marketplace, Islamic banks must become experts in market micro-segmentation. Tailoring the various elements of their value proposition to resonate with the needs, wants, and desires of people within demographic subgroups is a fundamental skill that many banks have yet to master. New technological innovations, such as the intelligent ATM machine that links with the bank's customer relationship management (CRM) system to provide a unique experience for each customer by tailoring products and services to the individual customer's needs, are a huge advance toward banking that focuses on lifestyles.

Strategy

To capitalize on the similarities and variations in the Islamic banking value proposition, Islamic banks have three distinct strategic options: cost leadership, market differentiation, and micro-segmentation.[1] Cost leadership centers on lowering operating costs to become the low-cost provider, thereby competing purely on price. In the case of SMEs, this option can only be achieved through collaboration or co-opetition with other banks to consolidate technology investment and reach sufficient transaction volume to lower the per transaction cost. Market differentiation focuses on identifying specific perceived differences in the product offering, and augmenting these differences so that they become the customer's choice. A micro-segmentation strategy identifies clearly defined market subsegments, harnessing resources to excel at providing exceptional service to these customers.

The Elements of the Global Variations

What we will see in this chapter is a small sample of the variety of organizations, each enabling Islamic banking in a unique way to either strive toward similarity or make the most of cultural differences in how *Sharia* principles are applied to their customers. Within the context of how these two factors influence the Islamic value proposition, one can clearly distinguish that under *Sharia* principles, there is a set of core values in the Islamic banking value proposition that is similar and applicable to all Muslims. The intrinsic value of these shared values can be embedded in a financial product that can also be appreciated by non-Muslims, such as buying a house and securing financing. The set of values holds the key to establishing a basic construct to standardized global practices. One of the main problems in the Islamic banking value proposition on a global scale is the lack of standardization, discussed in detail in Chapter 5. The second part of the value proposition centers on what issues are cultural variations, such as what constitutes *haram* and *halal*. Combining the similar aspects of *Sharia* principles with the various aspects of cultural interpretation gives Islamic banking sufficient flexibility to make possible a wide degree of mass customization. The degree of variation in the interpretation of applied *Sharia* principles can be set across a spectrum, from fundamentalism to liberalism.

United Kingdom: Islamic Bank of Britain

One of the most significant examples of the need for banking and financial services that can be used by Muslims under *Sharia* principles is the creation of the UK's Islamic Bank of Britain (IBB). Having opened its doors in 2004, the Islamic Bank of Britain caters for both Muslims and non-Muslims, providing banking services that are compliant to *Sharia* principles. The Islamic Bank of Britain brings the latest technology, delivery channels, and management systems to serve Muslims in a way that is efficient and not against their faith. The uniqueness of the Islamic Bank of Britain's start in Britain is that it is the first European bank to offer Islamic banking that is *Sharia*-approved. However, in order to do this something quite extraordinary had to happen: British banking laws had to be changed. So as to provide *murabahah* mortgages that do not violate the Islamic faith and offer *Sharia*-compliant savings, the bank had to work with the Financial Services Authority (FSA) and other government agencies to amend British banking laws to gain authorization to operate in the UK.

As said before, the fact that money itself has no intrinsic value in the Islamic faith has made Islamic finance a complex issue for Westerners to understand. Only legitimate trade and investment in assets are allowed, so that money can be made in a proactive way and used in a productive way. The principal means of Islamic finance are based on trading. It is essential that a shared risk should be involved in any trading activity. Any gains relating to the trading are also shared between the person providing the capital and the person providing the expertise. In order to demonstrate its degree of trustworthiness to customers, the Islamic Bank of Britain defines its value proposition in a way that communicates the high degree of fidelity it aspires to as a financial intermediary, stating that its main values are faith, value, convenience, and trust (Figure 3.1).

The idea of creating a *Sharia*-compliant bank in the UK was conceived in 2002, when several Middle Eastern bankers, who today form the non-executive board of directors of the Islamic Bank of Britain, saw the need for a stand-alone Islamic bank in the UK to cater for the 1.8 million Muslims in England and Scotland. The Islamic House of Britain was then formed in 2002, and it appointed consultants and advisers who carried out an initial feasibility study and confirmed that a *Sharia*-compliant bank was indeed needed and even welcomed by the FSA, the UK's banking regulator. Key potential investors in the Gulf were invited, and they put together a private placement document, enabling the Islamic House of Britain to raise US$25

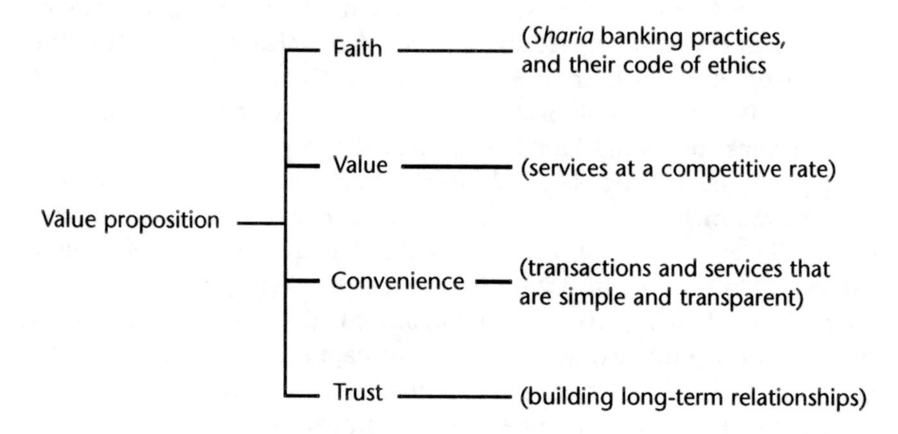

Figure 3.1 Islamic Bank of Britain's value proposition

million in start-up capital. To achieve FSA authorization, the Islamic House of Britain – changing into a bank with a bank's brand name – had to solve a number of initial regulatory issues. For example, Islamic savings based on the principle of profit and loss do not guarantee the depositor's capital; this was not consistent with UK principles regarding bank deposits. The solution was to develop layers of protection for depositors by offering to compensate the customer on any capital loss; when the bank needs to make a capital payment to offset the loss, customers can choose to accept or decline the offer. Other issues centered on problems such as business taxation, value added tax (VAT), the Sale of Goods Act and stamp duty on mortgage transactions. In August 2004, the FSA granted its authorization and the Islamic Bank of Britain, the first purely Islamic bank in the UK, came into being.

The bank's strategy is initially simple: attract Muslims who, until then, had to belong to unbanked sectors or violate their faith by using traditional banking. Once these customers have joined the bank, the second part of the Islamic Bank of Britain's strategy becomes more interesting: how to attract customers, Muslims or not, away from conventional banks and/or people with no commercial banking relationship? Sophisticated early adopters were easily attracted, although they were not simply migrating on faith alone; competitive pricing played a big part in the decision-making process. In the customer attraction and migration strategy, a subsegment of Muslims was aware of their faith's requirements in financial practices in theory, but was unfamiliar with the level of compliance to *Sharia* principles of the members of the Islamic Bank of Britain's *Sharia* board. To attract sufficient numbers of these people, the bank needed to build trust between its own image and brand and the potential customers. To do this, the Islamic Bank of Britain embarked on a program of customer education by visiting mosques and developing a dialogue with local *imams*, who customers regularly turned to for guidance. The Islamic Bank of Britain states its own interpretation of *Sharia* principles on its website:

SHARIA-COMPLIANT BANKING – BACKGROUND

Under Islamic principles:

- All money must be invested in purely ethical industries – so Islamic Bank of Britain will not invest in businesses dealing with interest, tobacco, alcohol, pornography, etc.
- The giving or receiving of interest is forbidden
- Money cannot be simply traded for money
- Money can be used to buy goods or services, which can then be sold for a profit.

For example, in an interest-based bank, when a customer is granted a loan, interest is charged on the use of that money. The Islamic Bank of Britain will not lend money but will deal in real items. So if a customer wants to buy a computer, the Bank would buy the computer and then sell it to the customer at a fixed price, or lease it to the customer and charge a rental fee until the item is fully paid for by the customer.'[2]

In early 2005, the bank also launched its "*halal* personal finance" product, a *Sharia*-compliant personal "loan" facility, making it the only provider of *halal* unsecured finance in the UK. The new unsecured loan facility allows customers to generate cash funds between US$1,700 and US$36,000, using *murabahah* with deferred payments. The result is that consumers are offered a financial facility of a non-interest-based loan in accordance with the Muslim faith, in which the use of interest is forbidden.

The principle behind the Islamic Bank of Britain's *halal* unsecured finance should be familiar to Islamic bankers worldwide: the bank buys commodities and then sells them to the customer for the cost plus the bank's profit. The customer then becomes the owner of the commodities. An independent agent (a broker) then sells the commodities on the customer's behalf for the market price and deposits the resulting cash into the customer's account for the customer to use to finance their purchase. The customer then pays the bank in monthly installments over a period

(12–60 months in this case). This new service is much needed by Britain's 1.8 million Muslims, who up to 2004 had no FSA-approved way to receive financing without violating their faith.

Another aspect of the Islamic Bank of Britain's range of services is the offer of special services to *masjids* and *madrasahs*. *Masjids* and *madrasahs* are extended free *Sharia*-compliant banking which allows them to earn profit on their funds for the first time in UK history. Because *Sharia* principles state that interest is *haram* (forbidden) and that wealth can only be generated through legitimate trade and the creation of assets, until then British *masjids* and *madrasahs* found it difficult to use banking products and services without going against their religious principles. In the Islamic Bank of Britain, however, *masjids* and *madrasahs* can place their funds in *Sharia*-compliant current and savings accounts, and earn *halal* profit which can be sent back into their work with the community. The *masjid* and *madrasah* package includes a *halal* current account, savings accounts, finance facilities, a free cash reserve of US$1,700, and support from a customer relationship manager who understands the specific needs of these organizations.

Developing a Growth Agenda

To grow as an institution, Islamic Bank of Britain will have to develop a three-tiered agenda for top-line growth: product width, market depth, and market breadth. To compete with conventional banks, the Islamic Bank of Britain will need to have a greater number of product offerings such as internet banking, a *Sharia*-compliant debit/credit card, and a wide range of investment options. As it introduces new products, it has two clear strategic options: to use products to attract new customers, and to cross-sell products to existing customers. The logic is simple: a suite of products that is similar to other high street banks makes it easier for customers to compare. Similarly, the logic for cross-selling is equally clear, as the bank builds trust, customers become loyal and in turn use more services from a reliable supplier.[3] Adding subsequent layers of products gives the bank greater flexibility in its approach to the market. Products can be targeted to specific demographic Muslim or non-Muslim market subsegments, giving the bank the opportunity over time to develop specific financing needs profiles for each micro-market segment. Profiling customer behavior in this way will eventually enable the bank to optimize its operating cost structure by identifying which products command higher transaction volumes and/or require less labor.

The second tier in a growth agenda is to increase market depth by identifying which Muslim communities constitute sufficient population density to warrant the opening of a new branch. A comprehensive branch strategy, coupled with other delivery channels such as internet banking and intelligent ATMs, will enable the bank to increase its brand presence in the marketplace. One can speculate on the Islamic Bank of Britain's third tier, an expansion of market breadth, perhaps starting operations in Germany, the Netherlands, or France. As a first-to-market mover, the Islamic Bank of Britain's ability to attract Muslim customers will grow as its brand matures and its value proposition becomes better known to customers.

The key to the Islamic Bank of Britain's growth strategy lies in its greatest resource, namely its employees, who come from a wide range of backgrounds and who are not all Muslims. In *The Discipline of Market Leaders*, Treacy and Wiersema describe companies that create "the cult of the customer", such as leading company Federal Express, where the operating ethos of delivery by the next day permeates every aspect of what employees say and do.[4] Employee attitude is by far the single most important aspect of what breeds success. During a recent visit to the Islamic Bank of Britain's branch in London, a customer was being served who was obviously having difficultly reading and understanding the forms and requirements for opening an account. The customer service representative (CSR) patiently helped the customer, explaining the exact process. Noticing that the customer was not as comfortable speaking in English, they quickly switched to a more comfortable Arabic and continued for 15 minutes past the closing time for the branch. The CSR steadfastly worked with the customer to make him feel relaxed and comfortable during the entire process, and this was recognized by the customer. As the door opened for him to leave, he remarked, "Thank you for taking the time to help me, I could not have done it without you." Once the customer was safely on his way and the door closed, the look of satisfaction on the face of the CSR told the entire story – "I am proud to work here."

Pakistan: First Women Bank

Pakistan is a nation rich in human resources and sparse in readily accessible natural resources. Like other nations, Pakistan must compete for goods and services in world markets as well as maintaining a robust domestic economy. To best understand the value proposition of Islamic banking in Pakistan, one must consider the following analogy: a nation is like a corporation, using raw materials such as natural resources and people to produce goods and services which are in turn sold on domestic and international markets. The prime resource under this scenario is people, an asset which can be considered raw material until an investment is made in education, skills or practical experience so as to transform the asset into productive assets or what is called "human capital". Human capital becomes the means by which the nation engages commerce to result in productive output. Like any other assets, people require periodic investment to maintain skill levels, develop insight to streamline business processes and intrinsically become the innovators of tomorrow.

When one typically breaks down the value proposition of a financial institution into its component parts, the activities of the firm, the products it develops, and the services it provides are inherently valuable to specific segments of the population. An examination of First Women Bank in Pakistan revealed something quite unexpected: a clear link to adding value to the nation state. Pakistan is a nation of 3.2 million SMEs, which represent 78 percent of the non-agricultural workforce. SMEs play an intrinsic role in generating 30 percent of the nation's GDP, 25 percent of the nation's export earnings, and 35 percent of the manufacturing sector's output.[5]

To pursue the analogy of the nation as a company, the environment in which people work, typically associated with a building or premises, on a macroeconomic scale is the legal system, regulatory statutes and tax structure – the business environment which enables commerce to flourish. The human capital of the nation is the work center that performs discreet tasks. The monetary system provides the lubricant to production. The central bank, banking institutions, and financial services act as the enablers or disablers of the production flow, providing lubrication when needed and retarding the flow of capital when economic conditions dictate that the pace of production will outstrip the nation's ability to maintain the rate of growth.

For Pakistan's SMEs to thrive, four basic factors must work in unison to create an environment where the number of SMEs can grow, produce higher output, increase their ability to generate jobs, provide workers with higher levels of disposable income, and produce commercial financial transactions that cascade throughout all levels of the economy. These are:

- a favorable national business environment
- greater access to capital

- a robust, technologically based infrastructure
- periodic investments in human capital.

Banks must therefore be willing to assess the needs of an SME within the context of a national agenda, not simply on an individual's ability to repay advanced capital.

SMEs are the lifeblood of Pakistan's economy; their success is imperative for the long-term viability of Pakistan as a nation. In our analogy of Pakistan as a corporation, SMEs act in a similar fashion to small operating groups within a firm. An SME's need for capital is small, they are a prime source of employment, they work in short cycles, the benefits they produce and shortfalls they experience are widely felt, and, perhaps most importantly, their reduced bureaucracy enables them to adapt to market conditions faster than their larger counterparts. Providing capital to SMEs is the catalyst required to establish a growth economy. Three key factors will shape Pakistan's economy in the future: a rise in the number of working age people, greater numbers of women entering the workforce as prime earners, and the migration of labor away from agriculture. Hence the forecast of a great need for small amounts of available capital to finance growth in the SME sector.

First Women Bank Ltd

The value proposition of First Women Bank Ltd (FWBL) is not simply that of a commercial bank that lends money to women at the lower end of the economic spectrum. The true value proposition lies in its operating ethos: to empower women and especially those from low and middle income groups by providing conventional banking services and non-traditional support services to enable them to identify and capitalize on opportunities that will enhance their socioeconomic status through self-development and the nurturing of an entrepreneurial spirit. According to Zarine Aziz, FWBL's president: "the goal of the bank is not to provide banking services to women at the lower end of the economic spectrum, our objective is to provide the means for women to reach their aspirations by supplying services that will enable them to live up to their potential."[6] Simply, First Women Bank measures its success by the number of customers it can move from being borrowers at the edge of poverty to entrepreneurial business owners. Unlike many other banking institutions, FWBL has learned that to migrate customers from one

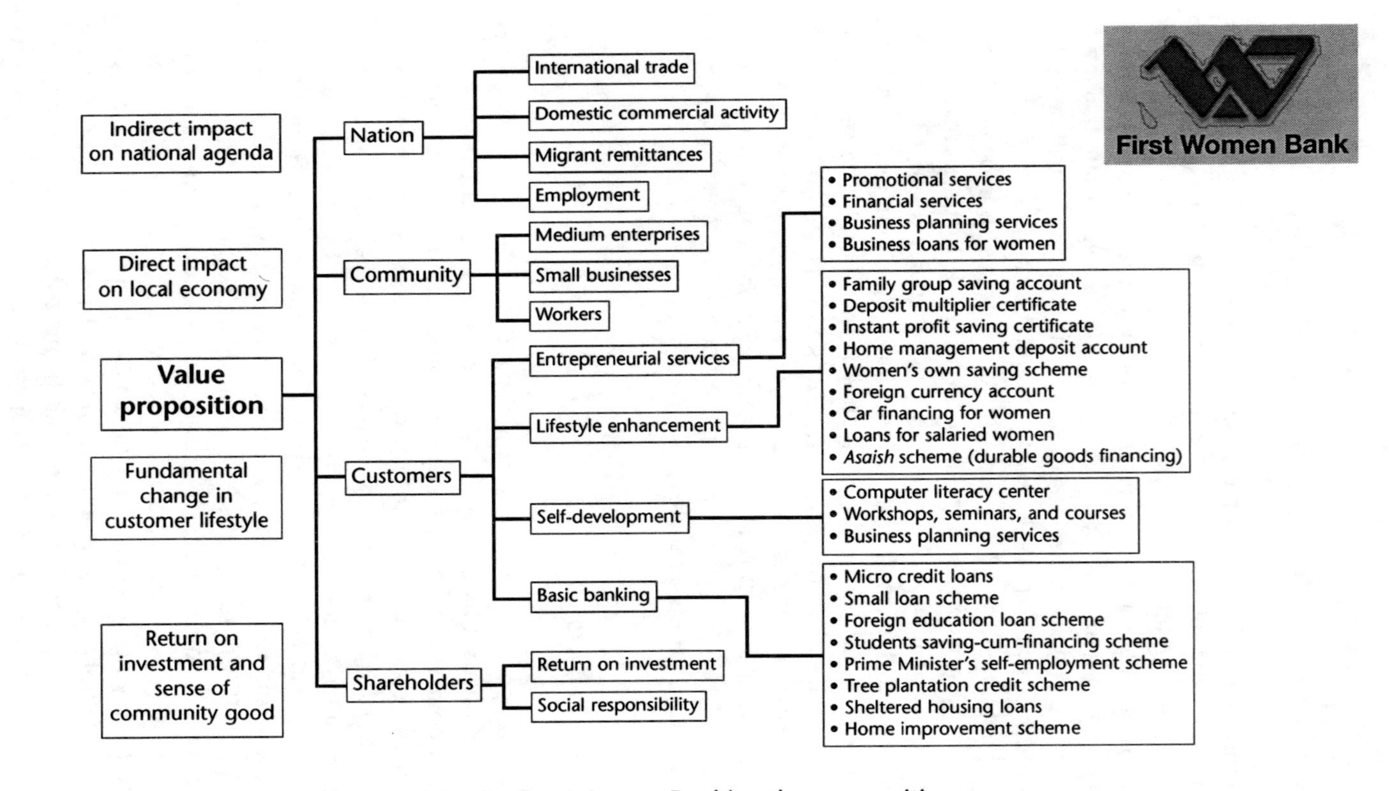

Figure 3.2 First Women Bank's value proposition

socioeconomic stratum to another, services must go well beyond the offerings of conventional banks to include educational support and start-up business advice services, such as business planning, management, sales and marketing, and export quality standards. The First Women Bank support also extends services to assist customers with product exhibitions at chambers of commerce, export promotion bureaux and other places at concessionary rates.[7] The traditional value proposition of a financial services provider is enhanced in the case of FWBL, when viewed from the direct and indirect effects on its customers, community, and nation, as illustrated in Figure 3.2.

FWBL has realized that education precedes entrepreneurs. Customers do not just walk in and ask to be businesses. Migrating from worker to business manager or owner is a process of learning how to both run a business and manage a firm's financial health. For women to make this transformation, FWBL has established three training facilities that offer a wide variety of educational courses, workshops and seminars, as shown in Table 3.1.

Table 3.1 First Women Bank educational offerings

Courses	Workshops	Advanced courses
fashion designing	general fabric painting	stained glass
garment construction	silk painting	candle making
fabric painting	toll painting	fashion designing
silk painting	stencil painting	
stained glass painting	glass etching	
pottery painting and decoration	rug making	
mire modeling	dry flower arrangements	
personality grooming	kitchen fabrics	
development & stress management	interior designing	
self-grooming	beautician	
herbal skin and hair treatment	pottery painting	
mehndi		
flower making		
dry flower arrangement		
candle making		
cooking		
banking		

Source: Adapted from First Women Bank website

The educational offerings center on self-improvement, personal development and a migration toward a basic understanding of learning what it takes to move from acquiring a skill to becoming an independent working woman. The aspiration of the FWBL is to kindle the entrepreneurial spirit in women so they can capitalize on opportunities that were non-existent less than a generation ago.

A Multidimensional Approach

Conventional banks operating in the larger economic zones of North America, Europe and parts of Asia develop a value proposition and subsequently struggle to find a customer demographic that will recognize the value of the product offering. FWBL's approach to market is fundamentally different from that of conventional banks, because the value proposition is created directly from community interaction and applies to a specific demographic profile. The FWBL's value proposition is so strong that the brand is synonymous with success for women. A lesson to learn for bankers developing retail strategies is that FWBL's value proposition sends a simple, powerful message to its target market. This operating ethos of "financial innovations to empower a woman" is visible throughout every operation of the bank, which is reflected in the bank's vision statement: "to be the lead bank for women: Dynamic, adaptive and responsive to their special economic needs, offering the best financial services and the best banking practices."[8]

Empowering women is only half the equation for FWBL. The second part is an active engagement with the communities in which they operate, such as participating in micro-financing programs designed specifically to reduce child labor in the carpet industry. FWBL worked with the UN's International Labor Organization International Program on the Elimination of Child Labor to develop viable income replacement schemes. FWBL provided micro-financing schemes accompanied with non-financial entrepreneurial support to assist mothers of carpet-weaving children to move from micro-borrowers to self-employed small enterprises. The result was the distribution of US$400,000 as micro-loans to 846 families, with a loan recovery rate of 100 percent.

From a strategic perspective, the essence of FWBL's brand is built one family at a time. The attention to detail is the hallmark of the bank's value proposition, because under its operating model the customer is at the heart of its banking activities. Customer loyalty is a byproduct of a relationship of trust built over time as a borrower develops an understanding of prudent financial management and as the bank gains respect for individuals who develop their financial acumen. Customer loyalty can be measured by repeat transactions, default rate (which is close to 0 percent), and conversion rate of micro-client to small business. Perhaps the real measure of FWBL's customer loyalty is in "lifetime value", the commercial benefit of the relationship with a customer over time.

Looking at FWBL from a tactical perspective, its success is not a simple act of lending money to the traditionally unbanked or semi-banked segments of the population. To facilitate its approach to the market, a significant amount of the bank's back office procedures had to be streamlined. To accomplish this objective, FWBL developed a three-tiered strategy: strengthening operations, improving management, and a focus on women development. The result of this strategy has begun to pay significant benefits to both the bank in rising profits and its customers in achieving a higher standard of living. The lesson learned for banks in other parts of the world is that the fundamentals of the Islamic value proposition are the essential ingredient in customer lifetime value. In the FWBL model, customer loyalty is earned by how the bank engages its customers, not as simple facilitators of transactions, but as concerned partners providing all the necessary mechanisms for success.

Iran: Banks Refah, Tejarat, Saderat, Sepah, and Keshavarzi

Iran is one of the most fundamentalist Islamic nations in the world, following the revolution in 1979. The banking system, like many other industries, was nationalized. During the following decades, the Iran–Iraq war, international sanctions, economic policy, and the structural weakness of the Iranian economy led to poor economic performance, as labor strikes, material shortages, and a host of contributing factors were detrimental to the national banking system.[9] During 1983, the law of usury-free banking was passed, switching banks to perform as profit-sharing entities operating under Islamic principles. Since this time, banks in Iran operate in much the same way as other Islamic banks, with a few idiosyncratic differences in *Sharia* interpretation and structural differences in their relationship with the government.

Background

As scholars for many years have noticed, the process of Islamization of

Islamic banking in Iran has proceeded in three phases: nationalization, restructuring, and reorganization of the entire banking system. Nationalization took place between 1979 and 1982. Although external and internal factors contributed to keep policy makers from creating a coherent plan for the Islamization of the banking system, several attempts were made toward this goal.

The second phase of the Islamization process took place between 1982 and 1986. This was primarily characterized by the adoption of several legislative and administrative steps to help the implementation of an Islamic banking model that was typical of Iran. In 1983, a law against interest was passed, and within one year all banks in Iran had to comply with this ruling where savings accounts were concerned, and three years for all other operations; basically, this meant that all banks in Iran had to become Islamic banks.

The reorganization of the banking system began in 1986, and continues until this date. The banking system now makes, with the Islamic government, a coherent entity. The government's role in the Islamic economy, much debated as it has been, has been defended in Iran, where the government's active role has been found to be valuable. The reorganization of Islamic banks has not been simply to facilitate the following of Islamic philosophy through *Sharia*-compliant banking. Rather, the banking sector has become an essential instrument to restructure the Iranian economy, firstly, by providing credit to the service sector, then to offer financing in rural areas; thirdly, to establish a cooperative sector spanning agriculture, industry and trade. Finally, the banking system and the government together engage in financing large industrial projects and investing in social overhead capital. The Central Bank of the Islamic Republic of Iran (CBI) was established in 1960, and it is responsible for the monetary policy that controls the value of money, inflation and overall economic development.[10] CBI is the Iranian government's official bank, and works with the government to ensure that Islamic banking principles are maintained.

Lending, Leasing, and Economic Growth

Leasing (hire purchase) has been successfully implemented in Iran to provide people with the equipment they need that they would not normally be in a position to buy. Banks lease them the equipment so that they can, in the longer term, eventually pay the final installment and therefore become the owners. The Iranian variation of hire purchase is based on the continued concern by Iranian Muslims that they may be in violation of

Sharia principles. In a more fundamentalist philosophical environment, the economy naturally needs to make adjustments, and Iranian banks have had to rethink their products and services to ensure compliance.

Banks such as Bank Refah, Bank Tejarat and Bank Saderat are specialists in lending and leasing in Iran according to *Sharia* principles and Iranian jurisprudence. Each bank focuses on specific niche market aspects for their value proposition. Bank Refah's loan products are designed for specific community and agricultural needs, each product approaching the value proposition in a distinctly different way:[11]

- *Jeoaleh* – a short-term credit agreement to develop a productive and commercial service, whereby a person is required to pay a given amount in return for doing a given business by an agent.
- *Mozaree* – a credit facility for meeting short-term financial needs in the agricultural sector, whereby the owner and the farmer agree to divide equally a prespecified product.
- *Mosaghat* – a credit agreement designed for agriculture for the protection and cultivation of fruit trees, whereby each party has an equal share.

Operating in Iran where customers have deep concerns over compliance to *Sharia* principles, the *Qarz-al-Hassaneh* loan by Bank Refah is a loan that complies with Article 16 of the usury-free banking constitution of Iran, which provides either equipment and facilities to begin work, or facilities to improve agricultural, livestock and industrial products, or facilities to meet essential needs. Another Bank Refah product, *Mozarebeh*, is a form of loan agreement, by which the owner is required to provide cash capital and the borrower should have a business with that capital in order to share the gained profit. One way or another, all loan types aim at helping the borrower and sharing the profit rather than burdening the borrower, who is of course in great need, with extra fees.

The Bank of Industry and Mine (BIM) is another example of a bank whose mission statement clearly identifies its commitment to Iranian society: "applying developing banking procedures and to invest for the economic growth of the country; to prepare suitable circumstances for the presence and participation of the private sector by the use of all potential facilities such as: organizations, processes and appropriate devices in the field of industries, mines, modern technologies, and their associated services."[12] A developing bank, defined as "financial associations which outfit capital by proper circumstances in order to reasonably invest in manufacturing activities, by themselves or others or a combination of them, along with the country's objective of an economical development program,"[13] the BIM aims to help foster economic growth, aiding the private sector so as to ensure a dynamic economy.

A bank that has extended its value proposition beyond Iran is the Bank Sepah, Iran's first bank, established in 1925. With branches in Frankfurt, Paris, and Rome, the bank provides regular accounts (current *Gharz-al-hassaneh* deposit accounts of many forms, including savings), and facilities such as *mudarabah*, civil partnership, *jeoaleh*, and *gharzolhasane*, as well as many forms of leasing.[14] The bank's leasing facilities are, as typical of Islamic banking, designed to lead to ownership once the last installment has been paid.

The Move to Innovate

Finally, we must consider Bank Keshavarzi, founded in 1933 as the Farming and Industrial Bank. Its value proposition is highly focused on serving the specialized financial needs of the agricultural sector; with over 1800 branches nationwide, it finances nearly 70 percent of the sector. During the past decade, the bank has been successful in meeting its mission and objectives, which is evident by year-on-year credit and savings growth. To add depth to its value proposition, the bank has increased its product mix to include a growing number of diversified products such as:

- international Forex services
- electronic banking (MEHR)
- membership of the SHETAB Network (along with Bank Refah, Bank Melli, and Bank of Industry and Mine), to provide ATM-based card services
- introduction of the MEHR credit card (Iran's first)
- telephone account access
- electronic queuing system, to reduce branch congestion.

Perhaps the most interesting aspect of Bank Keshavarzi's approach to its value proposition is the continual process of innovation, such as establishing a 24/7 call center to serve people and farmers in the agricultural sector. Other innovations are the Kids Bank special windows at branches, designed to educate young people on the concept of savings, and financial planning and special services for women such as Iran Plan, *Hazrate Zaynabe Kobra* Plan (Atiyeh Investment Account), and Easy Deposit Plan.[15]

In the past, specialized services and product innovations targeted at specific market subsegments were typically found in Europe, the UK or the US. Technology and ingenuity have enabled Iranian banks to compete for customers in a closed Islamized economic system. The nature of competition in the Iranian banking sector coupled with the strategic adaptations of each bank's value proposition to remain competitive provide insight for Islamic banks operating outside an Islamized economy. Toutounchian describes the Islamic economic system as "a grand cooperative" system, whereby the attribute of cooperation is fundamentally incorporated into Islamic banking.[16] What is clear is that the monitoring cost of implementing Islamic banking in general, and leasing in particular, is high compared to a loan-based, conventional system. In Toutounchian's view, loans, borrowing and lending have their origins in individualism, not in a cooperative usury-free system that aims to avoid developing money markets and focuses on cultivating social benefits, reducing unemployment and other socioeconomic goals.

Clearly, in a closed Iranian economic system, financial institutions compete on service, quality and price among themselves as competition is limited by the total number of Islamic banks in operation. Competition in the Islamized banking environment is purely a process of customers assessing the overall value proposition of a financial services provider and comparing each element of value to make an informed selection of which bank best fits their needs. However, what the banking system in Iran makes evident is that Islamic banks operating in an interest-based economy or mixed or hybrid economy, where Islamic banks interoperate and compete against conventional banks, are more likely to be at a competitive disadvantage. The source of this weakness is in the creation of new financial instruments. Islamic banks can develop innovations, which can quickly be copied by conventional banks and offered at a lower price point because they do not have the added layer of the cost of compliance to *Sharia* principles.[17] However, the reverse is not true; conventional banks can develop new financial innovations which may not be compliant to *Sharia* principles, or the compliance may not be cost-effective. For our present purposes, let us label this phenomenon the "limited value switch", whereby a competitor can identify and isolate one aspect of a bank's value proposition and realize that their competitive advantage lies in the fact that the competitor can do little or nothing to make themselves more competitive. In the case of Islamic banks competing against conventional banks, the added layer of costs associated with *Sharia* compliance must be addressed or it will over the long term make Islamic banks operating in interest-based economies lose their competitive edge.

Bangladesh: Islami Bank Bangladesh Limited

The socioeconomic conditions in Bangladesh, as in many other Islamic nations, have created the need for micro-financing as a viable long-term tool in national economic development. Gaining popularity as a means to alleviate poverty by creating work opportunities which improve the living standards of the poorest people, micro-financing offers new opportunities to build a value proposition based on four key attributes: trust, loyalty, risk, and reward. Put simply, a financial institution takes a risk by extending an implied trust to a customer by providing them with capital; the customer in return repays the use of capital and rewards the institution with an even more valuable commodity: loyalty. In many cases, micro-financing is the loan of last resort for many people, and as a result loyalty becomes a byproduct of a relationship that is built over time by a series of trust-enhancing transactions. Small sums lead to larger sums; repayment leads to greater trust, a mutually beneficial relationship evolves, and the various elements of a bank's value proposition are executed and refined to meet the needs of economically disadvantaged customers.

Banks around the world are aware that in order to survive, to work, to buy a home, a car, sometimes appliances, to get an education, to start a business, and many other activities, people need to have access to capital. In a world where globalization makes what used to be considered chaos theory a reality, banks and other financial services institutions as well as non-financial organizations are only too aware of the need for micro-finance programs. Often seen as banking for the poor, these programs are extremely relevant because they can help the poor become less poor and rejoin society as productive individuals.

Earlier in this chapter, we saw the case of First Women Bank in Pakistan, a bank specializing in helping women on the edge of poverty to become entrepreneurs. Now we turn our attention to the Islami Bank Bangladesh Limited (IBBL). Bangladesh is one of the largest Islamic countries in the world, with an estimated 145 million inhabitants. Bangladeshi people are deeply committed to the Islamic way of life as taught in the Holy *Qur'an* and the *Sunnah*, and they naturally prefer not to violate their faith by using banking products and services that are not approved by their religion.

The Islami Bank Bangladesh Limited was established in 1983 as the response to the needs of millions of Bangladeshi Muslims. It was the first of its kind in Southeast Asia, being thoroughly committed to conducting all banking and investment activities on the basis of *Sharia* principles (interest-free, profit and risk-sharing services and products). The bank's mission statement, as outlined on its extremely comprehensive and informative website, is:

- To conduct interest-free banking
- To establish participatory banking instead of banking on a debtor–creditor relationship
- To invest on a profit and risk sharing basis
- To accept deposits on *mudaraba* and *al-wadeah* basis
- To establish a welfare-oriented banking system
- To extend cooperation to the poor, the helpless, and low-income groups for their economic upliftment
- To play a vital role in human development and employment generation
- To contribute toward balanced growth and development of the country through investment operations, particularly in the less developed areas
- To contribute to achieving the ultimate goal of an Islamic economic system.[18]

With 151 branches and over 4,000 employees, the IBBL employs a full *Sharia* council to ensure that all the bank's transactions are valid and allowed according to Islamic law. Micro-credit programs offered by the IBBL started in 1990, and the Rural Development Scheme (RDS), a pilot scheme supervised by the bank, started in 1996, with a view to providing micro-financial services to the agricultural and rural sector to create the opportunity for employment and income generation for rural people. The IBBL's viewpoint is that it should help the poor by offering them capital, so that they can start progressing, generating capital, and, having shown progress, increasing the need for capital. Instead of seeing the need to help the population as one of the government's tasks, the IBBL has worked with the government to achieve one of the goals of Islamic banking: the betterment of people's lives.

The main objectives of the Rural Development Scheme as it was conceived were:

- to extend investment facilities to agricultural, farming and non-farming activities in rural areas
- to finance self-employment and activities which brought income to poor people in rural areas, especially women

- to help alleviate rural poverty through an integrated approach, focusing on development of the area and people's capabilities
- to provide education and health facilities.

Those eligible to join the RDS were persons who were destitute and distressed, who had liabilities with other banks and as such were not eligible for financing. The scheme ran from one to three years, depending on which activity the bank was financing (for example production of crops would be financed for one year, whereas pond fishing would last three years; a rickshaw van would be financed for two years for the price of the van). The bank invested following *Sharia*-approved modes of investing, such as *bai-muajjal* (deferred payment sale), *shjrkatul meelk* (hire purchase), *bai salam, murabahah,* and others. Those who received financing paid the bank (via branch) in installments.

Rural development through micro-financing in Islamic banking is not the same as development and micro-financing in the Western world. First of all, Islam's commitment to the poor is based not only on making people's lives better in this life, but also in a spiritual sense and post-life. Therefore, helping someone better his or her life helps not only the poor person's soul, but the helper's as well. The Islamic concept of development comes from four key concepts in Islamic philosophy: *tawheed* (unity), *rabubiyah* (sustainer), *khalifah* (representative), and *tazkiyah* (purification). Together, these concepts offer a wide view of human life, taking into account the purpose of a man's life, why man is in this world and what is required of men so that there is spiritual improvement. In Islam, social life is supposed to be dynamic, with everyone's goal being a positive one. Human relationships are viewed on the basis of right (correctness) and justice (fairness). Injustice occurs when resources are denied or when those with readily available resources do not share them, as stated in the Holy *Qur'an* [59:7 and 51:19]. The attachment in a symbiotic manner of moral and material values to the concept of development in Islamic philosophy represents the gap between Islamic banking and its products and services and those offered by traditional banks.

However, IBBL is not alone in developing a value proposition that caters to people at the extreme end of the socioeconomic spectrum. The Arab Gulf Programme for United Nations Development Organizations (AGFUND) was established in 1980 as an initiative of HRH Prince Talal Bin Abdulaziz of Saudi Arabia, supported by Arab Gulf states to assist sustainable human development efforts, targeting the neediest groups in developing countries, particularly women and children, in cooperation with the organizations and institutions active in this field.[19] The AGFUND is engaged in similar micro-finance efforts such as:

- Al-Amal Bank for Microcredit in the Republic of Yemen
- Syria Bank for Micro Projects
- Al-Rajaa Bank in Lebanon
- Fund for Funding Poverty Projects in Sudan (requires setting up a bank)
- The Bank for the Poor in Morocco
- Bank for the Poor in Mauritania
- Bank for the Poor in Djibouti.

What Islamic banks can learn from these initiatives and others in micro-finance is that the greater the specificity in the target customer group (in this case a specific segment of society), the greater the need for a flexible and adaptable suite of products and services. During the next decade, the interconnected global economy will present four key challenges for most nations: job creation, attracting foreign direct investment (FDI), access to capital (micro-financing) for SMEs, and financial education. Islamic banks have the opportunity to play a vital role in community development, national economic growth and above all providing services to more diverse demographics than their Western counterparts do in reality.

Malaysia: AmBank Group

Business gurus will tell you that building a strong value proposition means designing products that resonate with customers. In multicultural environments, finding one set of products with universal appeal is often difficult, due to the wide variations in personal and social preferences, generational differences, and contrasting values. In banking, multiculturalism presents additional challenges where Islamic banking is concerned because of the need to comply with *Sharia* principles. Banking products and financial services cannot simply be cloned from their interest-based counterparts. In complex multicultural environments, financial institutions must employ a process of adaptive product design, what Baghai et al. describe as "active adaptation".[20] To tailor products and services to best serve the needs of multicultural communities, banks must do more than iteratively refine their interest-based products. Islamic banking requires a fundamental change in how transactions are processed, handled, and settled. In some cases, a process of active adaptation requires creating a hybrid approach to the banking model, whereby Islamic banking and conventional banking coexist within one institution but operate under two dynamically different business models.

The AmBank in Malaysia is an example of bank that provides services and product offerings for Muslims as well as non-Muslim customers. Innovation and customer focus are the two pillars of AmBank's value proposition. In 2005, AmBank and AmFinance merged, making AmBank the sixth largest bank in Malaysia. In terms of a hybrid approach to Islamic banking, it is definitely a case to be studied, as it provides products that are not only *Sharia*-compliant, but also very innovative. For example, in terms of *Sharia*-compliant credit cards, as outlined in Chapter 2, AmBank offers the Al-Taslif Credit Card-i, with a points reward and a low "profit rate of 1.25% per month on your outstanding balance". The Al-Taslif credit card is designed to bring peace of mind. Although some scholars have considered this type of card in which interest (by any name) can be charged if a balance is kept as *haram*, so far the Al-Taslif advantages have been seen as more significant than the disadvantages, and the card is being implemented with success.

In line with broader Muslim family values, AmBank's savings GANG Account-i is short for Great Activities 'n' Games, and it is a product designed specifically for families. With the account, based on the principles of *wadiah yad dhamanah* (savings with guarantee), the depositor receives interest on money deposited and an internet account with all eBanking facilities. The account also offers activities, excursions and a magazine for children and youngsters. The current account-i is also based on *wadiah yad dhamanah*, with cheque book, internet banking and ATM cards valid worldwide.

AmBank's investment accounts are based on *mudarabah* (profit sharing), and funds are used in accordance with *Sharia* and Bank Negara Malaysia rules and principles. The Value Plus Investment account-i offers these plus a higher possible return, which as advertised can change without prior notice and better risk management. A third type of investment account, the Afdhal Investment Account-i, is also based on *mudarabah*; the period of investment is flexible, with a minimum of one calendar month. Withdrawals can happen at any time provided that a minimum is kept.

Small and medium-size banks have a distinct advantage over larger competitors when it comes to innovation, due to three key factors: ability to redeploy resources rapidly, management flexibility, and a shorter decision-making process. A less discussed factor is that innovation is a product of evaluating customer need and constructing products to fulfil those needs, using a process that adjusts the product mix until the attributes of the products align themselves with customer needs. For example, an AmBank innovation in investment accounts, the Am50Plus Investment Account-i, offers profit-sharing ratio and automatic renewal for value-added investments. The investor receives free Takaful Group Personal Accident Plan as insurance. Likewise, AmQuantum Investment Account-i features the same advantages of the others but on a longer term investment account. These accounts are linked and automated so that the customer only revisits their selected options if their circumstances or lifestyle change.

For car financing, AmBank uses the *Sharia*-approved concept of *ijarah thumma al-bai*, that is, an agreement of leasing to purchase later, to offer its product Arif Hire Purchase-i. Loan approval is advertised to be fast, and up to 90 percent of the cost of the vehicle can be "borrowed" and paid for in up to nine years.

For home financing, AmBank offers the equivalent to a Western mortgage based on the principle of *bai bithaman ajil*, that is, deferred payment sale. The margin of financing is high (up to 90 percent) and loans can be taken for a period of 30 years or up to the age of 65. Legal fees and stamp duty are waived for completed and refinancing units, and a Takaful Mortgage Plan can be taken at the time of agreement.

AmBank offers personal financing at a flat rate of 7.3 percent on an annual basis, and repayments can be spread over 1 to 10 years. Guarantors are not required, and the maximum is a deduction of 60 percent of the individual's salary.

AmBank's products for Islamic banking are created to facilitate lifestyles. Although they are perhaps less strictly bound to principles which forbid profit based on money earned on time, they are *Sharia*-compliant in the bank's advisers' *Sharia* interpretation. As always, with Islamic banking, one has to interpret the word of the law, and it is up to customers to accept the interpretation or not.

Adaptation Strategy

AmBank's approach to the market is by active adaptation, whereby a continual assessment of the market, customers, and socioeconomic behaviors enables them to reframe products to capitalize on a wide range of opportunities. Each permutation of Islamic products has an associated cost of operations; at the same time, the new product provides AmBank with a new area of fee income and transaction-based revenues. To establish market credibility and quality of service in the highly competitive retail banking market, these opportunities require a clear value proposition. Banks such as AmBank, wishing to compete in the market based on active adaptation of products, must have an equally dynamic strategy that spans a host of business, technology, and organizational issues, the fundamentals of which are centered on the following actions:

- Know your value added and how it complements the market it serves
- Create mechanisms for market sensing
- Rebrand products to reflect your identity
- Build capabilities for rapid market reaction
- Develop competencies in customer relationship management (CRM)
- Leverage technology to facilitate transactions
- Get good at managing relationships
- Change offerings and approaches as the markets mature and evolve
- Develop relationships with providers of technology and services.

To take advantage of new opportunities as they emerge, AmBank's approach to the market must remain flexible, mirroring the stages of market maturity and the rate of product adoption by customers. In December 2005, AmBank was preparing to launch a new wave of innovation, with property and motor vehicle auctions, designed as a practical experience for AmBank's techno-savvy customers. As the environment for electronic banking services matures, a bank must be able to adapt to the changing conditions. Some products will come and go as customer attention waxes and wanes, so a bank must look at the product offerings in their entirety in order to assess the long-term trend. As electronic banking products and financial services evolve rapidly to meet customer demand, they will follow a predictable pattern that in turn provides new opportunities for banks:

1. *Inception* – Partnering, experimentation, definition of an operating model, exploration of new channels (customer acquisition), branding, portal establishment, new product definition, bill presentment.
2. *Growth* – Refinement of the operation model, core banking services, rebranding of products and services with maturing partnerships,

revenue/profit-sharing model with channel partners, consolidation of retail services, wealth management, anticipatory payments.

3. *Maturity* – Driving down cost, optimization of processes, customer relationship management, customer order fulfilment, comprehensive wealth generation strategies.

Most internet banking offerings by Islamic banks are still in the inception phase, although a few early leaders have entered the growth phase. In the strategic agenda for action, the three most critical components are creating a value proposition, developing core competencies based on technology, and selecting the right partners. Developing a clear and understandable value proposition is paramount in establishing any comprehensive internet banking offering and critical for the long-term viability of any product. Developing appropriate competencies traditionally has been understood as creating compartmentalized and discreet activities that incrementally add value. In providing multi-channel banking products using combinations of the internet, ATMs, mobile phones and other innovations, financial services institutions must provide a suite of services that center on activities like originating, brokering, and passing transactions; aggregating, consolidating, and managing transactions; and providing extra-market interchange. Providing products and services to banking customers is only half the challenge though, the more significant challenge being "innovation mobility" – being able to harness resources quickly to capitalize on technological change. Essentials are rapid deployment; building infrastructure capabilities that can be quickly connected and integrated for complete product offerings; and technology enabling mass "customization" so that consumers can readily select product options designed to suit their lifestyles.

The final component of an internet strategy is the selection of partners to perform or support the value-added service. Today's internationally focused business climate allows few companies the luxury of performing all aspects of the services that need to be delivered to customers. A key feature of the new banking model is that it can be readily disaggregated into its components, making specialization a viable strategy. Insurance companies are effectively product specialists, relying on a network of brokers and agents to distribute their product. Credit card companies are good examples of infrastructure specialists. The lesson is to develop a network of capabilities that fulfil a value-added service to the customer as part of a network of value-added relationships that must be managed just as any other performing asset.

Although conservative Islamic scholars may not be in agreement with the Malaysian approach to Islamic banking in general and the use of interest specifically, it is important to understand their approach to put the future of Islamic banking into a historical context.

The Islamic banks discussed in this chapter represent a very small sample of the ways in which banks are defining their value propositions to customers. Although each bank opted for a different approach to the development, implementation, and long-term delivery of products, they all realized that Islamic banking is their market and is more than simply providing financial services. To their credit, each bank identified a specific need in the market and developed a strategy to fulfil that need as a means to establish a base value proposition, which later could be amended to include additional banking products, other specialized financial services, educational services, and services designed to support entrepreneurs. In total, these banks have been successful because they have an in-depth understanding of what their customers find valuable. Their value propositions reflect a simple and direct response to a market need. However, in the next generation of competition for Islamic banks, they must supplement this by shifting from a reactive approach to a proactive methodology in order to manage and build on the value they have created. Developing a proactive strategy requires a comprehensive understanding of the Islamic banking value proposition, to which we now turn.

Notes

1 Nicholas, Trevor *Strategic Management of Technology, Competition & Co-operation in World Banking*, London: The Institute of Bankers, 1985, p. 107.

2 Islamic Bank of Britain, November 2005, available at http://www.islamic-bank.com/islamicbanklive/PressRelease1/1/Home/1/Home.jsp.

3 Davis, Stephen *Excellence in Banking – Revisited!* Basingstoke: Palgrave Macmillan, 2004, p. 60.

4 Treacy, Michael, and Wiersema, Fred *The Discipline of Market Leaders*, Reading, MA: Perseus Books, 1997, pp. 179–80.

5 Khan, Aftab Ahmad, Importance of SMEs and Future Development, Institute of Bankers Pakistan, November 2005 available at http://www.ibp.org.pk/tdetail.asp?sno=115.

6 Telephone conversation with Zarine Aziz on December 29, 2005.

7 First Women Bank, Pakistan, December, 2005, available at http://www.fwbl.com.pk/businesscenter.htm.

8 First Women Bank – Special Edition, The News International, Pakistan, available at http://jang.com.pk/thenews/spedition/firstwomebank/#a1.

9 Brörklund, Iréne, and Lundström, Lisabeth, Islamic Banking an Alternative System, Kristianstad University College, FEC 685, Dissertation, December 2004, pp. 51–3.

10 Central Bank of Iran, available at http://www.cbi.ir.

11 Loan Services and Facilities, Bank Refah, December, 2005, available at http://bankrefah.ir/en/services/default.asp.

12 Objectives and Mission, Bank of Industry and Mine, December 2005, available at http://w3e.bim.ir/ourbank/target-mission.asp.

13 Definition of Developing Bank, Bank of Industry and Mine, December 2005, available at http://w3e.bim.ir/ourbank/DevelBank.asp.

14 Services (Rial), Bank Sepah, December, 2005, available at http://www.banksepah.ir/EN/Services/Default.aspx?type=r.

15 Overview of the Bank, Bank Keshavarzi, December, 2005, available at http://www.agri-bank.com/Static/English/About/Profile.asp.

16 Toutounchian, Iraj, Islamic Leasing and its Impact on Islamic Banking in Iran, Paper presented at International Conference on Islamic Leasing, February 13–14, 2005, Kuwait, p. 19.

17 Al-Omar, Fuad, and Abdel-Haq, Mohammed *Islamic Banking: Theory, Practice and Challenges*, London: Zed Books, 1996.

18 Aims and Objectives, Islami Bank Bangladesh Limited, December, 2005, available at http://www.islamibankbd.com/page/glance.htm.

19 AGFUND Mission, The Arab Gulf Programme for United Nations Development Organizations, November, 2005, available at http://www.agfund.org/english/about.htm.

20 Baghai, Mehrdad, Coley, Stephen, and White, David *The Alchemy of Growth*, London: Texere, 2000, p. 108.

4

THE ISLAMIC BANKING VALUE PROPOSITION

In the past five years, there has been a meteoric rise in books, conferences and seminars aiming to understand Islamic banking, Muslim financing, and the economic system that operates independent of interest. The study of Islamic banking is no longer confined to a network of *Sharia* scholars or a minority of academics. Organizations such as the International Monetary Fund, the World Bank, many Western central banks, and centers of higher education like Harvard and Rice universities, the London School of Economics and Loughborough University have all allocated resources to understand Islamic commerce in greater detail.[1] Numerous Western nation states now recognize that Muslim populations within their borders are seeking financial intermediaries that enable them to interact with the world financially while observing their faith. One of the key drivers in this sudden interest in Islamic banking is the realization that a significant number of financial transactions between Muslims occur outside the formal banking systems.

The value proposition for Islamic banking is multidimensional, as it must offer more than a simple alternative to interest-based economic activity. Because of the size of many Islamic institutions, which is small compared to their conventional banking counterparts, the value proposition must be more comprehensive because they must compete against foreign Islamic and conventional banks in a rapidly globalizing market.

According to Mohamed Ariff, perhaps the one single market differentiator that is most telling in the Islamic banking value proposition is that "unlike conventional banking, it [Islamic banking] is concerned about the viability of the project and the profitability of the operation but not the size of the collateral."[2] Islamic banks are more willing to assess a project based on its potential to be a success rather than its collateral, and they often hedge their risk by taking on shorter term projects. Ariff highlights that this strategy sometimes poses a problem due to two key elements of the Islamic banking value proposition: the insufficient numbers of highly qualified people who are needed to assess and manage the risks associated with long-term projects, and a lack of back-up institutional structures such as secondary capital markets for Islamic financial instruments.[3]

An essential element in the Islamic value proposition is the desire to play a greater role in the community; in many cases, banks working on their own or in concert with government agencies, central banks, and NGOs endeavor to be the catalysts for economic development.

If one examines the basic tenets of the Islamic banking value proposition from a Western perspective, one aspect becomes surprisingly clear: the vast majority of the value proposition should also appeal to conservative Christians and people with a concern for ethical investing. The rise of ethical investing in the West is basically a realignment of awareness in social responsibility by people with a strong commitment to their community. We could argue that there is not a similar sudden rise in Muslim communities because the concern over what is morally responsible has never waned as it did in the Western world. The key similarity between Western socially responsible investing and the rules of investing under Islamic *Sharia* principles is that in each case investors' concerns center on how, where and in what their money is invested. Islamic investors are prohibited from providing capital to corporations that deal in products such as tobacco, alcohol, or military hardware, while Western ethical investors focus on corporations that meet the criteria of environmental sustainability, or do not produce products such as pornography and other investments similar to those prohibited by *Sharia* principles.

Another parallel between the Islamic banking value proposition and the ethical investors in the West is the overlap in time. During the past 30 years, both have grown from small beginnings to appeal to larger and larger portions of society. Islamic banking in the 1970s was a fledgling

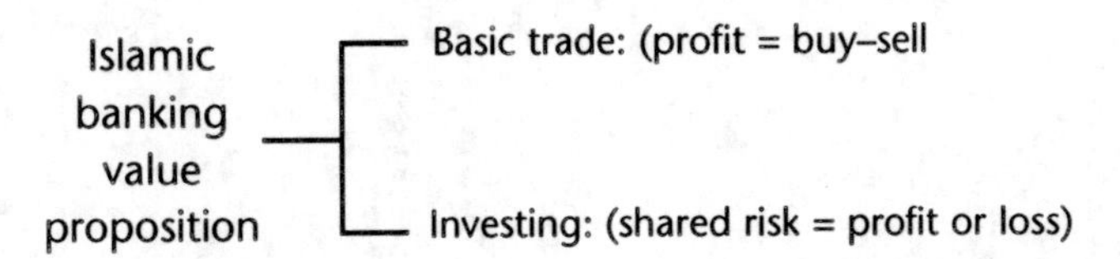

Figure 4.1 The fundamentals of the Islamic banking value proposition

Mudarabah (silent partnership) (profit-sharing agreement)
- **Investor** – provides capital, pre-agreed share of profit, absorbs any loss
- **Entrepreneur** – provides time, pre-agreed share of profit, sole control of enterprise

Musharakah (partnership) (equity participation)
- **Partners** – provide capital under joint venture, pre-agreement to share profit and loss, partner has right to co-manage

Murabahah (resale contract) (cost plus financing)
- **Supplier** – markets to customer, sells asset to bank, receives payment from bank
- **Bank** – buys asset, adds mark-up
- **Customer** – receives goods, makes deferred payments

Commodity *murabahah* (short-term deposit placement)
- **Broker A** (seller) —— **Broker B** (buyer)
- **Conventional bank** – acts as agent to buy commodity from broker
- **Islamic bank** – stands as guarantor behind the transaction

Quardhul hassan (good loan)
- **Lender** – provides capital
- **Borrower** – receives capital, obligated to repay the capital; reward to lender left to judgment of borrower

Ijarah (simple leasing agreement)
- **Bank** – buys asset, leases at fair market rate
- **Lessee** – rents asset, pays rent (sometimes option to buy is built into deal)

Bai al-salam or *salam* (post delivery sale) (deferred delivery)
- **Manufacturer** – sells goods before they are produced
- **Bank** – buys asset, at discount

Istisna (work in progress)
- **Entrepreneur**
- **Financier** (bank)
- **Manufacturer**

Bai muajjal (deferred payment)
- Considered trade not loan, property financing on deferred basis with pre-agreed mark-up

Sukuks (Islamic bonds) (proportional beneficial ownership)
- ***Sukuk* holder** – holds a proportion of the asset
- **Entrepreneur** – special financing need
- ***Sukuk* issuer**

Figure 4.2 The topology of Islamic banking

Source: Adapted from Bahrain Monetary Agency, and Tlemsani and Matthews

set of operations, while ethical investing was met with liberal doses of skepticism and derision. The key differentiator between these two similar principle-based lines of thinking is that under the Islamic value proposition, investors are concerned with the way activities are financed as well as simply what kinds of products are produced. As we shall see in this chapter, many products and concerns of Islamic banking are similar to those of the West, although the approach and commitment of the bank to the customers and employees is sometimes quite different. Having looked at global specificity in Chapter 3, we shall now focus on some similarities between Islamic banking and aspects of traditional Western banking.

Islamic Knowledge Capital

Now, in the early years of the twenty-first century, business gurus, academics, government and the media have universally decreed that the world is based on a knowledge economy. Human capital is rapidly becoming recognized by Islamic and conventional financial services corporations as an organization's most valuable asset. The knowledge inherent in the people employed by the firm will determine the organization's competitive edge. Until recently, technology was thought to be the means to achieve market differentiation in banking products; now, senior bank managers are discovering that it is people who make the big difference. The reason for this is simple: as technology continues to be commoditized, the components needed to modernize a banking institution become more affordable to all banks. Technology managers are buying ready-made solutions, resulting in greater numbers of banks using the same tools, technologies and templates as their competitors. Thus, given that many institutions are now using the same or similar technologies to deliver banking services, the relative value of technology between competitors is zero. It is the people in the bank who are using technology who have become the key to providing higher levels of customer service as the industry shifts from selling customer banking products to providing services, such as advisory, planning, and lifestyle management. Human resource managers in all banks are realizing that acquiring and retaining qualified talent is more than a challenge for their bank; talent has become a national problem.

Islamic banks like their conventional counterparts must consider the pitfalls of a global marketplace; the demand for talent and the availability of talent pools shift like sand in the wind. Talent is the prime ingredient of knowledge capital because knowledge becomes self-regenerating under the right business conditions (bring enough talented people to work together and you create an environment of experimentation, innovation, and entrepreneurism). The power of knowledge capital is important for Islamic banks for three distinct reasons: the potential for innovation, excellence in customer service, and the development of customer intelligence. Islamic banks today are bereft of talent in many cases – the Achilles heel for numerous institutions – as the focus in providing Islamic banking services shifts to profitability, top-line growth, and expansion into new markets. Shortages in knowledge capital, talent, and innovation are becoming so acute that the subject is one of widespread concern. Proactive advocates of talent view it in the context of a national resource which requires continual investment, and this is debated throughout the Islamic world. This is Jordan's Queen Rania Al-Abdullah's view on the subject:

> Human capital is every country's most valuable asset. Whether the goal is promoting access to technology, education, health, meaningful jobs or civil services, our efforts should maximize the human potential of all citizens, enabling them to lead lives of dignity and independence.[4]

It is vital that Islamic banks realize the implications of Queen Rania Al-Abdullah's observation that human capital does not simply appear; skilled labor is the result of continual investment in people to acquire new skills and knowledge. Human capital, like any other asset of a bank, must be managed with an investment strategy that assesses the potential relative value of the individual and makes periodic investments in his/her skill base. Unlike other assets, human capital requires motivation. Banks must offer career opportunities in an environment to which people want to belong. For Islamic banks operating in all parts of the world, attracting and retaining qualified talent will become a bigger problem as increasing numbers of banks and financial institutions begin to offer Islamic services to Muslim customers. One question that comes to mind is: what constitutes Islamic knowledge capital for banking and finance?

Knowledge – the New World Currency

We could argue that knowledge has been the currency of the world for centuries; only now have we discovered how to capitalize on the tools to make us more aware of the exchange of ideas and concepts that result in products. Innovation is a product of knowledge capital. Innovative thinking has a long tradition in the Islamic world. Dibooglu describes how, during the Middle Ages, as Europeans engaged with Muslim communities, they discovered that in certain areas Islamic commerce had advanced beyond the means of what was then conventional commerce, using mechanisms similar to bills of exchange (*sutfaya*) and devised forward contracts (*mohatra*).[5] Another example is the use of the zero as a numerical placeholder that derives ultimately from the Arabic *sifr*, meaning empty or vacant. The zero was in wide use by Islamic mathematicians in the early medieval period and made its way to Europe in the eleventh century, via Andalusia. Astronomical instruments such as the astrolabe brought Arabic numerals into common use. Innovators such as the twelfth-century mechanical engineer Badi' Al-Zaman Abull-Ezz Ibn Ismail Ibn Al-Razzaz Al-Jazari have used technical innovations to seek practical solutions. Today's senior Islamic business managers can learn several key lessons about the innovative process from Al-Jazari, as Chowdhry observes; in order to be innovative, an organization must learn to read the practical needs of customers and capitalize on market trends, and to innovate people must be in command of their skills in order to leverage the potential of a new idea.[6] The influence of Islamic innovation and medieval Islamic knowledge capital can be observed throughout Europe in the architecture of cathedrals.

With a long history of Islamic innovation, the knowledge economy in the Islamic world is as yet an untapped resource. However, to uncover the value of Islamic knowledge capital, financial institutions must do two things: invest in continuing education to build on the knowledge base, and provide an environment in which innovation, creativity, and experimentation can flourish so as to keep employees (human capital) satisfied and motivated. Having an in-depth understanding of knowledge capital is vital for Islamic banks because the application of knowledge generates profits and long-term viability for the institution. As was true in the medieval period, the applied use of a technology, such as the zero, letters of credit, or stonework, is where economic gain is derived. In Strassmann's view, knowledge capital can be defined as the economic value added by an organization divided by the price of capital or the associated cost of the organization.[7] For Islamic banks, Islamic knowledge capital has one key value: the potential to generate profits, which in turn will sustain them as competition increases for Muslim-based financial services.

Senior bank managers instinctively know that the knowledge held by people within the organization is similar to a treasure box. However, they often struggle to find the key that will open the treasure box, or tap the potential of the organization to do things that are more productive,

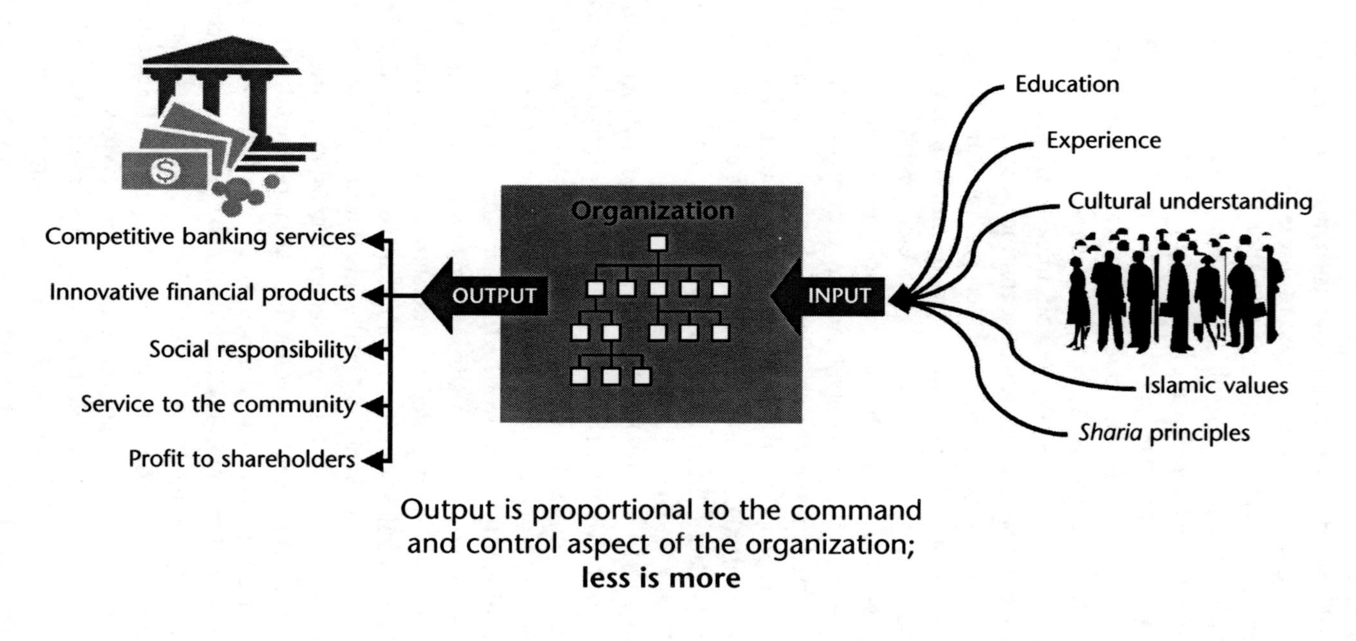

Figure 4.3 Applied Islamic knowledge capital

invent new products or occasionally create new businesses. Moreover, once they have opened the box, it becomes increasingly difficult to retain the knowledge and talent, as people may be approached by other employers and take their knowledge with them. The topic of what constitutes Islamic knowledge capital and how it is distinctly different from other forms of applied knowledge is worthy of study in its own right. For our purposes, let us give the following definition in order to understand how the application of knowledge has both direct and indirect consequences for the value proposition of Islamic banks. Islamic knowledge capital is the potential (tapped and untapped) value that can be generated by the skills, training, experience, values, beliefs, and wisdom inherent in the people who make up an organization, reduced by the cost of using their resources, multiplied or divided by the working environment in which they operate. This is illustrated in Figure 4.3.

Senior banking managers realize that one of the challenges faced by Islamic banks is the acquisition and management of knowledge capital. Like most types of business in the twenty-first century, financial services companies in Islamic countries struggle to capitalize on knowledge, while trying to cut down on investment in education and training. As access to talent pools becomes increasingly difficult, can banks in the Islamic regions gain knowledge or create knowledge capital without going through the traditional means of educating people?[8]

Perhaps the best way to gain knowledge is through another ancient Islamic value – collaboration. Middle Eastern banks are in a unique position to gain knowledge through collaboration due to the longstanding collaborative nature of regional relationships at the microeconomic business activity level. Fundamental Islamic principles such as sharing risk mean that collaboration between Islamic banks and financial services institutions is seen as favorable to both (or all) parties. Therefore, intrabank or transborder collaboration is a natural choice for organizations wishing to grow knowledge capital internally.

One way to remain competitive while acquiring knowledge is by using the latest technology to develop an agenda that positions cultural interests (local) into a global perspective to better understand Middle Eastern banking objectives. First, Islamic banks must apply their knowledge capital and *think global*, that is, they must adapt to the global market by offering products, services, and solutions that are found in the global marketplace in order to remain competitive. Strategically, Islamic banks can accomplish this by partnering with other banks in various regions or by starting operations in other regions using locally available talent.

Secondly, Islamic banks must *act regional*, in other words, they must keep in mind the interests of the regions and populations they serve by collaboration or in association with other financial intermediaries. Knowledge capital must be applied to brands, services, and product offerings in order to tailor or adapt offerings to cater for regional customers. In a regional context, banks have the opportunity to co-brand services while collaborating on the non-differentiating aspects of their operations such as shared infrastructure. The result of this co-branding collaboration is co-opetition, whereby several banks share a common set of services and/or cross-sell each other's products in a competitive environment through alliances and affiliations.

The third and most underestimated aspect of applied knowledge capital in Islamic banking is to *look local,* that is, to serve local customers and develop an agenda for long-term viability. A key learning from conventional banks for Islamic banks with global ambitions is that when banks aim for a more global market, they often forget to cater for the immediate population they serve or have served in the past. In numerous cases where banks are growing rapidly into new markets or have grown through mergers and/or acquisitions, they tend to ignore their customer base until customer retention becomes a major problem. Islamic banks today enjoy a customer base that exhibits a higher degree of loyalty than their conventional counterparts. To maintain the relationship with customers, Islamic banks must be careful not to repeat the mistakes of conventional banks by losing sight of the importance of local customers in global growth. One way or another, in order to have loyal customers, Islamic banks must be loyal to them; a bank must look local and offer products and services that cater for the lifestyles of the people in the community they serve. Knowledge capital plays an intrinsic part in executing these three strategic views; Islamic knowledge capital is instrumental in capitalizing on the opportunities that are present at all three levels.[9]

Islamic knowledge capital is invaluable to banks that must strike a balance between cost of delivery and total potential value of a specific demographic market subsegment. Knowledge of local values, traditions, and economic problems is paramount to brand building on all three levels. Global banks such as HSBC have learned this, as reflected in its marketing slogan: the world's local bank. In the case of global banks, they must learn to blend in, in that they must gain an understanding of their customers' needs and wants before they offer them new products and services. Islamic banks have a greater bond with the communities they serve and have a clear but rapidly fading competitive advantage as conventional banks and new competitors gain local knowledge.

In order to compete against institutions with a lower operating cost structure, Islamic banks must collaborate to compete – known as *co-opetition*.[10] Co-opetition provides a means for Islamic banks to establish a network of value-added suppliers of Islamic-based financial services. In order to be in this state of co-opetition, Islamic banks must be particularly aware of their own value proposition, so as to establish the relative value of what they have to offer to potential partnering organizations. To do this, Islamic banks may find it helpful to use Treacy and Wiersema's model, found in *The Discipline of Market Leaders*, which postulates that companies must discipline themselves to select one key area (or value discipline) where they alone can provide unique value to targeted customers, thus directing their energy and resources to excel consistently in their chosen discipline.[11] The three value disciplines are product leadership, operational excellence, and customer intimacy. Each discipline represents a targeted customer base and method of providing services and/or goods. The value discipline model provides a framework for discovering the value of a bank's products and services against the management team's operational goals and objectives, the firm's operating ethos, and the needs of customers. For many Islamic banks, developing an understanding of their knowledge capital is a prerequisite to exploiting the inherent potential locked in their overall value proposition. Senior managers must focus on assessing and managing their knowledge capital and work toward an intimate understanding of how to convert knowledge capital to specific characteristics of their value proposition.

Innovations, Traditional Values, and Value Propositions

It is almost impossible to mention or list all the new products which have come to market during the past few years that cater to Muslims looking for Islamic banking and investment solutions that express their values and beliefs. If the laws of probability are any benchmark, by the time this book is published, the list of Islamic-based products will have doubled again. That said, although the list of individual products is rising rapidly, the commonality of characteristics in these financial instruments provides a means to systemize the individual elements of value, as the differences provide insight into the cultures in which they emerge.

Delivering products and services requires organizing work into discrete activities which can be discussed as disciplines. The disciplines of how Islamic banking and non-Muslim financial services organizations engage their resources to meet competitive pressures share striking similarities, especially when considered independently of geography, demographics, and access to technological infrastructure. Regardless of where in the world a financial services company operates, issues such as the adoption rate of technology by local populations drive the type, style, and number of financial services products offered to the marketplace. Reduced operating cost, speed or availability of information, and the exploitation of channels to serve customers better or to acquire new customers are factors that drive the design and delivery of banking products and the organizations providing financial services. In all cases, competitive strategies that leverage technology will center on a continual reduction of cost for long-term viability and mechanisms to establish clear product and service differentiation to attract new revenue sources.

Customers are eager to be offered new products, and they are constantly demanding a broader suite of financial services. However, delivering these services profitably is one of the challenges in the twenty-first-century financial services agenda. Traditional banking organizations are threatened by a plethora of new market entrants coupled with emerging trends like personalized customer services, mobile banking, and internet-based technologies that are transforming the nature of how customers in all demographic profiles rationalize money. This convergence results in a need for financial services organizations continually to develop new capabilities to fulfil the market demand. As a direct result of technological innovation, the disciplines of banking systems, their operations, development, and infrastructure are undergoing tremendous change, exacerbated by the rise in computer literacy in the world population. Exciting times, for sure, but costly.

Market trends like the management of personal wealth and ubiquitous technologies are rapidly converging, creating the opportunity for financial services companies to discover innovative approaches to delivering services. Islamic banks may not all mirror exactly the service offerings of Western conventional banks, due to social idiosyncrasies that reflect strong traditions indigenous to the region's rich cultural history. However, in the Islamic banking industry overall, market pressure is intense and banks face forces that present a greater level of challenge as compared to their Western counterparts.

Financial services organizations around the globe are faced with the complex task of balancing the delivery of even more services with a continual technology investment that is seemingly endless. To complicate the technological landscape, innovations such as internet banking, biometrics, mobile banking, intelligent ATMs, customer relationship management, and a growing list of multiple delivery technologies are pushing what were technology decisions a few years ago onto today's business agenda. In the new competitive landscape, technology is no longer divorced from issues of brand, service delivery, cooperative ventures, and other items on the business agenda. Currently, technology is often the factor that determines what, how, where, and when organizations will meet competitive challenges. In many organizations, technology decisions are now business decisions that will make or break a firm's ability to compete.

Almost as numerous as grains of sand in the desert, a new generation of Islamic banking products is being brought to the market, seemingly on a daily basis. The greatest challenge will be to maintain the principles of Islam as banks adapt products, exploring the various elements in their value proposition. Innovations fall into three broad categories: Islamic banking products, financial services, and technological innovations in distribution. Innovation in the context of Islamic banking products is the creation of new financial instruments, such as Islamic debt funds, commodity (*murabahah*) funds, lease (*ijara*) funds, Islamic equity funds, Islamic hedge funds, Islamic equity REITs. These instruments are innovations that spring from combining customer/market feedback with business/*Sharia* knowledge to produce a new instrument that is tailored to suit a specific demographic profile, such as Dubai Bank's Royal Banking,[12] or to match a particular market situation, such as the Bahrain Monetary Agency's Al-Salam Government *Sukuk*.[13] Innovations also take the form of financial services, where customers are given access to highly specialized services to facilitate their lifestyles such as wealth management or microfinance or services for specific life events, such as mortgages.

However, the plethora and growing level of complexity of new products also present new problems for Islamic banks, as Obaidullah observes:

> An example of a product that scores high on complexity in terms of financial characteristics is the Islamic Multi-Investment Fund by AMEX-Faisal Finance, which consists of five portfolios: 1. Islamic Market Opportunities (investment in Islamically acceptable options, futures and forward contracts 2. Emerging Markets Equity 3. Global Equities 4. Trade Finance, and 5. Parallel Purchase and Sale of Currencies and Commodities. Investors may invest in the entire portfolio through a predetermined asset allocation formula or choose to invest in an individual portfolio or develop unique portfolio allocation. The issue of Islamically acceptable options, futures and forwards is not fully comprehensible even by Islamic scholars, not to speak of the Muslim investor community. It is one of the most controversial issues in Islamic finance. The additional feature of stipulation of an option of determination or *khiyar al-tayeen* in *Shariah* parlance only adds to its complexity.[14]

Obaidullah's observation brings into context three key issues that influence an Islamic bank's value proposition: customer education, brand identity, and product clarity. Although the technical aspects of these banking products may be complex, the explanation of the product to the customer must be simple, clear, and concise. Two additional concerns must be considered as Islamic banks formulate their competitive strategies: market hesitation and market saturation. Market hesitation is the time lag between the introduction of the product and the customer's awareness and understanding of the product relative to their lifestyle or use of the product. Islamic banking products, as all other products, must be introduced with the management team's realization that the time associated with market hesitation is directly proportional to marketing and customer education. Market saturation, on the other hand, is the confusion in the mind of the customer when faced with too many choices by numerous suppliers. In the case of market saturation, Islamic banks must carefully monitor the competition and alter their value propositions in such a way that accentuates the elements of value that make their offerings unique.

With a growing number of new products and services, the number of choices for Muslim customers is increasing daily. The following are just a few examples of innovations that have come to the market in recent years, each with a distinctly different approach to their underlying value proposition.

Bank Islam: Tourist Friend Card

Designed as a *Sharia*-compliant alternative to cash, while promoting domestic tourism for customers who travel throughout Malaysia, the co-branded Master Card enables members to receive discounts of up to 50 per cent at over 200 participating outlets, ranging from restaurants, hotels, and shopping centers to places of interest throughout the country.[15] The card offers *takaful* insurance coverage, a competitive profit rate and bonus profit rebate of 0.5–2.5 percent that will be credited directly to the accounts of cardholders who pay on time every month. The success of this project is evidenced by the statistics: the bank has been issuing approximately 10,000 new cards a month, bringing the total to some 105,000 credit card holders to date, with the number expected to double to about 220,000 by mid 2006.

United Arab Emirates: Emirates Islamic Bank – Islamic Credit Card

A truly *Sharia*-compliant credit card designed for Muslims who need to travel and make purchases globally. The Emirates Islamic Bank's Credit Card works by allowing the customer to pay a quarterly fixed fee, which enables transaction activity up to an approved limit.[16] The customer receives a monthly statement detailing the transactions for the month and can pay as much or as little as they want above the minimum amount required. There is no interest on the outstanding balance.

Cayman Islands: Al-Tawfeek Company – Children Investment Fund

The objective of the Children Investment Fund is twofold: to encourage young investors to learn about their financial obligations as Muslims and to save by earning returns on investments according to *Sharia* rules.[17]

Bahrain: Noriba Bank – Range Murabaha Investments

Sharia-compliant wealth management firm Noriba Bank has developed the Range Murabaha Investments (RaMI). These are short-term *Sharia*-compliant investment products offering capital preservation with higher than average returns. Investors select a benchmark commodity or currency and a selected band of performance from a list of price ranges, thereby planning for a higher overall return within a given time period, typically one to three years.[18] The bank executes periodic *murabahah* trades over the life of the investment, with deferred sales proceeds and profits paid to the investor. The original amount of the investment is rolled over or reinvested in subsequent *murabahah* trades. The goal is to offer capital preservation while presenting the investor with opportunities to earn higher rates of return.

The Next Generation of Islamic Innovation

All new Islamic banking innovations have one thing in common: their underlying degree of risk. Some Islamic banking products are more conservative in their approach and others more liberal in their application of *Sharia* principles. The diversity reflects the markets in which the product is to be offered and the attitudes of the target customer segments. Risk is yet another interesting facet of Islamic innovation. The word itself is believed (although debated by various academics) to come from the Arabic *rizq*, roughly translated as "what God and fate provide for your life". Other uses of the word risk also reflect cultural attitudes toward the current innovations in the Islamic banking market, such as the proverbs "Nothing ventured, nothing gained" or "God helps the brave". Therefore, what is clear is that each variation of an innovation is primarily designed to first deconstruct an existing conventional product, and subsequently address one or more elements in a bank's value proposition.

It has been argued that the majority of these innovations are simply conventional banking products that have been reverse engineered to accommodate *Sharia* principles.[19] Although this may be true from a purely technical point of view, the process itself is the real innovation, because it sets in motion a progression of continuous product development. Another advantage of this approach is that by dismantling conventional products and reassembling them as *Sharia*-compliant offerings, Islamic banks gain the advantage of now having something for consumers to compare on a basis of equality. The next generation of Islamic financial product innovation may be more diverse in its approach, but then again the market and customers will be better educated by that time and more receptive to non-traditional products.

The Human Capital Agenda

A substantial portion of an Islamic financial institution's value proposition is based on the talented people they employ. Human resource (HR) managers in Islamic banks (and all Islamic corporations) are faced with a unique set of problems: they must interact with – or in some cases they find themselves part of – Western corporations while remaining engaged with Islamic values and beliefs that are their cultural inheritance. One could argue that HR managers with multicultural workforces have twice the work of their Western counterparts because they must adhere to cultural values that define their character and, at the same time, they must be tolerant of Western ideals regarding the application of labor to corporate activities.

Within this context, HR managers in Islamic organizations have a distinctive role when it comes to managing the human capital of the organization. Forward-thinking HR managers appreciate that the human capital of the firm is what drives the company's value proposition, comprising the intellect, skills, experience, values, beliefs, and knowledge of the people employed. This makes people the organization's primary asset. Innovation, high levels of customer satisfaction and, ultimately, profits are all direct results of how human capital is applied to customer demands. Typically, the tangible outcomes of an effective human capital strategy are evident in the banking products and financial services that are offered to customers and in turn used to generate profits.

Theoretically, everyone in the organization is an asset contributing to the mission of the firm by applying his or her skills to specific activities derived from the business processes used to support a product or service. In an Islamic bank, as in any other bank, people are abundantly available; however, competent workers with the relevant skills are often in short supply. Just as in Western labor markets, shortages occur for two primary reasons: skilled workers are located in the wrong place at the wrong time, and/or insufficient numbers of people exist with the skills required for the specialized tasks or operations required by a bank's business processes. This issue of having the right skills to meet the desired output of an organization is a growing one for HR managers in Islamic banks, who realize that attracting and retaining talent is a problem of huge proportions (see Figure 4.4). Forward-thinking HR managers are now looking at

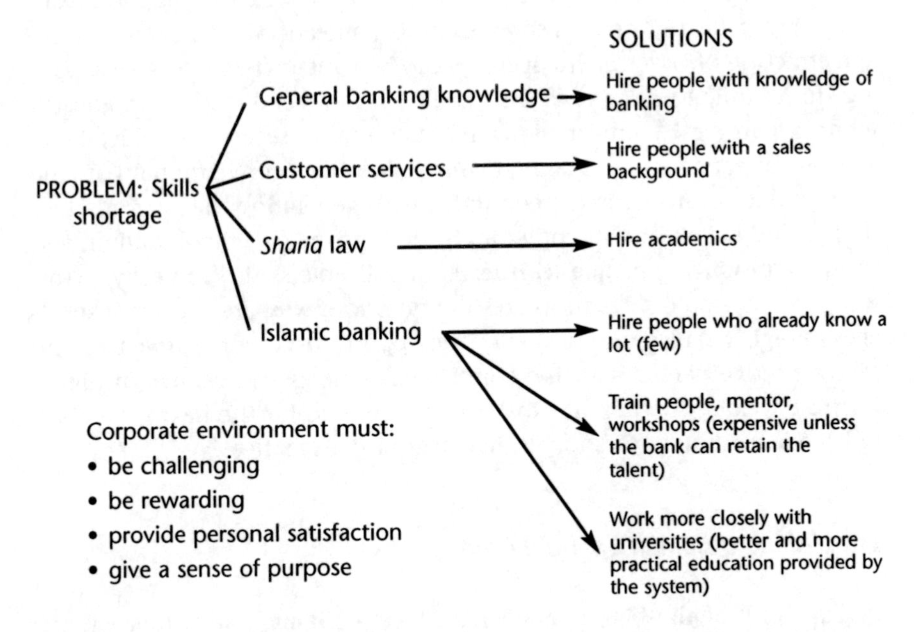

Figure 4.4 Skills attraction and retention – problem and solutions

their organizational shortfalls within the greater context of the industrial output of a nation, region or local community. For many HR executives, finding the right talent is a problem that is no longer confined to local talent pools, because the activities of organizations are no longer confined to operating in simply one region; increasingly, Islamic banks are delivering services that span many nations.

On a national level, senior managers in Islamic banks are realizing that human capital, or more specifically talented people with skills that enable positive economic growth and who act to enrich society in general, comes from three distinct sources: primary and secondary educational sources, continuing education, and mentoring. Therefore, it is not surprising to see Islamic (and conventional) banks beginning to study and evaluate the supply lines of human capital. In the vast majority of nation states, the fundamental problem of human capital is not always recognized by corporations, and to a greater degree is almost completely ignored by banks in general. Financial institutions vying for talent rarely examine the bigger long-term problem of where tomorrow's talent will come from.

Islamic banks and financial services companies operating in nations with predominantly Muslim populations have a unique opportunity, unlike their counterparts in larger nations, to influence the generation of talent in their local/national economies. Because of the size of many nations in which Islamic banks operate, the layers of government bureaucracy are smaller but not less complex or less bureaucratic. The reduced size and structure of government agencies can be a distinct competitive advantage for Islamic banks, due to their ability to interact directly with government departments, universities and, potentially, secondary educational sources. In many cases, Islamic banks – like their conventional banking counterparts – can become preoccupied with generating the next quarter's profits, and believe, rightly or wrongly, that secondary schools and universities are producing people with readily applicable skills. Ironically, if this were true, it would raise an interesting question: why are there still shortages in highly skilled professionals? The opportunity is for Islamic banks to take an active part in assisting educational sources and centers of higher learning to identify the skills that will be required for the next generation of Islamic banking professionals, managers and executives.

Establishing a Human Capital Agenda

Perhaps one of the biggest challenges facing Islamic banks today is the realization that the career path for banking professionals has become significantly different from what it used to be in the 1990s. Professionals in the banking and finance industry in many countries are experiencing career mobility, moving from one set of responsibilities within a firm to another role in the same company or, increasingly, moving to another institution entirely. The mobility of employees presents a new problem for an Islamic bank's value proposition: as people change institutions, they take with them their experience in operating the bank's many processes, banking product knowledge and an understanding of the services required for specific customers. This can be extremely damaging to a bank's long-term value proposition, perhaps not immediately after the departure of any single individual, but through the fulfilment of a process similar to "death by a thousand cuts". Each departure reduces the overall capability of the bank by a fractional amount, gaining momentum over time. Therefore, HR managers must play a pivotal role in managing human capital as any other valued corporate asset. It would be unthinkable for a bank to have an asset like an investment portfolio without an asset manager who monitors, changes, upgrades specific equities, assesses economic trends, and provides direction on the overall performance of the assets. HR managers rarely have that level of responsibility within a financial institution where their day-to-day activities are tied to the productive output of the bank or directly to the profitability of the institution in total. So as to leverage the knowledge assets in a bank, the HR manager must have a discernible human capital plan. Exploiting knowledge is a complex activity with no simple, universally accepted method, as evidenced by the increasing number of books on the subject.[20]

Devising a plan to leverage the human capital of the bank is not as difficult as it may appear at first. HR managers have an important tool at their disposal, namely, the company's value proposition. Plans of this magnitude cannot be created in a vacuum; well-informed HR managers must establish a process that engages many people within the bank to participate actively in the creation and updating of the human capital strategy. For Islamic banks, a human capital plan should comprise four essential parts: a method of value proposition alignment (matching today's skills to activities and tomorrow's skills to upcoming innovations), a means for dynamic resource application, a process for knowledge and skill enhancement, and a mechanism for performance measurement.

The first activity is to take an inventory of the skills that currently reside in the bank and understand the overall knowledge base that this represents. Next, the skills should be matched to the various elements and/or characteristics of the corporate value proposition to customers. At this point, many human capital strategies fall short because they attempt to match skills to the far too numerous business processes in the bank, not to the value proposition. Matching skills to the value proposition is a far easier task and a better use of resources, because, in the vast majority of banks (Islamic and conventional), business processes typically lag behind how the firm is delivering value and, more importantly, how it wants to satisfy customers in the future. One can equate the process of matching skills to processes as driving down the road continually looking in the rear-view mirror instead of looking at the road in front.

The second challenge in human capital strategy development is to institute a means for dynamic resource application. People are mobile, people look for challenges, people desire job satisfaction, and people want to feel engaged in solving problems and serving customers, so why do we try to place them in a singularly defined job? In a number of large US multinational corporations, people are rotating with greater frequency between jobs, departments, and corporate divisions. There are four lessons that Islamic banks can learn from these multinationals:

- job rotation promotes worker satisfaction by exposing them to new challenges
- it trains people to know more about the firm and how to apply its many products to changing customers needs
- rotating jobs fosters innovation by giving employees in-depth knowledge of the many business processes in the company
- moving across the various divisions of the bank creates diversity of knowledge in problem solving.

The third aspect of a human capital strategy centers on a process for knowledge and skill enhancement which can be accomplished cost-effectively by putting in place a program of active mentoring. Mentoring is not a complex process. A mentoring strategy should be equally free of complexity, almost like matchmaking. By using technology, HR managers can create an environment whereby people with skills to share can be linked to people who want to acquire new skills. Invariably, it becomes an environment where people new to a career in banking are looking for new skills which people who are more senior never have the time and aptitude to teach. Mentoring is a power tool because it enables the firm to leverage its knowledge across a broad base of people. Senior managers (like everyone else) need to be motivated to participate in an active mentoring program, simply because their skills are the ones in shortest supply. In

Islamic banks, senior bankers can supply three necessary skills that most banks desperately need: knowledge on general banking operations (not "how to" knowledge, but experiential knowledge that can be applied to current management objectives, such as bottom-line improvement or top-line growth), *Sharia* principles and, more importantly, Islamic banking, such as how to serve the needs of Islamic customers, the management of a multicultural workforce, risk management, and dealing with regulatory agencies and other external entities such as the media.

For the final aspect of a human capital strategy, the HR manager must engage his or her business counterparts and establish a mechanism for performance measurement. In most Islamic banks, this already exists in one form or another, but typically the performance measurement mechanism is out of date and its success as a measure is rarely used as an indicator of banking personnel performance. Strategists must ask themselves: if the business environment is continually changing, our products are always changing, customer demands are changing, regulatory statutes are changing, and technology is always changing our capabilities, why are our performance measurement mechanisms not changing?

Developing an agenda for human capital is not a huge task. It is, however, a continuous one and HR managers must be familiar with all aspects of the bank's value proposition. As the managers of the firm's largest asset for long-term, potential profit generation, HR managers must take a leadership position in making Islamic banks diverse in their knowledge capital, flexible in their approach to business challenges, and adaptive in their application of resources to business activities. Perhaps the single most important challenge for HR managers in Islamic banks today is to actively work toward creating a corporate culture that encourages innovation and change.

SMEs: Funding Working Capital Needs

We have turned our attention to human capital and innovation as integral parts of the value proposition of Islamic banking. Now, let us examine the other side of the value proposition equation, a productive output of Islamic banking that differs from most conventional banks and holds opportunities to make the most of Islamic values and beliefs. Financing the working capital needs of SMEs through the Islamic banking system may provide an avenue to appreciate and understand the intrinsic value of Islamic ideals. During the next decade, the interconnected global economy will present four key challenges for most nations:

job creation, attracting foreign direct investment, access to capital (micro-financing) for SMEs, and financial education. Islamic banks operate in many nations that have emerging economies. Facilitating the financial needs for capital, business transactions, and financial education presents Islamic banks with an opportunity for organic growth that will not be available to conventional banks of the same size in North America and Europe. The flexibility of *Sharia* principles enables Islamic banks to be innovative in their approach to providing services to SMEs. Innovation is the key to market differentiation in the area of micro-finance and SME banking, as noted by HRH Prince Talal Bin Abdulaziz of Saudi Arabia: "tackling poverty does not need money more than it needs the ideas which innovate beneficial means."[21] Therefore, innovation in financial services aimed at providing capital to people and aspiring businesses at the lower thirty percentile of the economic spectrum holds a vast new set of opportunities for Islamic banks.

The Fundamentals of SME Financing

To start a company, individuals need working capital. Working capital can come from many sources. For the scope of this discussion, we will focus on the role Islamic banks will play in SME financing relative to the institutions' value proposition. The Islami Bank Bangladesh defines working capital as:

> assets held for current use within a business, less the amount due to those who await settlement in the short term for value supplied in whatever form. A business enterprise has to maintain an adequate amount of working capital to ensure its liquidity so that the firm does not face any difficulty in meeting its current obligations.[22]

How are the working capital needs of SMEs and the financial offerings different in conventional banks and Islamic banks?

The capital requirements for SMEs exist in two forms: gross working capital and net working capital. As SMEs grow, they need to expand both their physical capital and their gross working capital. In this context, a company's capital requirements might be (but not limited to) to purchase additional inventory, expand operations or buy additional capacity from another source. Managing working capital is often an area that leads an SME into financial difficulties; therefore, another opportunity for banks is to provide education to SMEs on the fundamentals of managing discounted cash flows and other financial controls. Working capital is a prerequisite for an SME to exist as a business entity. SMEs can turn to a number of sources for working capital funding, such as government loans, venture capitalist, and conventional banks, who offer working capital in the form of loans, overdrafts, credit cards, cash credits, discounting and factoring bill receivables, among others. In most cases, interest is charged as the means for the provider of capital to realize any return on investment. In the case of venture capitalists (rare as a source to SMEs in many emerging economies), return on investment is not in the form of interest, but rather as a percentage of equity.

Islamic banks have three basic offerings for SME financing: as an investor, as an agent for commodities and trade, and as the facilitator of commercial transactions. As an investor, an Islamic bank can provide capital in many forms on a profit/loss-sharing basis, utilizing financial instruments based on the structures of *mudarabah*, where the bank incurs the entire loss, or *musharakah*, where the entrepreneur shares the loss with the bank. As an agent, an Islamic bank can purchase the goods on the SME's behalf in exchange for repayment in a lump sum or installments. Once again, using *Sharia*-compliant financial instruments of *murabahah*, a bank purchases the goods and retains possession until the firm can pay the bank in full, or the bank can offer a *muajjal* agreement, where the bank buys the goods, allowing the firm to take possession of the goods in exchange for a deferred payment. The third role an Islamic bank can play is that of a facilitator of commercial transactions by providing accounts receivable financing (although discounting is not permitted). Under *Sharia* principles, when the bank accepts the responsibility for the receivable, it can charge a commission for facilitating the transaction based on the amount of the receivables, not on the period of payment.[23]

There are various examples of Islamic banks providing micro-financing and therefore contributing to the economy of a particular nation state. In Chapter 3, we outlined the approach of selected banks in Pakistan and Bangladesh toward the problem of micro-financing. Aden Microfinance Foundation in Yemen, as yet another example, has a program which started in 2001 with the purpose of fostering a sense of community and solidarity as well as employment and creativity in the society. The program also endeavors to improve the standard of living in Yemen, and provide sustainable micro-finance services to selected segments, especially women, for income-generating activities. Similar to the First Women Bank of Pakistan, Aden Microfinance Foundation is working to transform women with talent and the capacity to work into business entrepreneurs.

The Islamic Development Bank of Brunei Berhad established the Small and Medium Enterprise Service Center to facilitate access to services for local entrepreneurs by providing not only capital in the form of microcredit financing, but also by offering services such as training, seminars, workshops, and a business forum to foster communication between entrepreneurs and funding sources. In addition, the Islamic Development Bank of Brunei Berhad created the Young Entrepreneurial Scheme to provide financing opportunities for young people, or university students who have creative business ideas.[24]

Another interesting case study is Lebanon's Makhzoumi Foundation. The foundation, which won the Lebanon Award for Innovation, works toward the enrichment of Lebanese society through enhancing the potential of human resources in the country, on the premise that all members of society must work toward a common goal which is independent of ideology, religion, or political stance. Encompassing an educational program, healthcare and awareness programs, and micro-credit, the Makhzoumi Foundation works to be a source of inspiration and ideas as well as a practical means to help those in need. It exists as part of a wider movement in Lebanon of NGOs trying to fulfil functions which were traditionally considered the government's domain.[25]

In Malaysia and Saudi Arabia, banks, in particular Islamic banks, are eagerly investing increasing amounts in SMEs in an effort to stimulate the private sector and alleviate rural and inner city poverty. Bank Negara, Malaysia's central bank, reported that in 2003 the financing for SMEs was US$1.6 billion, the amount increasing to US$2.2 billion in 2004. The market share of Islamic banking financing as a percentage of total financing for SMEs in the country (a strong 7.5 percent in 2003) increased to 13.9 percent in 2004. Islamic banking is clearly investing quite a lot of its capital into SMEs in an effort to make people's lives better and provide them with a means to generate income through many types of activities.

In Saudi Arabia, National Commercial Bank, the country's largest bank, launched a *Sharia*-compliant financing scheme in early 2005, targeting small businesses and self-employed professionals. The Al-Ahli Program for Free Tradesmen offers Islamic banking and *Sharia*-approved loans repayable over three years to small businesses and professionals such as doctors, engineers, and accountants who have small businesses. With the small business sector making up 80 percent of the Saudi market, there is clear need for such initiatives in Saudi Arabia to provide additional jobs through a self-supporting system which brings benefits to the country.[26]

In February 2004, the UN Economic and Social Council produced a paper on human rights and extreme poverty written by an independent researcher, who compared the situations in Sudan and Washington, DC. With reference to Sudan, the report outlines that although a lack of statistics makes it harder to map out the true situation of poverty and the need for specific amounts of capital, a few NGOs have been working hard to provide micro-financing through the channels available to Islamic banking in the country. *Zakat* (charitable donation) sometimes seems to be the predominant form, together with *hawala* (remittance). *Zakat* is taken proportional to a person's wealth, and can only be given without prejudice of any kind.[27] As with the problem of remittances, the lack of control and formalized channels is a potential problem with the *zakat* system in Sudan, which, despite alleviating poverty, does not leave sufficient audit trails. As we will see in Chapter 5, regulation and transparency are issues facing Islamic banking today, as they determine compliance to international markets and therefore the viability of the system in the global economy.

Moving from Possibility to Reality

The establishment of a financial infrastructure in which all government, business and private services are delivered is critical to the success of any national economic agenda. To build a platform for economic success, nations must establish a stable, predictable, and dynamic financial infrastructure in which a broad range of banking and financial services can be distributed. This is a prerequisite for providing the services that SMEs need in order to have a direct impact on a national economy. Collaboration between Islamic banks, central banks, conventional banks and financial institutions in other nations will be the key to providing widespread services to SMEs and people at the lower end of the economic spectrum. However, providing financing is only part of the challenge, as financial education for SMEs is also in short supply. The case of Iran is representative of this shortage, as stated by the United Nations Industrial Development Organization: "Many of the Iranian industrial enterprises, notably SMEs, may not posses the technological and financial strength and managerial capabilities needed to compete globally in an effective way."[28] This problem is not limited to Iran, as many emerging economies face the same shortfall in SME knowledge. We could argue that perhaps more valuable than the financing is a fundamental business knowledge about sources, uses and the management of capital, which Islamic institutions are in an ideal position to provide either by themselves or in collaboration with local educational institutions. Financial knowledge enables SMEs to manage their businesses more effectively; access to capital provides them with the means to grow their businesses.

Launched in 2000, organizations such as the Microfinance Gateway supported by the Consultative Group to Assist the Poor, a consortium of 28 public and private development agencies operating together to expand access to financial services for the poor, are working to aggregate the knowledge of micro-financing and provide pathways to funding sources.[29] Another organization is the Egyptian-based Sanabel Microfinance Network for Arab Countries, which was established in 2002 to provide micro-finance institutions with a forum for mutual learning and exchange, capacity-building services, and advocacy for best practice micro-finance.[30]

Thus, the opportunity for Islamic banks to leverage their value propositions in a way that explores and capitalizes on new markets is evident. Providing services to SMEs using financial instruments based on *Sharia* principles enables Islamic banks to engage with entrepreneurs in ways that make them more that a simple source of capital. However, as the State Bank of Pakistan rightly points out, for many banks, providing SME services and the extension of SME services will depend on the extent to which banks can develop internal procedures and controls in risk appraisal and mitigation.[31]

Notes

1 Zaher, Tarek S. and Hassan, M. Kabir, A Comparative Literature Survey of Islamic Finance and Banking, *Financial Markets, Institutions & Instruments*, **10(4)**, November 2001, Oxford: Blackwell, p. 169.

2 Ariff, Mohamed, Islamic Banking, *Asian-Pacific Economic Literature*, **2**(2), September 1988, pp. 46–62.

3 Ariff, Mohamed, Islamic Banking, *Asian-Pacific Economic Literature*, **2**(2), September 1988, pp. 46–62.

4 Queen Rania Al-Abdullah of Jordan, Big challenge to close the hope gap, *Financial Times:* Special Report – Investing in Young People, January 23, 2004, p. 12.

5 Dibooglu, Selahattin, On Commerce, Institutions and Underdevelopment: A Comparative Perspective, *Knowledge, Technology and Policy,* (Winter 2003), **15**(4), p. 12.

6 Chowdhry, Sajjad, Al-Jazari: A Case Study in Innovative Thinking, *Dinar Standard,* October 1, 2004, available at http://www.dinarstandard.com/innovation/aljazari100104.htm.

7 Strassmann, Paul, Software Expense or Asset?, San Francisco: Sun Microsystems and Business 2.0 conference, The Art of the Return on Investment, June 14, 1999, p. 28.

8 DiVanna, Joseph and Rogers, Jay *People – The New Asset on the Balance Sheet* (Basingstoke: Palgrave Macmillan, 2004), especially pp. 70–3.

9 See also DiVanna, Joseph *Redefining Financial Services: The New Renaissance in Value Propositions* (Basingstoke: Palgrave Macmillan, 2002).

10 Brandenburger, A. M., and Nalebuff B. J. *Co-opetition*, New York: Doubleday, 1996.

11 Treacy, Michael, and Wiersema, Fred *The Discipline of Market Leaders*, Reading, MA: Perseus Books, 1997.

12 Royal Banking, Dubai Bank, December 2005, available at http://www.dubaibank.ae/html/consumer/Royal_Banking.htm.

13 Sukuk Al-Salam bonds fully subscribed, press release, Bahrain Monetary Agency, January 2, 2006, available at http://www.bma.gov.bh/cmsrule/index.jsp?action=article&ID=1691.

14 Obaidullah, Mohammed, *Islamic Financial Services*, Jedda: King Abdulaziz University, 2005, p. 255.

15 Zanina, Putri, Bank Islam Card for Tourists, New Straits Times Press: *Travel Times*, December 8, 2005, available at http://www.nst.com.my/Weekly/Travel/article/TravelNews/20051108110158/Article/index_html.

16 Credit Cards, Emirates Islamic Bank, December 2005, available at http://www.emiratesislamicbank.ae/eib/retailbanking/creditcards/default.htm.

17 Children Investment Fund Prospectus, Al-Tawfeek Company, December 2005, available at http://www.altawfeek.com/.

18 Range Murabaha Investments (RaMI), Noriba Bank, October, 2005, available at http://www.noriba.com/rami.htm.

19 Drawing a Roadmap for Islamic Banking, *Banker Middle East*, December 2003, http://www.bankerme.com/bme/2003/dec/islamic_banking.asp.

20 See, for example, Aldisert, L. *Valuing People: How Human Capital Can Be Your Strongest Asset*, Chicago: Dearborn Trade Publishing, 2002; Andreissen, D. and Tissen, R. J. *Weightless Wealth: Find Your Real Value in a Future of Intangible Assets*, Prentice Hall, 2001; Ashkenas, R., Todd Jick, D., Kerr, S. *The Boundaryless Organization: Breaking the Chains of Organizational Structure*, San Francisco: Jossey-Bass, 2002; Becker, G. *Human Capital: a Theoretical and Empirical Analysis, with Special Reference to Education*, Princeton, NJ: Princeton University Press, 1964; DiVanna, J. and Rogers, J. *People – The New Asset on the Balance Sheet*, Basingstoke: Palgrave Macmillan, 2004.

21 Prince Talal Bin Abdulaziz: Tackling Poverty is Restrained by Lack of Ideas More than the Shortage of Money, *AGFund News*, Riyadh: Arab Gulf Programme for United Nations Development Organizations, December 7, 2005, available at http://www.agfund.org/english/news_d.asp?id=8.

22 Concept of Working Capital, Concept and Ideology: Operational Techniques of Islamic Banks, Islami Bank Bangladesh, November 2005, available at http://www.islamibankbd.com/page/ih_4.htm#WCI.

23 Concept of Working Capital, Concept and Ideology: Operational Techniques of Islamic Banks, Islami Bank Bangladesh, November 2005, available at http://www.islamibankbd.com/page/ih_4.htm#WCI.

24 Financial Facilities: SME Service Centre, Islamic Development Bank of Brunei Berhad, November 2005, available at http://www.idbb-bank.com.bn/finance.htm.

25 Micro-Credit Program, Makhzoumi Foundation, December 2005, available at www.makhzoumifoundation.org

26 Financing for SMEs by Islamic Banks on the Rise, GlobalPro Training and Development, October 3, 2005, available at http://www.globalpro.com.my/03Oct05-FinancingforSMEsbyIslamicBanksontheRise.rtf.

27 Lizin, A. M. *Economic, Social and Cultural Rights*, United Nations Economic and Social Council E/CN.4/2004/43, February 29, 2004, available at http://www.unhchr.ch/

Huridocda/Huridoca.nsf/e06a5300f90fa0238025668700518ca4/
67750bb7d0eb1004c1256e7b002c4a10/$FILE/G0411124.pdf.

28 Strategy document: To enhance the contribution of an efficient and competitive small and medium-size enterprise sector to industrial and economic development in the Islamic Republic of Iran, United Nations Industrial Development Organization, February 2003, p. 82.

29 The Microfinance Gateway, Washington DC, January 2006, available at http://www.microfinancegateway.org/.

30 Sanabel, Microfinance Network of Arab Countries, Cairo, January 2006, available at http://www.sanabelnetwork.org/.

31 Banking System Review for the Year ending December 31, 2003, Karachi: State Bank of Pakistan, June 4, 2004, p. 3.

5

THE LOOK AHEAD

Islamic banking today is at a crossroad: banks must provide services to Muslims globally while simultaneously interfacing with the conventional economic activity between nations. Providing services to Muslims in all parts of the world has been the ambition of many Islamic bankers, simply to show that Islamic banking can stand in the industry on equal terms with conventional banking. However, within the spotlight of today's popularity comes the microscope of scrutiny; regulatory bodies around the world will examine Islamic banking with greater interest looking for activities that might be construed as financing terrorism, money laundering, political corruption and more of today's societal enemies. In developing their strategic plans, Islamic banks must consider two distinct sets of factors that have direct implications on their value propositions: issues that are beyond their control, and issues that are also, for the most part, beyond their control but whose direction can be influenced by their actions.

Beyond the control of most institutions are issues such as political instability, the imposition of global regulatory conditions, barriers to trade and commerce, the introduction of a single Islamic currency, economic monetary union, and other national agenda items. A bank's competitive strategy must incorporate an increasing number of factors to formulate a wider range of scenarios with a greater number of optional pathways. Islamic banks in particular must become more agile in the organization's ability to devise strategies. More importantly, Islamic banks must advance their capabilities in rapidly assessing the changes in the competitive landscape and selecting an appropriate competitive response. Beyond the companies' direct control, but within the direct influence of many financial institutions, are issues such as emerging customer trends, the changing financial needs of the community, increasing numbers of SMEs requiring access to capital, attracting foreign direct investment, and other services that either reflect the current or future needs of their customers.

Banks, insurance companies and other financial institutions operating in what the International Finance Corporation of the World Bank calls an emerging or developing market economy are typically smaller than the financial intermediaries in the US and Europe. The smaller size is a double-edged sword: it can be seen as an advantage because smaller organizations are more agile when responding to rapidly changing priorities to best meet customer needs; nevertheless, at the same time, smaller institutions will face greater challenges from the continued internationalization of the marketplace as new regulatory guidelines favor larger global financial institutions.

We can argue that the current economic climate, coupled with the media's new infatuation with all things Islamic, has fostered a sudden rise in notoriety for Islamic banks as they are categorized as an alternative financial/investment system. We can only hope that this hype will not lure Islamic banks into a false sense of competitive security because, as most Western companies have learned, once media attention wanes, Muslim customers, like their non-Muslim counterparts, will still demand performance. This in turn means that in the current market, Islamic banks will need to cope with the sudden surge of new business while keeping a watchful eye on new competitive challenges looming on the horizon. In short, Islamic banks must become adept in assessing new opportunities to reduce their cost structure, offer new products, enter new markets, and meet an ever changing set of regulatory requirements. Moreover, Islamic banks must be prepared to adjust rapidly the characteristics and attributes of their value proposition. In some cases, the modifications to the value proposition will be severe, as competitive pressures will force banks into creating market differentiation that is clearly understood by customers. Strategically, this translates into one thing: Islamic banks need to make significant investments in technology to leverage their organization's abilities into distinct competitive capabilities and lower cost structures.

In this chapter, we examine the macroeconomic factors that will invariably alter, in varying degrees of severity, the value propositions of Islamic banks. These factors are important for banks to consider because they impact Islamic banks universally, just as *riba* is a universal concern of Islamic banks in general. Macroeconomic factors, such as Islamic monetary and economic union, regulatory and compliance issues, and others, bring the people of Islam closer together psychologically.

As Islamic banks provide equity capital or *riba*-free debt capital in the form of trade credit or leasing, the financial institution shares the commercial risk with the users of their capital. This connection between the financial intermediary and the community through a set of shared values is different from the one found in the relationship between conventional banks and the community, as traditional banks often have an adversarial relationship with borrowers (for example when banks turn customers over to collection agencies). The engagement of a bank with its community has a propensity to ease tensions between social classes by connecting the fortunes of capital providers and labor more closely.[1]

It is not the intention of this chapter to speculate on the validity of the underlying arguments on macroeconomic factors that will shape the future of Islamic banking. Frankly, the discussion would add thousands of pages to this book. However, the implications of these factors on the value propositions of Islamic banks are not in the distant future; banks must assess the relative impact on their value proposition and take deliberate steps to remain competitive. Since no one can accurately predict what will happen, Islamic banks must have strategies that reflect the actions they take while managing operational risk, taking into account options that will put them in the best long-term position.

Establishing an Agenda for Action

Few banks or financial institutions operate without a strategy that reflects their value proposition. However, even with a solid value proposition that represents good value for money, many strategies have been known to fail or seem to stray from preset operating targets. Islamic banks have extra layers of complexity added to their strategies in order to address issues such as *Sharia* principles, macroeconomic factors, and microeconomic concerns such as illiteracy and extreme poverty. In many cases, strategy comes with a connotation of a grand plan that has little real value to individuals. The perception of strategy as aloof, detached from the realities of operating a financial institution on a daily basis, has led us to rethink the use of the term and instead opt for creating an "agenda for action". Senior executives in Islamic banks should assess their strategies by keeping the following six ideas at the forefront of their thinking:[2]

- A clear value proposition
- Do no confuse customers with choices for choices' sake
- Brand identity must be distinct and identifiable
- Brokered services must show value added
- Mature markets are often areas of great change
- Market changes create many new opportunities.

We now turn to the macroeconomic trends that impact a bank's agenda for action by identifying the key issues that must be addressed during strategy development.

The Development of *Sharia* Standards

If we consider the diverse nature of the four schools of Islamic thought in the context of conventional banking regulations, the lack of uniformity in *Sharia* law is seen as a weakness in the Islamic banking value proposition. However, we could argue that from the perspective of value overall to global customers, both Muslims and non-Muslims, the diversity of *Sharia* law and the lack of a global standard is its strength because *Sharia* scholars can use the adaptive nature of Islamic principles to best serve regional and local communities. Moreover, in today's world there are a number of disparities in operations and practices among Islamic banking institutions in various parts of the world, which standards could clarify but may also retard interpretations of *Sharia* principles. Countries offering Islamic banking have tended to adopt their own standards in legislation, terminology, regulations, and other aspects of Islamic banking practices. The problem of terminology, for example, is a complex one, as Arabic is a language which has evolved differently in different areas. Different words can mean the same thing depending on where they are used, and the same word can mean different things. For example, in Malaysia, *wadiah* refers to deposits or savings, whereas in Indonesia it also includes loans. Clarity in terminology is critical in conveying the characteristics of a bank's value proposition to customers. Islamic banks must consider clarity in terms in the development of product definitions, brand identities, and overall corporate image in this fundamental area.

The challenge at the current time is for Islamic institutions and nations with growing levels of Islamic economic activity to develop the means to interoperate seamlessly with conventional economies and international regulatory statutes without compromising Islamic principles. The Delors Report, which has been widely used as the defining source for the EU, notes four principal features of economic union:

- A single market within which persons, goods, services and capital can move freely
- Competition policy and other measures aimed at strengthening the market mechanisms
- Common policies aimed at structural change and regional development
- Macroeconomic policy coordination, including binding guidelines for budgetary policy (upper limits on deficits).[3]

If we examine these prerequisites for economic union, there are several issues where a coordinated framework of universally accepted *Sharia* principles would galvanize an Islamic banking network as a precursor to economic and monetary union. The widespread use of a basic framework for *Sharia* law would provide local Islamic scholars with a template in which rules can be benchmarked. The framework would in turn aid the image of Islamic banks as to the fidelity of their adherence to universal *Sharia* principles. The customer's reaction to a set of universal principles, accurately reflecting the interpretations of their local *Sharia* scholar, is a matter yet to be debated. That said, there are several organizations that are addressing these issues from various angles, many of which have direct implications to an Islamic bank's value proposition.

The Accounting and Auditing Organization for Islamic Financial Institutions (AAOIFI) in Bahrain has issued 56 standards on accounting, auditing, governance, ethical, and *Sharia* standards, including a statement on capital adequacy. Producing high-quality standards coupled with an approach that is part of a process of enlisting joint operations between interested parties, the AAOIFI's standards are now used by regulators in Bahrain, Sudan, Jordan, Malaysia, Qatar, Saudi Arabia, Dubai, Lebanon and Syria.[4] In a global context, the standards set by the AAOIFI fulfil a key component of the Islamic banking value proposition, that is, they provide accuracy in financial reporting and transparency in the global marketplace, as illustrated in the case of the Bank of Beirut's value proposition in Figure 5.1.

International recognition and consistent application of international standards will strengthen the credibility of Islamic banking. The use of internalized Islamic standards by the Islamic banking and finance industry will enable the industry to realize the full benefits of accurate and transparent financial reporting. In addition, as the AAOIFI states, it is only through international recognition that Islamic banking will complete its undertaking of bringing credible solutions to Muslims.

To facilitate the development of Islamic financial services, a number of international Islamic organizations have been established in the past few years. One of these is the Islamic Financial Services Board (IFSB) in Malaysia, which aims to harmonize the regulations and supervision of the global Islamic financial industry. Its objectives, as expressed on its website, are:

- To promote transparency in the Islamic financial services industry through the introduction or adaptation of international standards consistent with *Sharia* principles and to recommend their implementation

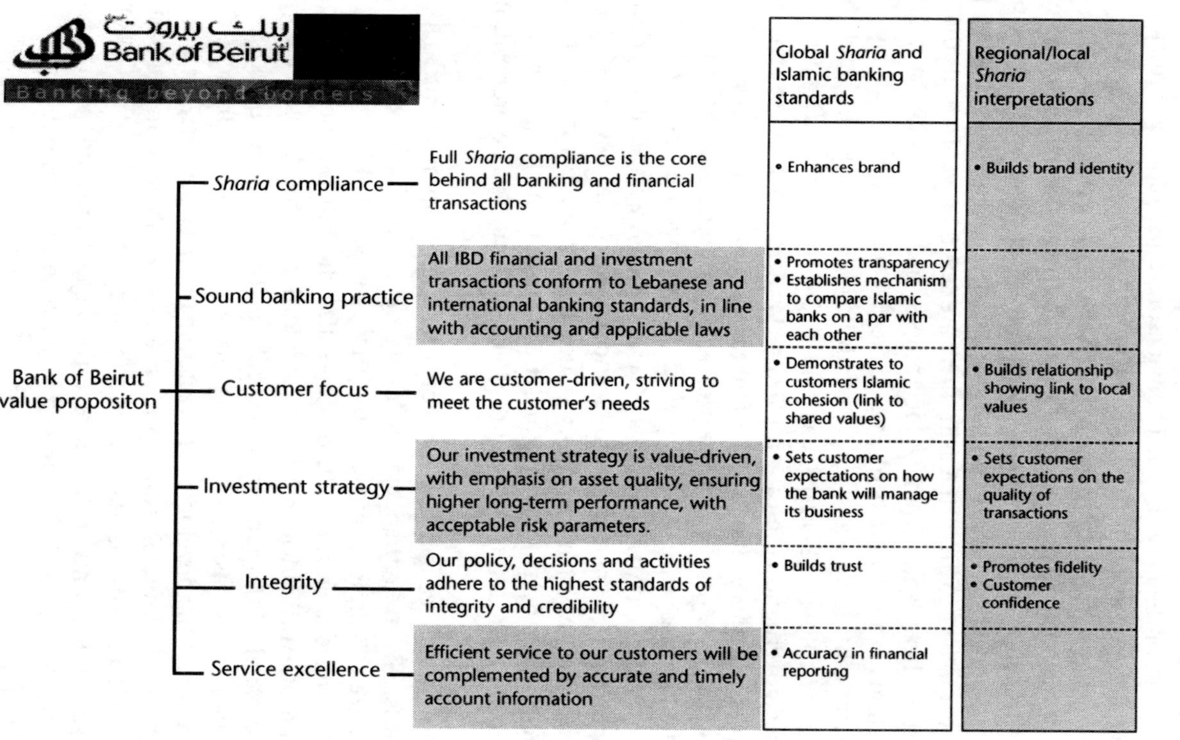

Figure 5.1 Global value proposition for Islamic banking standards

- To provide guidance on the effective supervision and regulation of institutions offering Islamic financial products and to create for the industry the criteria for identifying, measuring, managing, and disclosing risks considering international standards
- To liaise with relevant organizations currently setting standards for the stability and soundness of the international monetary and financial systems and those of member countries
- To coordinate initiatives to create instruments and procedures for efficient operations and risk management
- To encourage cooperation among member countries
- To facilitate training and personnel development of human capital
- To undertake research and produce publications and surveys on the Islamic financial services industry
- To create a database of Islamic banks, financial institutions. and industry experts.[5]

The IFSB was officially opened in 2002 as the culmination of a two-year consultative process initiated by a group of governors and senior officials of central banks and monetary authorities of various countries, coupled with the support of the Islamic Development Bank, the IMF, and the AAOIFI.

Another organization created to provide assistance in the development of *Sharia* standards is the Union of Arab Banks (UAB). Founded in 1974 under the umbrella of the Arab Administrative Development Organization, the UAB was created to work within the framework of unions affiliated to the League of Arab Nations. The goals of the UAB are to consolidate relations and foster mutual aid between its members, coordinating their activities and calling attention to their Arab character to secure the common interests of the region. In addition, the UAB seeks to help the development of the banking and financial sector in Arab countries, and boost the role of Islamic banking and financial institutions in strengthening social and economic development in the Arab region. Basically, the UAB is seeking to be the main source of support for common Arab economic practice and the development of an environment of banking cooperation for the benefit of economic, financial, and banking development in the Arab world.[6]

In Malaysia, the National Syariah Advisory Council for Islamic Banking and Takaful (NSAC) was established in 1997 and set up at Bank Negara, the central bank of Malaysia. The NSAC advises the central bank on *Sharia* issues regarding operations, services and products offered by Islamic banks. Islamic banks and banking institutions that offer Islamic banking products and services are required to establish *Sharia* advisory committees and/or consultants to advise them and ensure that the operations and activities of the bank comply with *Sharia* principles.[7]

In Bahrain, Ezzedine Khoja, secretary-general of the General Council for Islamic Banks and Financial Institutions, explains that Islamic banks in the region are still relying on the first generation of scholars who learned their financial skills when the industry was born in the 1970s. As she stated:

> Now is the time for the industry to take a step further. The scholars on the *Sharia* boards are not enough, and we're now seeing banks start to hire permanent *Sharia* auditors who can become the board scholars of the future. It is crucial that they do this because we expect continued fast growth over the next 20 years. Although the Accounting and Auditing Organisation for Islamic Financial Institutions (AAOIFI) has set out *Sharia* standards for all banks to follow, there will always be a need for scholars who can issue *fatwas* on new solutions.[8]

Because Islamic *Sharia* is not a set of codified laws, but rather a set of interpretations based on sources as varied as the Holy *Qur'an*, the *Sunnah*, judgments by other scholars, and consensus agreement, it follows that religious rulings are affected by personal beliefs and cultural influences. Naturally, any rulings in any given system, be they based on one law or several, are always subjective and ultimately personal. However, Islamic banks seek to make the rulings seem less personal by having boards which all act to achieve a consensus. It is to the consensus regarding regulation and supervision that we now turn.

Regulation and Compliance

The inherent differences in regulatory issues, how Islamic banks are supervised, financial reporting, and issues such as accounting standards are a continual source of confusion to banks within the Muslim financial services community and, even more so, to global fund managers and Western banking supervisory authorities. We can argue that the lack of clarity is also a prime contributor to confusion for Muslim and non-Muslim investors. That said, there are a number of issues centering on the standardization of Islamic financial products that are being addressed by several key organizations, which must be mentioned because of the implications they may bring to the overall value proposition of Islamic banking over the next decade. Two questions are at the nexus of the general debate on the standardization and supervision of Islamic banking and finance:

what are the roles of the various international organizations in establishing standards, and what is the applicability of the emerging standards within various nation states?

Islamic banking was formally born in Egypt in the 1960s, although the first Islamic bank did not come into full operation until the late 1970s. Due to the nature of each nation state, their policies, their government and their openness or reticence to Western values, each country has naturally evolved its own set of rules and regulations. Similar to conventional banking supervision where each country has its own regulatory systems, Islamic banks operating in Muslim and non-Muslim countries must also adhere to the same variability in regulatory practices in addition to their own *Sharia* principles. To understand the variability in regulatory control in the context of how it influences an Islamic bank's value proposition, let us begin by examining a few countries' monetary agencies' regulations and principles to identify their similarities and differences.

The key difference in regulatory environments on the value proposition of Islamic banks is, firstly, the central authority; secondly, the impact on the construction of banking products and financial services; thirdly, the limitations on what constitutes compliance, and fourthly, the implication of international transparency. Perhaps the factor with the greatest long-term potential effect on a bank's value proposition is the primary structure of the regulatory environment, as illustrated in Figure 5.2.

At the current stage of development in Islamic banking as an industry, the seemingly minor differences in structure may not be a major concern. However, a nation with a regulatory structure based on Islamic values has the potential to give Islamic banks more latitude in the construction of products for two reasons: it can encourage experimentation as a stimulus for economic growth, and it can act faster to amend regulations and introduce new laws because it does not see Islamic banking as something that must fit into a conventional regulatory framework. These factors can ultimately affect the time to market for banks to introduce new Islamic financial innovations.

The first country we examine here is Bahrain and the Bahrain Monetary Agency (BMA). Stating that Islamic banking is based on one principle, profit and loss sharing, the financial authority stipulates that in order to comply, all transactions offered by banks in Bahrain must be based on a partnership whereby profits (and loss) are shared according to a predetermined ratio. *Mudarabah* (profit sharing) is the main form of investment.[9] The regulation of Islamic banks in Bahrain according to the BMA is relatively simple: banks cannot charge or pay interest (*riba*). *Mudarabah* is the only way to bring return on investments. In addition, banks must employ

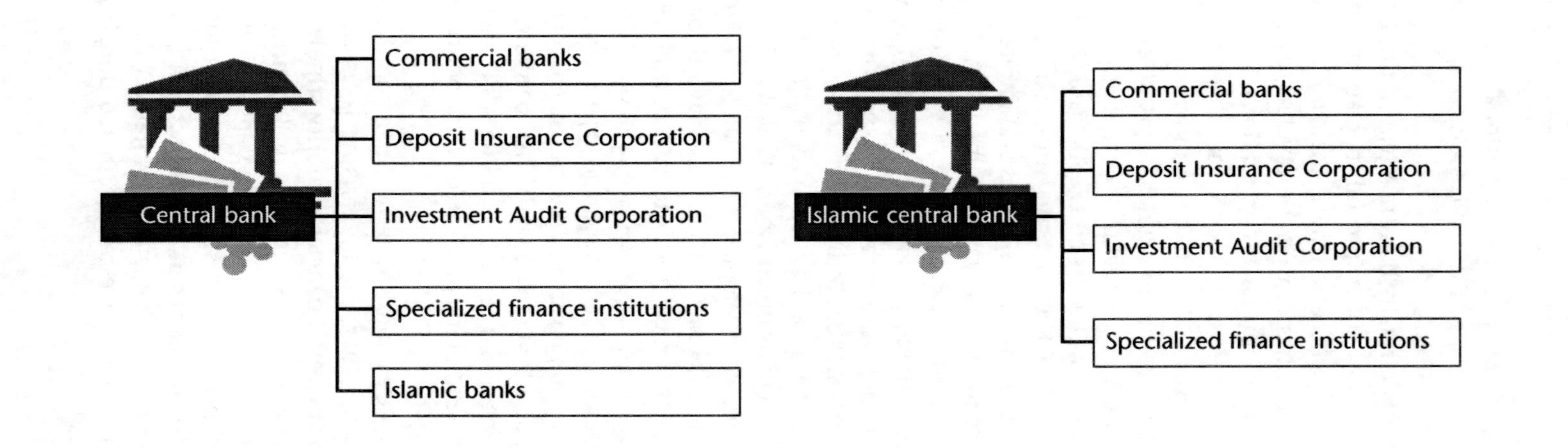

Figure 5.2 Regulatory structures
Source: Adapted from McCann

a *Sharia* supervisory board and all investments in banks and companies must be made according to *Sharia*-approved rules (no investments must be made in companies concerned with tobacco, gambling, pornography, alcohol, and other activities that are *haram*). Investments can be classified as restricted or unrestricted, and as long as they are *Sharia*-compliant, there is no impediment. Retail banks tend to work with unrestricted investment accounts, whereas wholesale banking corporations work with restricted accounts to high net worth individuals. In both cases, what is passed on to customers is based on a predetermined ratio.[10] These BMA regulations are essential in constructing an Islamic bank's value proposition because of their direct influence on the design of products. As in any bank or investment enterprise, in Bahrain banking, investment in companies must be asset-backed; in Islamic banking, only tangible assets are considered where investment is concerned, and the BMA regulates that banks take this into account. As Islamic banks are under great pressure to deliver returns to shareholders, one area of risk is, of course, large withdrawals of investment funds. The BMA is working under Basel II regulations to ensure that risk is minimized and mitigated.[11] Transparency and full disclosure are also on the set of rules produced by the BMA, which emphasizes the importance of annual reports and full information about the banks in the country.[12]

Likewise, the Central Bank of Kuwait passed Law 32/1968. In section 10, the bank states that in its Islamic banking regulations, all transactions must be *Sharia*-compliant, and that means having contracts such as *murabahah, musharakah* and *mudarabah,* which are non-interest making and that are risk and profit sharing. A *Sharia* board must exist in-house to supervise all activities and products offered by the bank. Any foreign bank providing Islamic banking must comply with the same rules.[13]

Indonesia is one country that provides a comprehensive set of guidelines for *Sharia* and international regulatory compliance for Islamic banking. In *The Blueprint of Islamic Banking Development in Indonesia,* developed in 2002, the Central Bank of the Republic of Indonesia outlines the role of Islamic banking in Indonesian society, its character of society building rather than profit making per se and the need for continual supervision by *Sharia* scholars. The Central Bank does not only look to international regulations for compliance issues, but also from the point of view of *Sharia* law to ensure that interpretations are widely accepted. One of the aspects that the Central Bank emphasizes is the ratio of non-performing loans in conventional banking and in Islamic banking, which has a much smaller ratio, showing that the Islamic banking system is better for the population as well as the bank.[14] One aspect which the

Indonesian Central Bank highlights is that *Sharia* banking can be as effective and competitive as its traditional counterpart. Building social stability rather than fostering inequality and exploiting those who are most in need, Islamic banking becomes the fair way to the future.

In Lebanon, law number 575, entitled Establishing Islamic Banks in Lebanon, provides a definition of Islamic banks and sets out rules for the licensing of domestic Islamic banks, the registration of foreign Islamic banks, applicable laws, permissible activities, exemptions from existing laws, powers pertaining to the Central Bank, minimum disclosure frameworks, and *Sharia*-compliance supervision. The Central Council of the Bank of Lebanon prescribes all conditions which must be met to gain authorization. According to the law, investments in Lebanon must account for at least 50 percent of the assets and rights included in the Islamic bank's balance sheet.[15] In addition, the Central Bank of Lebanon has issued four circulars on Islamic banking. They are available on the Central Bank website, under "laws and circulars": Circular 94 8/26/2004, Practice of Islamic Banking in Lebanon; Circular 95 8/26/2004, Conditions of Islamic Banking Establishment in Lebanon; Circular 96 10/20/2004, Interest Operations Carried Out with/or through Islamic Banking; Circular 97 1/19/2005, Operations of "Musharaka" or Sharing Executed by the Islamic Banks. However, these circulars are available in Arabic only.

In Malaysia, through the Islamic Banking Act of 1983, banking regulation is defined, including an article concerning foreign banks wanting to establish Islamic banking in the country. Regulation establishes minimum assets to be owned by the banks, but it does not mention investments outside Malaysia.[16]

In Pakistan, the State Bank of Pakistan has established the Islamic Banking Department. One important document, published in 2004, is *Policies for the Promotion of Islamic Banking,* illustrating the State Bank's policies for the promotion of Islamic banking in Pakistan, which was established in 2003. The strategy involves three pillars: first, the establishment of fully fledged Islamic banks in the private sector; secondly, the setting up of subsidiaries by existing commercial banks for Islamic banking; and thirdly, allowing stand-alone branches for Islamic banking in existing commercial banks.[17] The document emphasizes the role of Islamic banking in the development of the country. Its interpretation that a debtor who is truly distressed and cannot repay the debt must not be penalized, but a debtor who is in a position to repay but does not do so must be penalized shows how fair the Pakistani Islamic banking system seeks to be.

In the Philippines, the Republic Act No. 6848, also known as the Charter of Al-Amanah Islamic Investment Bank of the Philippines, acts as a manual of regulations for banks. It contains rulings and principles for Islamic banking approved by the monetary board through Resolutions 161 and 244 on February 14 and March 6, 1996. The regulations apply to many banking topics, such as the overall purpose of the bank, functions of the *Sharia* advisory council, powers of the bank, return on investment funds, authorized operations, investment risk funds, accounting and training of personnel and others.[18]

In Saudi Arabia, in 2003, the Saudi Arabia Monetary Agency produced a document entitled *A Case Study on Globalization and the Role of Institution Building in the Financial Sector in Saudi Arabia*. This comprehensive set of regulations offers an overview of the main regulations introduced in the past few years to consolidate the banking industry in Saudi Arabia, in particular concerning Islamic banking. Technology, supervision, globalization, corporate governance, and other issues are discussed.[19]

In October 2004, the Bank of Sudan joined other nation states' central banks to discuss the emerging topic of regulation and transparency. The document, entitled *Issues in the Regulation of Islamic Banking: the Case of Sudan* by Sabir Mohamed Hassan, reflects on the applicability of Basel II regulations to Islamic banking that is also *Sharia*-complaint. The matter of capital adequacy is seen via risk management practices as stated in international banking regulations. For Islamic banks with strategies that call for transnational growth, Hassan rightly points out a key issue that must be considered in the formulation of a bank's value proposition: "various supervisors interpret capital adequacy regulations differently, the capital of Islamic banks operating in different countries may not be measured on a level playing field."[20]

In 1985, the United Arab Emirates, via the Dubai International Finance Center, created federal law number 6, entitled Regarding Islamic Banks, Financial Institutions and Investment Companies. This law, as expected, provides the rules and principles for Islamic banking in the country, including applicable laws, incorporation, financial activities that are allowed, and *Sharia* audit (articles 5 and 6).[21] The Dubai Financial Services Authority (DFSA) also creates laws regarding Islamic banking in the country, such as law number 13, 2004.[22] A third document regulating the presence and activities of Islamic banks in the UAE is the *Islamic Financial Business Model* of the DFSA *Rulebook*,[23] which defines the conduct of an Islamic financial business, and outlines the fundamentals of profit-sharing investment accounts.

As we can see, the majority of regulatory issues center on what constitutes solvency in a bank and its operations, the adherence to *Sharia* principles and their subsequent ability to be audited, the disclosure of risks to the customer, and the fundamentals of those activities for which a bank can call itself Islamic. The variations in regulatory constructs in some cases reduce the capabilities of an Islamic bank to lower its cost structure as it attempts to provide similar products across borders. Over time, standardization of Islamic practices will act to reduce the incremental costs of operations brought on by the idiosyncrasies of regulations in each nation state. That said, banks can only hope to operate at lower costs by leveraging technology in a way that enables them to provide a core product that can be altered to comply with local regulatory conditions. Therefore, technology is the key ingredient in taking a bank's value proposition beyond a local market presence.

Islamic Monetary Union

The global economy is like a nuclear energy source: it consumes fuel to generate energy in various forms. Control rods moving in and out of the nuclear core control the reaction and subsequently speed up or slow down the rate of the reactants. In the global economy, the cacophony of business activity, government expenditures, banking transactions, consumer spending, trade and commerce, and all other forms of economic activity that cost money or generate revenue are similar to the multitude of small uranium pellets that make up a nuclear pile. Governments use mechanisms such as interest rates to act as control rods to stimulate economic activity or slow down the rate of inflation (consumer overexuberance). Money is the prime medium of exchange in the global economy, and in turn is the fundamental building block of any financial institution's products and services, and so of direct consequence to a bank's value proposition.

As Rodney Wilson pointed out, one problem facing Muslim economies is the fact that their currency is pegged to the dollar, suffering the same fluctuations as the dollar and the same trade deterioration, as the dollar is the currency of international exports.[24] Since 2002, the idea of implementing the Islamic gold dinar has been in the minds of Middle Eastern governments, banks, and people in the Gulf region. If fluctuations on the price of gold make this idea, although backed up by history, almost impossible to realize today, the idea of an Islamic dinar that can do what the euro did, offering a unified currency for all Islamic countries, is not so disturbing. Dr. Mahatir Mohammed, former prime minister of Malaysia, for example, is one of the most enthusiastic advocates of the single currency.

The six currencies of the Gulf Cooperation Council (GCC) area have experienced a good degree of stability over the past 25 years, as their currency was pegged to the dollar and the economies of Jordan, Lebanon, Syria and Malaysia remained stable. In December 2001, the GCC announced steps to "create a single market and currency no later than 1 January 2010."[25] In March 2005, a meeting of GCC central bankers proposed that the Gulf monetary union must meet five criteria of convergence as a part of their monetary and financial policy integration: budget balance, foreign reserves, public debt, interest rates on deposits, and inflation rates.[26] In Rutledge's view, the theoretical benefits of a monetary union in a unified GCC currency are lower transactions costs, increased levels of trade between member nations, greater regional-wide competition, and a revolutionizing effect on financial markets.[27] Rutledge makes a key point, however, identifying that the benefits of monetary union may not be as great for those nations that already peg their currencies to the US dollar, because of the relatively low levels of regional trade between nations. This is an important distinction when applied on a macroeconomic scale to a transnational Islamic currency, because the key beneficiaries are more likely to be companies with smaller market capitalizations looking to expand into larger regional and global markets. However, Rutledge also identifies that a critical element in a monetary union is the need for a single independent central bank and a monetary authority. Economic union, as was possible in Europe to varying degrees before the introduction of a common currency, makes the Islamic monetary union theoretically possible under the right conditions and given that there is sufficient political will to carry the unification toward a single monetary conclusion. In Wilson's view, a first step toward monetary union may be the introduction of the GCC dinar, which introduces critical questions, such as whether to peg the dinar to the dollar or allow the dinar to float free. The GCC dinar may act in the long term to stabilize oil and gas prices between oil-importing Muslim countries, providing a means for states to peg their currencies against the new Gulf dinar, and creating the means for monetary union within those Muslim states able and willing to participate.[28] Wilson also makes an important observation that a unified Islamic dinar may become the currency of choice for the issue of Islamic *sukuk* securities.[29]

Outside the GCC, in central Africa and Turkey, for example, depreciation of currency and inflation have occurred in the past few decades. Controlling currency fluctuations and inflation is a problem of managed interest, which is of course unacceptable for Islamic banking. So there lies the challenge – to find a solution to the problem of currency fluctuations, thereby bringing one strong currency to the region.[30]

A single currency, whether on a regional scale (such as the GCC dinar) or on a transnational scale (as the Islamic dinar), presents new opportunities for Islamic banks to create new products and services to facilitate cross-border commerce. The introduction of any monetary union (regardless of currency) will enable Islamic banks to rethink their value proposition across a wider range of customer needs, such as SMEs or micro-capitalization companies desiring to partner with complementary businesses in another Muslim nation. However, the problem of adoption of a common currency is a complex one. Scholars and government officials have argued its impossibility. In order for the single currency to work, there must be a single effective currency (one currency operating as legal tender in all member countries) and a single effective exchange rate (one single exchange rate between the united currency and that of each individual country). One single monetary policy to regulate the money supply, exchange and interest rates, and inflation rates is also fundamental. In addition, the issue of Turkey seeking to be a potential future member of the EU poses a theoretical challenge to the union of all Muslim countries.[31]

The argument presented by Jaffery notes several historical examples that provide insight into Islamic Monetary Union (IMU). The Colonial New England Union failed due to lack of centralized control. Likewise, a member-partner that is too strong (as was the case of Germany, France and Belgium in the success of the Zollverein, CFA Franc Zone, and the Belgium–Luxembourg Union respectively) can lead to success but at the risk of one partner taking over what should be a community of interests. The Latin Monetary Union collapsed due to this inefficiency and the diversity of governments and peoples in the region.[32] Taken as a group, when considering why so many monetary unions fell short of expectations and ultimately collapsed, Jaffery's conclusions are as follows:

- The non-existence of a strong partner for administering centralized control
- The existence of a dominating partner controlling monetary policy
- One common currency without a common monetary policy, or a common monetary policy without a common monetary authority
- A bimetallic currency standard, with the official exchange rate between the two currencies varying from that in the open market
- The dumping in one or more member states of debased and low-value subsidiary coins, which are legal tender across the union

- The fixing of the official price of gold in the wake of depreciated paper currencies which were issued without adequate gold reserves.

Numerous examples of failure in one or another sense may follow. Although an interesting debate between academics, governments, and economists, we do not intend to speculate here on whether the unified Islamic dinar would or would not follow the path of failures or success (the euro, for example). The purpose of this section is to examine the possible implications of a unified economic environment and the creation of a single currency from the point of view of the value proposition of Islamic banking. Hassan argues that the downside to economic union is that each country relinquishes its ability to set monetary policy and use it to influence its economy or adjust its exchange rate with regard to the others.[33] In Hassan's view, currency trading can be considered *haram* and if the world shifted back to a gold standard, there is essentially one currency.

Perhaps the most significant move toward monetary union was expressed by Pakistan's Prime Minster Shaukat Aziz, in his 10-point road map to leverage the potential of the Ummah, which resonates clearly with many of the elements of the Islamic banking value proposition, as stated below:[34]

- Promote greater unity, cohesion and cooperation within the Muslim Ummah by addressing and resolving dissensions within Muslim societies
- Ensure good governance through people's participation, transparency, and accountability
- Implement reforms to restructure our economies through deregulation, liberalization and privatization to leverage the full potential of productive capacities
- Improve delivery of social services especially health and education to create an environment of quality education and higher learning, especially in the scientific and technical fields
- Encourage cooperation to share best practices with each other, acknowledging that by helping each other we can help ourselves
- Create complementary relationships between us in the economic and trade fields so as to ensure a win–win situation for all
- Financial and commodity surpluses should be shared to promote development and progress through institutional mechanisms
- Restructure and redefine the role of Islamic Development Bank and enhance its capacity not only for development but also to promote investment and trade
- The Organization of Islamic Conference has to be reorganized, reinvigorated, and repositioned as a forum for the empowerment of Ummah to meet the challenges of the new millennium

- Create the necessary intellectual environment for a renaissance of the Muslim world through achieving intellectual revival, academic excellence, and a spirit of enquiry.

An examination of Prime Minster Aziz's plan reveals many of the inherent values that are characteristic of the value proposition for Islamic banking. For Islamic banks, the 10-point plan identifies opportunities to innovate many new banking products, financial services, and ancillary community services, such as partnerships with higher education to support SMEs. Regardless of the timing, structure, political will, and other factors that will shape or hinder Islamic monetary union, one thing is clear: the implications of either fate create opportunities for Islamic banks to provide a uniquely branded suite of financial services across an increasingly wide economic region. Lack of a monetary union leads banks to provide services that assist customers in fundamental transactions, which are typically encumbered by geopolitical borders, such as remittances and attracting foreign direct investment, to name a few. In this case, banks must concentrate on building their brand image and highlighting transparency, fidelity, and other characteristics that instil in customers a sense of trust and stability. In the case of eventual monetary union, the opportunities for Islamic banks fall into the categories of developing banking services that foster economic cooperation, such as SME financing, between international trading partners and other mechanisms to provide economic gateways for entrepreneurs and investors such as *sukuks*.

Electronic Money

On August 18, 1991 Muslims in Granada issued a *fatwa* on the use of paper money as a medium of exchange because, under their interpretation, paper money represents a debt. In their examination, the nature of paper money as a promise to pay for merchandise (or the representation of a merchandise when used as an instrument of debt) makes the transaction usurious. In Granada's *fatwa,* it is ruled that under no circumstances must paper money be used or accepted as a medium of exchange, regardless of the idea that paper money is backed up by gold or silver. The money cannot be used outside the closed circuit of depositor and receiver. On a private scale, paper money can be transferred, but it may not circulate. As the *fatwa* in Granada stated:

> After examining all the aspects of paper money, in the Light of the *Qur'an* and the *Sunnah,* we declare that the use of paper money in any form of exchange is usury and is therefore *haram.* It is not permitted for the Muslim to accept or to give paper money in a commercial transaction. It is an obligation on the Muslims to abandon usury and to introduce new media of exchange, or money, and the best way is to follow the *sunna* of the Messenger of Allah, *salallau alaihi wa salaam,* by using gold and silver, or any other merchandise commonly accepted as a medium of exchange.

Although the Grenadian ruling is not shared universally by Muslims (in fact, we can argue that this is indeed a minority opinion), it does, however, raise several interesting questions on what monetary trends may have in store for the value propositions of Islamic banks. It could be argued that nowadays paper money has been reduced to a pure symbol, with no reality attached to it except the imposition of the law.

Cases like the Granada *fatwa* provide the media with a negative impression of what is, in fact, a well-developed and extremely complex philosophical structure, encompassing every aspect of life, society, economy, and politics. Rather than being seen as the rule, cases such as the anti-paper money condemnation must be viewed as an exception. If some groups within Islam seem to be moving back to a past ideal of currency, there are groups who are actually focusing on the utilization of current technology as a mechanism to foster new ways of exchange. This is the case of eMoney.

The treatment of money, and the subsequent transactions required to utilize the intrinsic value that money represents, is at the core of the value proposition for Islamic banking. Therefore, understanding the issues of an eCurrency is imperative for bankers. Electronic Money, eMoney, and eCash are the various names for intangible money, that is, money that only exists in virtual space. Instead of trading using cattle, salt, gold, or silver (as in the past) or paper bills and coins (as today), people exchange goods and services through payment via eMoney. Electronic Money is made possible by using public key cryptography and digital signatures (both blind and non-blind signatures); banks and merchants/customers have public keys which come in pairs, so that the transaction can be processed. Instead of signing or typing in a PIN, banks and customers use their keys to encrypt (for security) and sign (for identification) blocks of digital data that represent money orders "signed" by the bank using its private key. These money orders become available to customers, and when a customer wants to spend money, the merchant verifies the "signed" money orders using the bank's widely published public key. Customers sign deposits and withdrawals using their own key and the bank uses the customer's public key to verify the signed withdrawals and deposits.[35]

Although we can imagine that physical currencies will eventually be replaced by an electronic representative (debit and credit transactions have surpassed cash ones since 2000 in the US, and 2004 in the UK), it is difficult to say when customers worldwide will decide that eMoney is a more convenient alternative. With its clear advantages and disadvantages, paper money and coins are at the heart of how we understand the economy, the shopping experience, and the means of payment available. For example, for someone who has lived in a country where currency devaluation was extremely high for decades, becoming acquainted with the use of coins is a challenge; likewise, for us, a move from paper money and coins to eMoney is likely to necessitate a period of transition. The point of this section is not to condone or condemn eMoney, but rather to investigate how Islamic banks and nation states are using – or are considering using – eMoney and how the existence of an eCurrency impacts the Islamic banking value proposition.

One purely Islamic eMoney product is the Dubai-based e-Dinar, an electronic payment and exchange system that facilitates online transactions, which is fully backed by a physical gold bullion repository.[36] In the e-Dinar scheme, each electronic unit corresponds to a fixed weight of 4.25 grams of pure 24k gold (e-Dirham corresponds to 3 grams of sterling silver). The e-Dinar is incorporated in Labuan, Malaysia, as e-Dinar Ltd, and in Dubai Internet City, UAE, as e-Dinar FZ-LLC.[37]

Launched in late 2000, the e-Dinar is backed by gold held in a vault in Dubai International Airport. Since then it has allowed many Muslims an alternative to Western currencies. The e-Dinar program is an electronic form of the historic Muslim gold dinar, which dates as far back as 700 AD and was in circulation until 1924, when the Ottoman Empire collapsed. The fluctuations in the US dollar in 2000–2002 made many governments in the Middle Eastern area concerned, as their currency is pegged to the US dollar, which made the use of the e-Dinar seem like a very feasible alternative for prices in the region, including, naturally, oil. However, the e-Dinar was never implemented on a large scale.[38]

The e-Dinar is the first electronic currency that shows the potential of worldwide eCommerce by enabling secure payments over the internet that are backed by physical gold, therefore eliminating uncertainty and risk. The principle of the e-Dinar is simple, secure, and open to all. In terms of Middle Eastern banking, the e-Dinar, in bringing back gold money, was expected to be well accepted, as transactions are seen as more legitimate if they are processed using real value instruments such as gold.[39] However, the introduction was not as successful as expected, and many still fear the lack of tangibility of the eCurrency. How did other countries implement the eCurrency, and how successful was the implementation?

For example, less than five years ago the Qatar National Bank (QNB) created a strategy to introduce the eCurrency to its customers, attempting to facilitate a transition to a cashless (or at least a less cash) society. QNB's strategy is to link a host of electronic services and initiatives with call centers, the Al-Watani line of home banking services and electronic payment gateway, with its co-branded credit card issued in partnership with MasterCard and the Ritz-Carlton Doha. In an effort to educate customers on the advantages of a cashless society to their lifestyle, the bank is linking several initiatives together to facilitate this transition.

Tunisia is another country which has started looking into virtual currencies. The government started a program called *e-tijara* hoping to increase eCommerce in the country. Its e-Dinar is also available through the post office as a prepaid rechargeable card with specific amounts. The customer has an account with the post office and a password, so that online transactions can be paid using the e-Dinar, which is in effect backed by the post office. No different from using a debit card, the method of payment nevertheless has the advantage of reducing the fear of theft and, of course, the card is not credit, as it is prepaid for the desired amount.[40]

As Mourad Touzani has shown, the adoption of the e-Dinar in Tunisia was mainly by the younger segment of the population who were eager to embrace the new technology, not having the prejudices of older groups, which is also true of Western and Asian attempts at eMoney. They see the e-Dinar as less risky than its paper counterpart. One interesting aspect is that, according to Touzani, most early adopters were well-educated young women.[41]

There are many internet solutions, including popular products such as eGold, PayPal, 2Checkout.com, LinkPoint, and iBill among many others. What these intermediaries do is take the money from someone's existing account (credit card, debit card or similar) and redirect it to someone else's account (again, credit card, current, and so on), charging a fee. The introduction and widespread use of eMoney would eliminate the intermediary and its associated administrative fee.[42]

All banks know that electronic transactions offer the benefit of lowering their operating costs.[43] A reduction in the cost of minting, circulating and tracking through the monetary system has made eMoney a future priority for governments, something to be considered carefully but not yet for implementation. As we discussed in the previous section, the

GCC is looking into the possibility of the establishment of a regional monetary union by 2010, which may result in a single currency like the euro or a variation of the e-Dinar. One way or another, the important point is that eMoney is a viable alternative, provided it can break through the early adopters so as to become a convenient and popular way to purchase commodities. Late adopters and laggards will always exist, but they are not a deterrent in this case. With the increased use of credit cards in Islamic countries, the idea of eMoney will gain in popularity, and then a future with a single eCurrency can become a reality.

Notes

1 Colburn, Jeff, Principles of Islamic Investment, gtNews.com, August 8, 2005, available at http://www.gtnews.com/article/6069.cfm.

2 DiVanna, Joseph *Redefining Financial Services: The New Renaissance in Value Propositions*, Basingstoke: Palgrave Macmillan, 2002, p. 242.

3 *Report on Economic and Monetary Union in the European Community*, Committee for the Study of Economic and Monetary Union, June 17,1989, Paragraph 25, p. 16.

4 Accounting and Auditing Organization for Islamic Financial Institutions, Bahrain, December 2005, available at http://www.aaoifi.com/.

5 Objectives of the IFSB, Islamic Financial Services Board (IFSB), January 2006, available at http://www.ifsb.org/index.php?ch=2&pg=2&ac=4.

6 Union of Arab Banks, Beirut, Lebanon, November, 2005, available at http://www.uabonline.org/default.htm.

7 http://www.bnm.gov.my/index.php?ch=174&pg=467&ac=371.

8 Wanted: More Sharia Banks, *The Banker*, 3 October 2005, http://www.thebanker.com/news/fullstory.php/aid/3480/Wanted:_more_sharia_bankers.html.

9 Islamic Banking & Finance in the Kingdom of Bahrain, Manama: Bahrain Monetary Agency, 2002, available at http://www.bma.gov.bh/cmsrule/media/Agency/Plbns/islamic_fi/ISLAMI_bank_2002.pdf.

10 Islamic Banking & Finance in the Kingdom of Bahrain, Manama: Bahrain Monetary Agency, 2002, p. 62, available at http://www.bma.gov.bh/cmsrule/media/Agency/Plbns/islamic_fi/ISLAMI_bank_2002.pd.

11 Islamic Banking & Finance in the Kingdom of Bahrain, Manama: Bahrain Monetary Agency, 2002, pp. 62–4, available at http://www.bma.gov.bh/cmsrule/media/Agency/Plbns/islamic_fi/ISLAMI_bank_2002.pd.

12 Bahrain Monetary Agency Rule Book; Vol. 2 (Part A) Islamic Banks, Manama: Bahrain Monetary Agency, Version 5, January 2006, available at http://www.bma.gov.bh/cmsrule/index.jsp?action=article&ID=1449.

13 Concerning Currency, The Central Bank of Kuwait and the Organization of Banking Business CBK Law 32/1968, Central Bank of Kuwait, Section 10, Articles 86–100 available at http://www.cbk.gov.kw/www/law.html.

14 The Blueprint of Islamic Banking Development in Indonesia, Jakarta: The Central Bank of the Republic of Indonesia, September, 2002, available at http://www.bi.go.id/NR/rdonlyres/9170EE41-7D9A-4376-B520-A6B3A0945153/1331/syariah_bprintengl.pdf.

15 Law no. 575 Establishing Islamic Banks in Lebanon, Beirut: Banque du Liban, February 11, 2004, available at http://www.bdl.gov.lb/circ/en/Law575e.htm.

16 Laws of Malaysia Act 276 Islamic Banking Act 1983, Kuala Lumpur: Bank Negara Malaysia, available at http://www.bnm.gov.my/index.php?ch=14&pg=17&ac=16&full=1.

17 General Information on Islamic Banking Department, Karachi: State Bank of Pakistan, September 2003, available at http://www.sbp.org.pk/departments/ibd.htm.

18 Manual for Regulation of Banks, Maynila: Bangko Sentral NG Pilipinas, 2004, available at http://www.bsp.gov.ph/downloads/2004/regs/MORB.pdf.

19 *A Case Study on Globalization and the Role of Institution Building in the Financial Sector in Saudi Arabia*, Saudi Arabian Monetary Agency, September 10, 2003, available at http://www.g8.utoronto.ca/g20/20030910_cs_sar.pdf.

20 Hassan, Sabir Mohamed, *Issues in the Regulation of Islamic Banking*, Bank of Sudan, Issue No. 5, October 2004, p. 16, available at http://www.bankofsudan.org/arabic/period/studies/issue_5.pdf.

21 Federal Law No. 6 of 1985 Regarding Islamic Banks, Financial Institutions and Investment Companies, Abu Dhabi: Central Bank of the United Arab Emirates, 1985, available at http://www.cbuae.gov.ae/LawNo6-1985-IslaminBanks.pdf.

22 Law regulating Islamic Financial Business DIFC Law No.13 of 2004, DIFC Dubai Financial Services Authority, available at http://www.dfsa.ae/NR/rdonlyres/F394A86D-1800-4AA2-9154-0005253DC327/0/Law_No13_IslamicFinancialBusiness.pdf.

23 Islamic Financial Business Model (ISF), *DFSA Rulebook*, Dubai: Dubai Financial Services Authority, ISF/VER1/250/09-04, available at http://www.dfsa.ae/NR/rdonlyres/F01602DE-8F17-4895-9B0F-7CDB7EE11B79/0/ISF_VER1_250_0904.pdf.

24 Wilson, Rodney, Exchange rate issues for Muslim economies, Conference paper, presented at the Gulf University for Science and Technology, Kuwait, 12 February 2005, available at http://www.gust.edu.kw/Workshop/docs/ExchangeratesWilsonGUSTKuwait.doc.

25 Gulf Cooperation Council steps closer to single currency, *Gulf Business*, Dubai: Motivate Publishing, November, 2002, p. 101.

26 Farooq, Sohail, Generic Risks Of Gulf Banks, *Middle East Economic Survey* Vol. XLVIII No. 34, August 22, 2005 available at http://www.mees.com/postedarticles/oped/v48n34-5OD01.htm.

27 Rutledge, Emilie, High time for a single GCC currency, *Aljazeera.Net*, October 3, 2005, available at http://english.aljazeera.net/NR/exeres/6472D68F-7D5D-4F37-A7AE-C345CEF5117B.htm.

28 Wilson, Rodney, *Exchange Rate Issues for Muslim Economies*, Gulf University for Science and Technology, Kuwait, February 12, 2005, pp. 14–16, available at http://www.gust.edu.kw/Workshop/docs/ExchangeratesWilsonGUSTKuwait.doc.

29 Wilson, Rodney, *Exchange Rate Issues for Muslim Economies*, Gulf University for Science and Technology, Kuwait, February 12, 2005, p. 17, available at http://www.gust.edu.kw/Workshop/docs/ExchangeratesWilsonGUSTKuwait.doc.

30 Wilson, Rodney, *Exchange Rate Issues for Muslim Economies*, Gulf University for Science and Technology, Kuwait, February 12, 2005, pp. 3–4, available at http://www.gust.edu.kw/Workshop/docs/ExchangeratesWilsonGUSTKuwait.doc.

31 Alpay, Sahin, Does Turkey have a B-plan?, Zaman Online, 5/11/2004, available at http://www.zaman.com/?bl=columnists&alt=&trh=20040511&hn=9064.

32 Jaffery, Sabir B., Unified single currency? A day-dream of the Islamic world, *Pakistan & Gulf Economist*, Issue 37, available at http://www.paksearch.com/page/2001/is37/!UNIFIED.htm.

33 Hassan, M. Kabir, The Gold, Dollar, Euro, Islamic Dinar and Endogeneity of Money: Conceptual Framework and Empirical Evidence, paper presented at the Islamic Economics Research Centre, King Abdulaziz University May 29, 2002, available at http://www.kantakji.org/fiqh/Files/Economics/005.doc.

34 Syed, Nadeem, PM's roadmap for Ummah uplift, *The Nation*, Karachi: Nawaiwaqt Group of News Papers, October 2, 2005, available at http://www.nation.com.pk/daily/oct-2005/2/index4.php.

35 See http://www.ex.ac.uk/~RDavies/arian/emoneyfaq.html.

36 E-Dinar, E-Dinar FZ-LLC, December 2005, available at http://www.edinar.com/html/2_1.html.

37 http://www.gold-pages.net/e-dinar2.htm.

38 http://www.gold-eagle.com/editorials_04/powers060304.html.

39 Zeidan Consultancy has become the first PR firm to accept payment by the new e-Dinar system, January 16, 2002, available at http://www.ameinfo.com/2461.html.

40 http://e-dinar.poste.tn/.

41 Touzani, Mourad, Profiling early adopters of a virtual currency: the e-Dinar case, available at http://www.csu.edu.au/faculty/commerce/jib/issues/issue01/iss01_touzani.pdf.

42 http://www.esvon.com/pg/products/p_payblock/www.e-dinar.com. See also http://www.black-stone.net/articles/Money_system.html.

43 DiVanna, Joseph *The Future of Retail Banking: Delivering Value to Global Customers*, Basingstoke: Palgrave Macmillan, 2003, pp. 79–81.

CONCLUSION

In five short chapters, we have covered a myriad of competitive, cultural, and international issues facing Islamic banks that will either enhance or weaken their value propositions to customers in a global environment. Islamic banks today are amidst a wave of popularity from the media that will be replaced by the harsh light of competition. Numerous factors provide opportunities for Islamic banks to develop their value propositions that will give them a discernable market value. Nevertheless, these same factors can hinder their competitiveness, if not carefully considered when defining their value proposition. Warren Edwardes points out that one of the problems of many of today's Islamic banks' value proposition is the terminology. Replacing Arabic terminology with easily comparable terms used in conventional banking will educate customers so they can compare and contrast Islamic products across financial services providers.[1] In Edwardes' view, Islamic clients would rather choose a bank with a brand name and a solid rating, which is why Western banking institutions are so successful at gaining Muslim market share in many countries where local banks should have the competitive advantage. Davis observes that there is a direct link between brand awareness and the ability to cross-sell to banking customers, which many banks (including Islamic banks) are only now realizing.[2] As the market for Islamic banking becomes more competitive, the ability to cross-sell is important for organic growth. Therefore, Islamic banks must focus on developing the attributes of their value proposition that foster brand awareness.

When we consider the future of Islamic banking, the strong attachment Muslims have to moral and ethical actions must be taken into account. As Levitt and Dubner say of social behavior in Western society:

> morality represents how we would like the world to work, economics represents how it actually does work.[3]

People struggling to understand the fundamental difference between Islamic banking and conventional banking do not have to turn to a discussion on interest, risk sharing or the division profit. Rather, one needs to observe Islamic values in action. For example, in October 2005, the Qatar National Bank (QNB) announced that it would defer all personal and vehicle loan installments due by customers in October as a *Ramadan* gesture.[4] Having studied the spending and savings habits of its customers during the Holy month of *Ramadan*, the bank saw that customers tended to overextend themselves during the period. The waiver was therefore designed to support those customers that needed assistance. Although, in conventional Western banking, this kind of gesture would seem to be cost prohibitive or simply not considered good business, the action by QNB exercised two key elements of the Islamic value proposition: compassion for individuals and a greater sense of purpose in the community. The net result of this action by QNB is simple: QNB practices the same values as its customers, and so people can relate to its value proposition because it reflects how they themselves want to behave; as a result, actions of this nature construct a greater bond with the community and build customer loyalty. When was the last time you heard a Western bank announce to customers, "if you cannot pay the interest on your loan this month, it's OK; it's on us – see you next month"? Clearly, actions speak louder than words.

As Islamic banks strive to meet the growing demand for products and services, they must practice thought leadership, a process in which senior managers bring together ideas, concepts, and models into a method whereby strategy formation becomes a synthesis of many things over a short and long-term planning horizon. Unfortunately, in many Islamic banks that are more financially secure than others, the competitive strategy sometimes consists of "doing it because everyone else is doing it". Oddly, this was the mantra of the dotcom companies in the late 1990s, and became a winning strategy for a handful of companies only, while for thousands of companies the strategy fell short of the mark.

In the context of Islamic banking, strategy must center on the development of the bank's value proposition consistent with their operating objectives followed by a plan of execution. Islamic banks, like their conventional counterparts, must derive their value proposition by first identifying specific market needs and then assessing the organization's ability to fulfil those needs. Inherent in all organizations is a potential for value creation, which is simply the ability of the organization to innovate new ways to provide services, minus the cost of the underlying capabilities to deliver services, as shown in Figure 6.1.

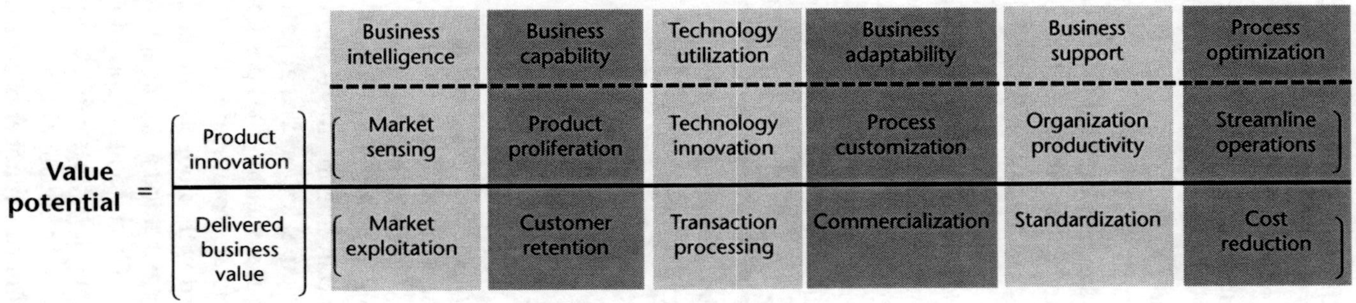

Figure 6.1 Value potential model

The value potential model consists of six core competencies, each comprising two distinct attributes which contribute to its execution in different ways. For example, technology utilization, which is the company's overall ability to apply technology to business challenges and market opportunities, is made up of technology innovations (the ability to come up with new ways to use technology) over transaction processing (the ability to use technology in a context that adds value to the business, either increasing revenues, improving quality, improving service, or reducing cost). To develop an effective value proposition, Islamic banks must construct a strategy that explores each component in the value potential model to assess their inherent ability to capitalize on the skills, talent, and knowledge of their organizations.

The strategy process itself is straightforward: identify a market opportunity; assess the organization's potential for meeting that opportunity; construct a value proposition that resonates with customers; and build an action plan to deliver on each element of value. Although this seems simple, many organizations get it wrong or – worse – never attempt it as a formalized process. Ironically, the time to do this type of planning is when the organization is growing and doing well because the choices and options are more numerous and resources are easier to acquire. Unfortunately, the time most organizations attempt to do this level of planning is once they realize they are in a competitive struggle or there is a downturn in the market.

The Relativity of Value

The creation of a value proposition and the organization's ability to deliver on that value are relative to the receptivity of customers to what is being offered by the firm. Anyone can make their products valuable to some segment of the marketplace by focusing resources on one or a few elements of value, and drastically altering those elements, for example by lowering the price to gain more sales, or changing the quality to appeal only to the wealthy. However, sustaining that position is often the more difficult part; cheap products are commoditized and margins diminish, wealthy people are inundated with products and become more selective. The key to using your value proposition as a strategic tool is to understand how to apply it relative to your customers. You can have a great value proposition with loyal customers, but if there are not enough customers to support your operating costs, eventually the company will no longer be viable. In Chapter 3, we examined a number of financial institutions that

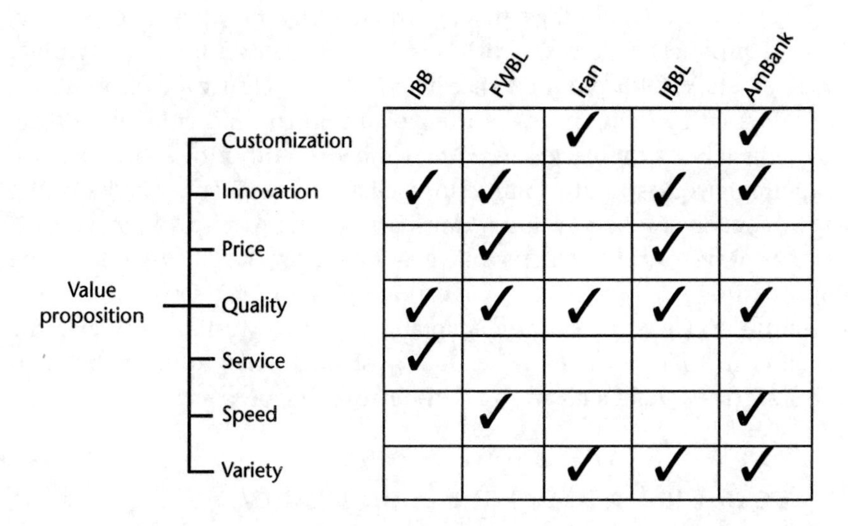

Figure 6.2 Comparison of Islamic value propositions
Source: Adapted from Champy

are using their value propositions in unique ways, based on the market opportunities in their respective countries. In Figure 6.2, we contrast the applied use of their resources against the elements of value described by Champy.[5]

Each organization emphasized a specific aspect of their value proposition to respond to the needs of a target group(s) of customers. One thing that they all have in common is a devotion to quality, which we could argue might be due to their underlying values and belief in Islam. The quality aspect is interesting because, in reviewing each organization, a dedication to doing the right thing for a customer was a recurring theme. However, to grow beyond their current operational limits, these banks will have to explore, experiment, and refine other attributes to attract new customers from existing markets or support expansion into other markets.

The future of Islamic finance seems bright, partly because of the privatization trend under way in some Muslim countries, such as Egypt, Jordan, and Morocco, and in high-growth Islamic countries such as Malaysia and Indonesia, where the demand for Islamic financial products is growing rapidly. Despite the rising popularity, success is dependent on how competitively and quickly Islamic banks can harness their ability to leverage their value propositions and resolve their shortcomings. To compete, Islamic banks need to expand their capabilities to innovate not simply by acquiring technology, but also by building knowledge capital which can apply technology in new ways. Also, the market for Islamic banking products is awash with products cloned from conventional banks, yet starved for products that demonstrate a clear value proposition for the many financing needs of the global ummah. Individually, Islamic banks must work more closely with regulatory authorities to develop a broad framework for uniformity in regulations and laws. Perhaps the biggest challenge is to develop a transnational approach to *Sharia* principles that provides consistency while enabling individual *Sharia* boards the proper latitude to interpret Islamic principles to best serve their local communities. Nevertheless, the adaptability of the Muslim spirit and the flexibility in Islamic values are enabling Islamic banks to meet the challenges of the twenty-first century with renewed vigor.

We Are at the First Step in a Long Journey

If the history of banking tells us anything, it is that socioeconomic trends, political agendas and their long-term effects on monetary policy will continue to create conditions that are strikingly similar to those of banking environments in the past. Although these previous incarnations of economic conditions are not specifically seen in the history of Islamic banking, the characteristics, attributes, and activities are reminiscent of other forms of banking that sprang from the same root. Therefore, we can surmise that the future of the competitive environment of Islamic banking will occur in three distinct phases: faith, price, and value.

Today, Islamic banks can compete for customers based on faith. In a market where few services are available for the devout Muslim, almost any product will fill the void. In many countries, the immediate future for Islamic banking services is bright, with new customers eager to have access to financial options that were non-existent just a decade ago.

On the horizon, as more institutions enter the market and existing Islamic banks add more and more products to their portfolios, competition will shift from product offerings to price and performance. The shift to a price-sensitive commodity will occur at different rates in the various economic regions, more rapidly in markets that have become saturated with competitors and slower in areas where the rate of customer adoption is low, such as in rural communities. In this market, small/regional banks will be at a disadvantage, as their cost structure may impede their overall competitiveness and they will struggle to maintain both customers and profitability. The added cost of compliance to international regulations such as Sarbanes-Oxley, Basel II, and any new *Sharia* standards will increase their overall cost structure, forcing them to seek innovative approaches to leveraging technology against their business processes, or establish cooperative partners to other institutions, or both. Under these market conditions, Islamic banks will learn to collaborate or evaporate.

If we can use past trends as an indicator of future consumer behavior, in the not too distant future there will be a third shift in Islamic banking, as customers become more sophisticated in their demands and seek out banks that can deliver value. In this context, the Islamic value proposition has a strategic advantage in that it can strengthen its relationships with existing customers by focusing on innovative approaches to facilitate their lifestyles and apply innovation to provide services to banking sectors like SMEs and the unbanked. While lecturing at Dubai University College, a student asked me: "If technology gives us the power to leverage what banks do at a lower cost, why can't they offer wealth management services for everyone?" Excellent question, I have often wondered this myself, as we see technology budgets rise and Islamic banks make bigger investments in technology. The answer must lie in the organization's ability to apply technology, not in the technology itself. Islamic banks must develop a technology agenda that comprises three interconnecting parts: infrastructure, intelligence, and delivery.

Eventually We Are All Bound to Talk about Technology

A predictable infrastructure is the key. The use of the word "predictable" to describe infrastructure is intentional because as line managers work closely with technology people in a process of innovation, the last thing they should have to consider is infrastructure. Technological infrastructure for a business should be invisible like electricity; you only notice it when it stops working. Numerous innovative projects are derailed when managers realize that the current infrastructure cannot accommodate the new product or service, and subsequently the project deteriorates into an IT infrastructure project, never being completed. One of the first items on the competitive agenda for CIOs is to get good at infrastructure in order to lay a foundation for future competitive levels.

The second aspect of a technology agenda in an Islamic bank is developing intelligence: customer, market, channel, product, and operational. As we have discussed, technology is changing the way a bank interacts with customers and facilitates their financial needs. Islamic bankers need to understand the new role of technology: to facilitate a dialogue with the customer, interactions that are the result of a two-way relationship between the customers and banking products, such as sending a customer an advice note for confirmation when transactions occur that do not match his or her historical profile. Technologies such as intelligent ATMs must also collect and analyze customer data, trends, behaviors, and interactions to develop profiles which can be used to have a more meaningful dialogue with customers and identify opportunities to cross-sell new products or services. Building organizational intelligence is the next big challenge of CIOs in Islamic banks to supply needed data, information, and knowledge that in turn can be used to alter the bank's value proposition.

The third aspect of the technology agenda is delivering products and services to customers. European banks learned a valuable lesson when they realized that although internet banking was a more cost-effective solution, using personal computers for banking only appeals to customers within certain demographic profiles. Hence, they realized – after alienating many customers – that branches play a vital role in maintaining the relationship with customers. When it comes to delivery, perceptive CIOs will engage people on the front line and the marketing department in a collaboration to develop a comprehensive understanding of how technology is applied to the customer dialogue. Next, this same group of bankers should focus on developing insight into which technologies bring the most value today and in the future by creating a channel management strategy. Without a comprehensive channel management strategy, Islamic banks are simply playing "follow the leader" with the competition. To become product innovators, a bank's senior management team must have an acute sense of the problems that technology must solve and the opportunities offered by technology. For a bank with global ambitions, technology is the only mechanism that will enable the institution to leverage its knowledge capital to innovate on a transnational scale.

Think Global, Act Regional, and Look Local

Conventional global banks see globalization as an opportunity to spread standardized low-cost products to all parts of the world. The expansion strategy of many institutions fails to consider that their value proposition is based on its appeal to local cultures. Islamic banks, on the other hand, may have a differentiating advantage, as the flexibility of *Sharia* principles enables them to adapt to local markets.[6] However, the adaptive nature of Islamic banking can only be realized by combining two key elements: infrastructure and human capital.

Specialized banks have demonstrated that by fine-tuning specific characteristics in their value proposition, they can provide unique service to niche markets at a profit. However, for the vast majority of Islamic banks serving the global ummah, the development of their products has been the result of direct market starvation for services, and not a decisive process of creating value-based services. In the global marketplace, Islamic banks need to compete on value, strategically looking at financial services and their associated banking products as they apply to Muslims and non-Muslims living in a wide range of economic conditions in various geographies and ask one simple question: what do these people have in common and/or what makes their circumstances unique? On a regional level, Islamic banks need to learn how to collaborate, building a bridge to other banks by sharing non-competitive resources such as card processing services and other infrastructure components that are invisible to customers. Regionally, Islamic banks have numerous opportunities to operate in a state of co-opetition by creating complementary services that can be used by customers such as a regional network for migrant remittances and payment services. Locally, Islamic banks must focus on services that best serve their communities and local values.

For the vast majority of Islamic banks, their local markets are located in nation states that are classified as emerging economies, that is, economic regions undergoing great changes where the playing field for business and banking is being redefined on a daily basis. This single fact is essential for Islamic banks to factor into their strategic thinking because as the market for Muslim-based banking continues its rise, conventional banks, academics, and the media will begin to measure the performance of Islamic banking with greater scrutiny. To measure Islamic banking performance, the industry will turn to the tools it knows best, such as market share, interest rates, and other traditional indicators of performance. As Islamic banks develop and refine their value propositions, they will by default become organizations that are much more process focused, concentrating their efforts on understanding how best to serve the customer and less oriented toward selling products.[7]

I have argued elsewhere that the real potential for Islamic banking is as a force to combine the cultural diversity of people within a nation state across a wide range of socioeconomic issues by providing them with an alternative to the conventional banking model.[8] Islamic banking is not simply a profit-making business or an automated mechanism to facilitate commerce as an intermediary in banking transactions; Islamic banking is a part of the social fabric of the community it serves, reflecting in its products and service offerings the values and beliefs of a culture based on fair play and a benevolent redistribution of wealth. The overarching principle to be more than a bank – to take an active part in providing services that have a direct value to the community – is clearly an element of value that is only resident in a minute number of conventional banks. This inherent Islamic principle of fair play, sense of community, and a conscious commitment to participate in the redistribution of wealth causes us to revise the Islamic banking value proposition with a new dimension, as shown in Figure 6.3.

$$\text{Value proposition} = \left\{ \begin{array}{c}\text{perceived value}\\ \text{(standardization/}\\ \text{customization)}\end{array} + \begin{array}{c}\text{value for}\\ \text{money}\\ \text{(price/cost)}\end{array} + \begin{array}{c}\text{convenience}\\ \text{(availability/time)}\end{array} + \begin{array}{c}\text{adherence to}\\ \text{principles (beliefs,}\\ \text{morals and ethics)}\end{array} \right\}$$

Figure 6.3 A twenty-first-century Islamic banking value proposition

Even if the world does not change from an interest-based to an equity/profit-based economy for global commerce and finance, the future of Islamic banking presents Muslims with an opportunity to demonstrate the power of their values. As Islamic banks expand their range of services to address the financial needs of all customers from wealthy to impoverished, from large multinational corporate finance to SME financing, from making markets more transparent to attract foreign direct investment or providing micro-financing, one thing is clear: the next ten years will be an exciting time which will test the endurance of the Islamic banking value proposition. Understanding how to apply their value proposition to address the financial needs of customers under a wide range of economic scenarios presents Islamic bankers with a challenge that can only be addressed through the application of knowledge contained within their human capital. It reminds me of an Arab proverb: "Knowledge without practice (or application) is a tree without fruit."[9]

Notes

1 Edwardes, Warren, Demystifying Islamic Banking and Finance, *Treasury Management International*, September 2001, p. 3.

2 Davis, Stephen *Excellence in Banking – Revisited!*, Basingstoke: Palgrave Macmillan, 2004, p. 60.

3 Levitt, Steven D. and Dubner, Stephen J. *Freakonomics: A Rogue Economist Explores the Hidden Side of Everything*, London: Allen Lane, 2005.

4 QNB Postpones Loans Instalments for October as Ramadan Gesture, Doha: Qatar National Bank, October 17, 2005, available at http://www.qnb.com.qa/news/news_101705.jsp.

5 Champy, James *X-Engineering the Corporation: Reinventing Your Business in the Digital Age*, New York: Warner Business Books, 2002.

6 DiVanna, Joseph *Redefining Financial Services: The New Renaissance in Value Propositions*, Basingstoke: Palgrave Macmillan, 2002, p. 143.

7 See, for example, Hammer's discussion on traditional performance measures in Hammer, Michael *Beyond Reengineering: How the Process-Centred Organization is Changing Our Work and Our Lives*, London: HarperCollins Business, 1996, p. 204.

8 DiVanna, Joseph *The Future of Retail Banking: Delivering Value to Global Customers*, Basingstoke: Palgrave Macmillan, 2004, p. 48.

9 Beg, Muhammad Abdul Jabbar *Wisdom of Islamic Civilization*, Kuala Lumpur: Percetakan Ban Huat Seng, 1986, p. 57.

GLOSSARY OF TERMS

All the terms in the glossary are shown in the Arabic form, and some include regional variations in spelling. The glossary is a compilation from many sources, including: AmBanking Group, State Bank of Pakistan, HSBC Amanah, and academic sources.

AAOIFI (Accounting and Audit Organization for Islamic Financial Institutions) – Established in 1991 in Bahrain, the AAOIFI is an Islamic international, autonomous and non-profit making corporate body that prepares accounting, auditing, governance, ethics and *Sharia* standards for Islamic financial institutions.

Advisory Board (Islamic Corporation for the Development of the Private Sector – ICD) – A group of renowned personalities who are experts in the field of ICD activities and provide expert advice in the conduct of ICD's business.

agency fees – An annual fee, calculated as a lump sum or per bank on a yearly basis, payable by a beneficiary to compensate an agent for the mechanical and operational work performed under a loan contract.

***al-ijarah thumma al bai* (hire purchase)** – There are two contracts involved in this concept. The first contract is called *ijarah* (see below) and the second contract is based on *bai* (see below); these two contracts are undertaken one after the other. For example, in a vehicle financing facility, a customer enters into the first contract and leases the car from the owner (bank) at an agreed rental over a determined period. When the leasing period expires, the second contract comes into effect, which enables the customer to purchase the car at an agreed price. This type of transaction is particularly reminiscent of *contractum trinius*, a complicated legal instrument used by European bankers and merchants during the Middle Ages, which involved combining three individually legal contracts in order to produce a transaction of a hidden interest-bearing loan (something that the Church made illegal). The *al-ijarah thumma al bai*, however, does not carry interest.

Amanah – Name of HSBC's Islamic face. It means trust, trustworthiness, faithfulness, reliability, and honesty. It includes the overall concept of a transaction in which one party keeps another party's funds or property in trust. *Amanah* in this sense has long been used in Islamic commercial law. By extension, the term can be used to describe financial or commercial activities such as deposit taking, custody or goods on consignment.

ar rahnu – Islamic pawnbroking services are popular with both financial institutions and consumers. Providing the customer with the option to obtain cash to fulfil any immediate financial needs, this service secures a loan through a personal surety or pledge. Islamic banks provide *ar rahnu*, meaning that customers will come to the bank for a "loan" and leave something tangible as collateral (jewelry, gold, or the like). From the bank's perspective, the risk of making a loss in this model is very small. The bank will retain the goods as collateral, charging for a safekeeping service. The gold will be valued at the current market price. The amount loaned by the bank will be slightly lower than the market value of the gold, and the safekeeping period is predetermined and agreed by both parties. When the period ends, the "loan" must be repaid to the bank and the collateral reclaimed. This service does not charge interest, and the bank retains the right to sell the goods used as collateral should the "loan" not be paid in time.

arranger – A bank or other financial institution responsible for originating and syndicating a transaction. The arranger may not necessarily be the agent or participant in the transaction.

arranger fees – Fees payable to an arranger in syndication for the origination of financing a deal.

at par *(sukuk)* – A *sukuk* (see below) issued at a price equal to its face (or par) value.

Awqaf Properties Investment Fund – A fund established by Awqaf ministries, Awqaf directorate, and Islamic banks including Islamic Development Bank (IDB) for the development of Awqaf properties around the globe.

bai – Contract for purchase.

bai al-dayn **(debt trading)** – Refers to debt financing, that is, the provision of financial resources which are required for production, commerce, and services through the sale and/or purchase of trade documents and papers. It is a short-term facility with a maturity of not more than a year. Only documents evidencing real debts arising from bona fide commercial transactions can be traded.

bai al-inah **(sell and buy back agreement)** – If a loan is needed, a financier sells an asset to the customer on a deferred payment, and then the asset is immediately repurchased by the borrower for cash at a discount, so that the borrower has extra cash in the transaction. The buying back agreement allows the bank to assume ownership over the asset in order to protect against default without explicitly charging interest in the event of late payments or insolvency.

***bai al-istijrar* (supply contract)** – This form of contract refers to an agreement between the client and the supplier, where the supplier agrees to provide a particular product on an ongoing basis and at an agreed price on the basis of an agreed mode of payment.

***bai al-salam, bay-salaam* or *salam* (future delivery)** – One of the basic conditions for the validity of a sale in *Sharia* law is that the commodity intended to be sold must be in the physical or constructive possession of the seller. This condition has three implications: firstly, the commodity must exist (advance payment is problematic, as something which does not exist cannot be sold); secondly, the seller should have acquired the ownership of that commodity in order to sell it; thirdly, ownership on paper is not sufficient. The commodity should have come into the possession of the seller, either physically or constructively. *Salam* and *istisna* are two special exceptions to *Sharia*. *Bai al-salam* is a sale whereby the seller undertakes to supply some specific goods to the buyer at a future date in exchange for an advanced price fully paid on the spot. It refers to an agreement where payment is made immediately while the goods are delivered at a later date. It is equivalent to an advance payment or retainer.

***bai bithaman ajil* (BBA or deferred payment sale)** – Typical of Malaysia and some other Southeast Asian countries, it is a form of *murabahah* in which payment is made in installments some time after delivery of goods. This form of sale is based on the selling of goods on a deferred payment basis at a price which includes a profit margin agreed by both parties. It is similar to *murabahah* (see below), except that the debtor makes only a single installment on the maturity date of the loan rather than on a regular basis.

dayn – Arabic term for debt.

fatwa – A legal pronouncement of Islam issued by a scholar specialist (*Mufti*) on the topic. It is typically an instrument used when part of the *fiqh* (Islamic jurisprudence) is open to interpretation, or is unclear.

fiqh – Islamic jurisprudence.

gharar – Uncertainty. With *riba* (interest) and *maysir* (gambling), the three forbidden elements of Islamic finance. The prohibition of *gharar* is based on certain aspects of financial transactions such as chance or risk.

halal – Arabic-speaking countries use *halal* to describe anything that is permissible under Islamic law. Non-Arabic-speaking countries generally use *halal* in the narrower context of Muslim dietary laws.

haram* or *haraam – Something that is forbidden by Islam, and indeed anything that is prohibited by the faith.

***hawala* or *hiwalah* (remittance)** – Refers to a transfer of funds/debt from the depositor's/debtor's account to the receiver's/creditor's account where a commission may be charged for such service.

hawaladar – An intermediary in the process of remittance (*hawala*).

***hibah* (gift)** – A token given voluntarily in return for loan given or benefit obtained. This is a token given voluntarily by a debtor to a creditor in return for a loan. *Hibah* usually arises in practice when Islamic banks voluntarily pay their customers interest on savings account balances rather than by agreement.

***hijra* year** – The Islamic lunar calendar system comprising 12 months: *muharram, safar, rabi al-awal, rabi al-thani, jumadal-awal, jumada al-thani, rajab, sha'ban, ramadan, shawal, dhul qa'da,* and *dhul hijjah.* It only contains 354 days, being 11 days shorter than the Gregorian calendar system.

***ijarah* (leasing)** – A medium-term mode of financing referring to an arrangement under which the lessor leases equipment, a building or other facility to a client at an agreed rental against a fixed charge, as agreed by both parties. It involves purchasing and subsequently transferring the right of use of the equipment and machinery to the beneficiary for a specific period of time.

imam – A respected Islamic scholar, especially a founder of a school of theology or law.

IRTI (Islamic Research and Training Institute) – Established in 1981 to undertake research, training, and information activities on Islamic economic, financial, and banking issues.

Islamic banking – A banking system where related transactions and activities are conducted in accordance with the tenets of *Sharia,* which allows asset-backed financing and prohibits interest-based dealings.

Islamic *dinar* – A unit of account of IDB which is equivalent to one special drawing right (SDR) of the International Monetary Fund (IMF).

istisna* or *istina'a – A medium-term mode of financing. Refers to a contract of sale and purchase of assets by specification or order where the price is paid in advance, but the assets are manufactured or produced and delivered at a later date. Also similar to a retainer. For the *istisna* to be valid, the price must be fixed with the consent of the parties and the necessary specification of the commodity (intended to be manufactured) fully settled between them.

***kafalah* (guarantee)** – Refers to the guarantee provided by a person to the owner of a good, who had placed or deposited his good with a third party, whereby any subsequent claim by the owner for his good must be met by the guarantor and the third party.

madrasah – Islamic school for the training of spiritual and legal leaders.

masjid – Muslim mosque.

maysir – Gambling, which is forbidden in Islamic law.

mode of financing – A *Sharia*-compatible instrument which is used by IDB to extend financing depending on the nature of the underlying project or operation and the party to which the financing is extended. For example: *murabahah*, loan, leasing, installment sale, equity participation, and so on.

modes of disbursement – Four major methods used for payment of funds under IDB financing: direct payment; reimbursement; irrevocable commitment; and imprest account.

mohatra – Arab devised forward contracts.

muajjal – A form of agreement for financing based on deferred payment to the financier, who purchases goods on behalf of the "borrower".

***mudarabah, mudaraba, mudharabah* or *modaraba* (profit sharing)** – The term implies an investment partnership contract, whereby the investor (the *rab ul mal*) entrusts money to the other party/entrepreneur (the *mudarib*) in order to undertake a business/investment activity. Profits of the *mudarabah* are shared in a pre-agreed ratio and losses in the proportion of the capital invested. While profits are shared on a pre-agreed ratio, loss of investment is born by the investor (*mudarib*) only.

***mudarabah* agreement** – A set of legal agreements signed between the parties to a syndicated financing, usually includes a financing agreement.

mudarib – A contracting party in a *mudarabah* financing who acts in a fiduciary capacity as the agent or fund manager.

***mudarib* fees** – Fees payable to a *mudarib* in his capacity as the fund manager.

***murabahah* or *murabaha* (purchase and resale)** – A sales contract between a buyer and a seller, whereby the selling price is based on costs plus a profit margin that is clearly stated to the buyer at the time of the agreement. In some cases, the payment for the purchase consists of installment payments specified in the initial sale agreement. Instead of lending out money, the capital provider purchases the commodity for which the loan would have been taken out from an independent third party and resells it to the person interested at a predetermined higher price to the capital user. By paying this higher price over installments, the capital user has effectively obtained credit without paying interest. This type of transaction is similar to "rent-to-own" arrangements for furniture or appliances that are very common in US stores. *Murabahah* is one of the most common types of mortgage-like agreements in Islamic banking.

***musharakah* or *musyarakah* (joint venture or profit and loss sharing)** – Refers to a partnership or joint venture for a specific business with a profit motive, whereby the distribution of profits will be apportioned as per the investment of each partner and according to an agreed ratio. In the event of losses, both parties will share the losses based on their equity participation. It is similar to a conventional partnership structure as well as the ownership of voting stock in a limited company. This equity financing arrangement is widely regarded as the purest form of Islamic financing as it is based on sharing risk and profits. It also appears as *mutanaqisa* (or diminishing/declining participation). There are many subdivisions of the concept, including: *sharikah al milk* (partnership based on joint ownership, which may be voluntary, for example in the purchase of an item, or involuntary, as in the case of inheritance); *sharikah al uqud* (partnership based on a contractual relationship), and others.

***qardhul hassan* or *qardhul hasan* (benevolent loan)** – A loan extended on a goodwill basis whereby the borrower is only required to repay the amount borrowed. At his discretion, the borrower may pay extra (without a formal agreement to that effect) as a token of appreciation. When the debtor does not pay an extra amount to the creditor, this transaction is a true interest-free loan. Some more strict Muslims consider this the only type of loan that does not violate the prohibition on *riba*, since it is the one form of lending that truly does not compensate the creditor for the time value of money.

***rahnu* or *rahn* (collateralized borrowing)** – Refers to an arrangement whereby a valuable asset is placed as a collateral for a debt. The collateral may be disposed of in the event of default.

***riba* (interest)** – Any return of money made on lending money, whether the interest is fixed or not, simple or compounded, and at whatever rate. *Riba* is prohibited under Islamic law.

riba al-fadl – One of the fundamental aspects of Islam is the aim to eliminate exploitation (seen as inherent in the concept of interest), as well as the abuse inherent in all forms of dishonest and unjust exchanges in business transactions. *Riba al-fadl* applies to hand-to-hand purchases and sales of commodities. It covers all spot transactions involving cash payment on one hand and immediate delivery of the commodity on the other. To avoid *riba al-fadl*, people have to exchange commodities equally. For example, gold for gold and silver for silver. Anything that is received as extra by one of the two parties to the transaction is called *riba al-fadl,* which can be defined as excess over what is justified by the counter-value.

riba al-nasi'ah – The term *nasi'ah* means to postpone, defer, or wait, and refers to the time that is allowed for the borrower to repay the loan in return for the addition or the premium. Hence *riba al-nasi'ah* refers to the interest on the loan. The term *riba* was used in this sense in the *Qur'an* in the verse "God has forbidden interest" [2: 275]. This is also the *riba* to which Mohammed the prophet referred when he said: "There is no riba except in nasi'ah." In Islamic banking, the prohibition of *riba al-nasi'ah* essentially implies that the agreement in advance of a positive return on a loan (interest-based profit) as a reward for waiting is not permitted by Islam. However, provided that the return on the principal can be either positive or negative (depending on the final outcome of the business) and not known in advance, it is allowed, provided that it is shared in accordance with the principles of *Sharia.*

salam – See *bai al-salam.*

***sarf* (foreign exchange)** – Refers to the buying and selling of foreign currencies.

Sharia, Shari'ah, Shari'a, Sharia'a – Islamic law, governing the life of Muslims, which is derived from the Holy *Qur'an* and *Sunnah. Sharia*-compliant products and services meet the requirements of Islamic law and are allowed.

***Sharia* advisory council/consultant** – Islamic banks and banking institutions that offer Islamic banking products and services are required to establish *Sharia* advisory committees/consultants to advise them and ensure that the operations and activities of the bank comply with *Sharia* principles. In Malaysia, for example, the National Syariah Advisory Council at Bank Negara Malaysia (BNM) advises BNM on the *Sharia* aspects of the operations of these institutions, as well as on their products and services.

***Sharia* committee** – An independent body comprising specialized jurists in *fiqh almua malat* (Islamic commercial jurisprudence) responsible for directing, reviewing, and supervising the activities of the Islamic financial institution to ensure that the company complies with *Sharia* rules and principles.

***Sharia*-compliant** – In agreement with *Sharia* principles and therefore permissible by Islamic law.

sukuk – Similar to a conventional bond, with the difference of being asset backed to comply with the no-*gharar* rule. A *sukuk* represents proportionate beneficial ownership in the underlying asset. The asset will be leased to the client to yield the return on the *sukuk.*

sutfaya – Arab bills of exchange.

takaful – Islamic insurance. It is characterized by a charitable collective pool of funds based on the idea of mutual assistance. This form of insurance is designed to avoid the elements of conventional insurance (interest and gambling) that are forbidden for Muslims.

tawarruq – Reverse *murabahah*. As used in personal financing, a customer with a genuine need purchases goods on credit from the bank on a deferred payment basis and then immediately resells it for cash to a third party in order to obtain cash. In this way, the customer can obtain cash without taking an interest-based loan.

***ujr* (fee)** – Refers to commissions or fees charged for services.

ummah – The global Muslim community.

***wadiah* (safekeeping)** or ***wadiah yad dhamanah* (savings with guarantee)** – An understanding whereby a depository (a person or institution such as a bank) is designated as a keeper or trustee of an asset in the form of a guaranteed trust. The depository guarantees refund of the whole amount of the deposit, or any part of the outstanding amount, at the point when the depositor demands it. The depositor, at the bank's discretion, may be rewarded with *hibah* (gift) as a form of appreciation for the use of funds by the bank. It is based on trust.

***wakalah* (agency)** – When a person appoints a representative to undertake transactions on their behalf. It is the equivalent of a power of attorney.

waqf – Endowment or charitable trust devoted exclusively to Islamic purposes.

Waqf Fund – A trust fund set up in Islamic year 1399H (1979) for financing special assistance operations, a scholarship program, a technical cooperation program, the Islamic Research and Training Institute, technical assistance, LDMCs Special Account, and the Adahi Sacrificial Meat Utilization Project.

zakat – A charitable donation proportionate to a person's wealth.

BIBLIOGRAPHY

Ahmed, A., Contemporary Experiences of Islamic Banks, *Journal of Objective Studies*, 1992.

Aldisert, L., *Valuing People: How Human Capital Can be Your Strongest Asset*, Chicago: Dearborn Trade Publishing, 2002.

Al-Omar, Fuad, and Abdel-Haq, Mohammed, *Islamic Banking: Theory, Practice and Challenges*, London: Zed Books, 1996.

Alpay, Sahin, Does Turkey have a B-plan?, *Zaman Online*, 5/11/2004, available at http://www.zaman.com/?bl=columnists&alt=&trh=20040511&hn=9064.

Altikriti, Anas Osama (translator), *First Collection of Fatwas*, Dublin: European Council for Fatwa Research, 1998, available at http://www.e-cfr.org/PDF/eng/Fatwa/Fatwa_e01.pdf.

Andreissen, D., and Tissen, R. J., *Weightless Wealth: Find Your Real Value in a Future of Intangible Assets*, New Jersey: Prentice Hall, 2001.

Arberry, Arthur, *The Koran Interpreted*, Oxford: Oxford University Press, 1964.

Ariff, Mohamed, Islamic Banking, *Asian-Pacific Economic Literature*, **2**(2) (September 1988).

As-Safadi, Al-Qadi Muhammad ibn Abd Ar-Rahman, *The Mercy: In the Difference of the Four Sunni Schools of Islamic Law*, London: Dar Al Taqwa, 2004.

Ashkenas, R. et al., *The Boundaryless Organization: Breaking the Chains of Organizational Structure*, San Francisco: Jossey-Bass, 2002.

Ayub, Muhammad, *Interest, Mark up and Time Value of Money*, Islamic Banking Department, State Bank of Pakistan, available at http://www.sbp.org.pk/departments/ibd/Interest_Mark_Up.pdf.

Aziz, Zeti Akhtar, Fostering Leadership Role in Islamic Finance, governor's speech at the launching of Hong Leong Islamic Bank Berhad, Kuala Lumpur, 19 July 2005, available at http://www.bnm.gov.my/index.php?ch=9&pg=15&ac=180.

Baghai, Mehrdad, Coley, Stephen, and White, David, *The Alchemy of Growth*, London: Texere, 2000.

Becker, G., *Human Capital: a Theoretical and Empirical Analysis, with Special Reference to Education*, Princeton: Princeton University Press, 1964.

Beg, Muhammad Abdul Jabbar, *Wisdom of Islamic Civilization*, Kuala Lumpur: Percetakan Ban Huat Seng, 1986.

Boyle, Leo, Is Usury a Sin?, Catholic FAQs: Morality, Kansas City, Missouri: Society of Saint Pius X, August 5, 2005, available at http://www.sspx.org/Catholic_FAQs/catholic_faqs__morality.htm#usuryasin.

Brandenburger, A. M., and Nalebuff, B. J., *Co-opetition*, New York: Doubleday, 1996.

Braudel, Fernand, *The Wheels of Commerce*, Vol. 2, London: William Collins Sons, 1982.

Brörklund, Iréne, and Lundström, Lisabeth, Islamic Banking: an Alternative System, Kristianstad University College, FEC 685, Dissertation, December 2004.

Bunt, Gary R., *Islam in the Digital Age: E-Jihad, Online Fatwas and Cyber Islamic Environments*, London: Pluto Press, July 2003.

Champy, James, *X-Engineering the Corporation: Reinventing Your Business in the Digital Age*, New York: Warner Business Books, 2002.

Chowdhry, Sajjad, Al-Jazari: A Case Study in Innovative Thinking, *Dinar Standard*, October 1, 2004, available at http://www.dinarstandard.com/innovation/aljazari100104.htm.

Colburn, Jeff, Principles of Islamic Investment, *gtNews.com*, August 8, 2005, available at http://www.gtnews.com/article/6069.cfm.

Coulter, Gary, *The Church and Usury: Error, Change or Development?*, Research paper, Emmitsburg, Mount Saint Mary's Seminary, 1999.

Davis, Stephen, *Excellence in Banking – Revisited!* Basingstoke: Palgrave Macmillan, 2004.

Dibooglu, Selahattin, On Commerce, Institutions and Underdevelopment: A Comparative Perspective, *Knowledge, Technology and Policy*, (winter 2003), **15**(4).

DiVanna, Joseph, *Redefining Financial Services: The New Renaissance in Value Propositions*, Basingstoke: Palgrave Macmillan, 2002.

DiVanna, Joseph, *The Future of Retail Banking: Delivering Value to Global Customers*, Basingstoke: Palgrave Macmillan, 2004.

DiVanna, Joseph, and Rogers, Jay, *People – The New Asset on the Balance Sheet*, Basingstoke: Palgrave Macmillan, 2005.

Edwardes, Warren, Demystifying Islamic Banking and Finance, *Treasury Management International*, September 2001.

el Diwany, Tarek, Step by Step You Shall Follow Them, *Education Exchange and Dinar Exchange Meeting*, 30 April 2004, available at http://www.dinar-exchange.co.uk/index.php?page=April_2004.

El-Gamal, Mahmoud A., *Can Islamic Banking Survive? A Micro-evolutionary Perspective*, Madison: University of Wisconson, 1997, available at http://vlib.unitarklj1.edu.my/pdf/islambank4.pdf.

El-Qorchi, Mohammed, *Hawala*, Finance & Development, *International Monetary Fund*, December 2002, **39**(4), available at http://www.imf.org/external/pubs/ft/fandd/2002/12/elqorchi.htm.

Fanning, David, Changing Times for Islamic Mortgages?, *Financial Services Review*, Association of Chartered Certified Accountants, (68), October 2003, available at http://www.accaglobal.com/publications/fsr/68/1016745.

Farooq, Sohail, Generic Risks of Gulf Banks, *Middle East Economic Survey*, XLVIII(34), August 22, 2005 available at http://www.mees.com/postedarticles/oped/v48n34-5OD01.htm.

Hammer, Michael, *Beyond Reengineering: How the Process-Centred Organization is Changing Our Work and Our Lives*, London: HarperCollins Business, 1996.

Hassan, M. Kabir, The Gold, Dollar, Euro, Islamic Dinar and Endogeneity of Money: Conceptual Framework and Empirical Evidence, paper presented at the Islamic Economics Research Centre, King Abdulaziz University, May 29, 2002, available at http://www.kantakji.org/fiqh/Files/Economics/005.doc.

Hassan, Sabir Mohamed, *Issues in the Regulation of Islamic Banking*, Bank of Sudan, (5), October 2004, available at http://www.bankofsudan.org/arabic/period/studies/issue_5.pdf.

Hunt, Edwin and Murry, James, *A History of Business in Medieval Europe 1200–1550*, Cambridge: Cambridge University Press, 1999.

Jackson, Wendy, Islamic Finance: Unlocking the Potential, *MoneyWorks*, January 2004, http://www.getyourmoneyworking.com/2004/JAN/03/Learn_About/Islamic_Finance/D040103967.html.

Jaffery, Sabir B., Unified Single Currency? A Day-dream of the Islamic World, *Pakistan & Gulf Economist*, (37), available at http://www.paksearch.com/page/2001/is37/!UNIFIED.htm.

Kahf, Monzer, Ahmad, Ausaf, and Homud, Sami, *Islamic Banking and Development – an Alternative Banking Concept?*, 1998, available at http://monzer.kahf.com/papers/english/Isbnkand%20dev%20alternative%20banking%20concept.pdf.

Khan, Aftab Ahmad, *Importance of SMEs and Future Development*, Institute of Bankers, Pakistan, November 2005 available at http://www.ibp.org.pk/tdetail.asp?sno=115.

Kandhlawi, Shaykh al-Hadith Muhammad Zakariyya, *The Differences of the Imams*, Santa Barbara: White Thread Press, 2004.

Kaye, Joel, *Economy and Nature in the Fourteenth Century*, Cambridge: Cambridge University Press, 2000.

Kuran, Timur, The Genesis of Islamic Economics: A Chapter in the Politics of Muslim Identity, *Social Research*, **64**(2) (summer 1997), available at http://www.mtholyoke.edu/acad/intrel/kuran.htm.

Levitt, Steven D. and Dubner, Stephen J., *Freakonomics: A Rogue Economist Explores the Hidden Side of Everything*, London: Allen Lane, 2005.

Lizin, A. M., *Economic, Social and Cultural Rights*, United Nations Economic and Social Council, E/CN.4/2004/43, February 29, 2004, available at http://www.unhchr.ch/Huridocda/Huridoca.nsf/e06a5300f90fa0238025668700518ca4/67750bb7d0eb1004c1256e7b002c4a10/$FILE/G0411124.pdf.

Lopez, Robert, *The Commercial Revolution of the Middle Ages, 950–1350*, Cambridge: Cambridge University Press, 1995.

Mangi, Naween, and O'Connell, Patricia (ed.), Pakistan Cripples the Money Movers, *BusinessWeek Online*, January 31, 2002, available at http://www.businessweek.com/bwdaily/dnflash/jan2002/nf20020131_6995.htm.

Ma'sum Billah, Prof. Mohd, *Islamic Credit Card in Practice*, Takaful Islamic Insurance, International Cooperative Mutual Insurance Federation (ICMIF), http://www.icmif.org/2k4takaful/site/documents/Islamic%20Credit%20Card.doc.

Molyneux, Philip and Iqbal, Munawar, *Banking and Financial Systems in the Arab World*, Basingstoke: Palgrave Macmillan, 2005.

Nicholas, Trevor, *Strategic Management of Technology, Competition & Co-operation in World Banking*, London: The Institute of Bankers, 1985.

Obaidullah, Mohammed, *Islamic Financial Services*, Jedda: King Abdulaziz University, 2005.

Passas, Nikos, *Hawala and Other Informal Value Transfer Systems: How to Regulate Them?* United States Department of State: International Information Program, available at http://usinfo.state.gov/eap/Archive_Index/Hawala_and_Other_Informal_Value_Transfer_Systems_How_to_Regulate_Them.html.

Prince Talal Bin Abdulaziz, Tackling Poverty is Restrained by Lack of Ideas More than the Shortage of Money, *AGFund News*, Riyadh: Arab Gulf Programme for United Nations Development Organizations, December 7, 2005, available at http://www.agfund.org/english/news_d.asp?id=81.

Queen Rania Al-Abdullah of Jordan, Big Challenge to Close the Hope Gap, *Financial Times*: Special Report – Investing in Young People, January 23, 2004.

Rice, Gillian, and Mahmoud, Essam, Integrating Quality Management, Creativity and Innovation in Islamic Banks, American Finance House: Lariba 8th Annual International Conference, Pasadena, California, June 16, 2001.

Rutledge, Emilie, High Time for a Single GCC Currency, *Aljazeera.Net*, October 3, 2005, available at http://english.aljazeera.net/NR/exeres/6472D68F-7D5D-4F37-A7AE-C345CEF5117B.htm.

Sachs, Susan, Pursuing an American Dream While Following the Quran, *New York Times Online*, July 5, 2001, available at http://www.islamfortoday.com/americandream.htm.

Siddiqi, Dr Muhammad Nejatullah, Islamic Finance & Beyond: Premises and Promises of Islamic Economics, Conference paper, Harvard University Forum on Islamic Finance, Islamic Finance: Challenges and Global Opportunities, October 1–2, 1999.

Skinner, Chris, Faith in Banking, *Finextra*, August 2, 2005, available at http://www.finextra.com/fullfeature.asp?id=645.

Strassmann, Paul, Software: Expense or Asset?, San Francisco: Sun Microsystems and Business 2.0 conference The Art of the Return on Investment, June 14, 1999.

Syed, Nadeem, PM's Roadmap for Ummah Uplift, *The Nation*, Karachi: Nawaiwaqt Group of News Papers, October 2, 2005, available at http://www.nation.com.pk/daily/oct-2005/2/index4.php.

Toutounchian, Iraj, Islamic Leasing and its Impact on Islamic Banking in Iran, Paper presented at International Conference on Islamic Leasing, Kuwait, February 13–14, 2005.

Touzani, Mourad, Profiling Early Adopters of a Virtual Currency: the e-Dinar Case, available at http://www.csu.edu.au/faculty/commerce/jib/issues/issue01/iss01_touzani.pdf).

Treacy, Michael, and Wiersema, Fred, *The Discipline of Market Leaders*, Reading: Perseus Books, 1997.

Ucko, Hans, *Communicating Identities and Valuing Differences in a Changing Europe*, World Council of Churches, WACC – European Region, Strasbourg, March 10–11, 2005, available at www.wacc.org.uk/wacc/content/download/1644/9364/file/identity.pdf.

Udovitch, Abraham, Bankers without Banks: Commerce, Banking and Society in the Islamic World of the Middle Ages, *The Dawn of Modern Banking*, Los Angeles: Center for Medieval and Renaissance Studies, University of California, 1979.

Warde, Ibrahim, *Islamic Finance in the Global Economy*, Edinburgh: Edinburgh University Press, 2000.

Wilson, Rodney, *Banking and Finance in Arab Middle East*, London: Macmillan – now Palgrave Macmillan, 1983.

Wilson, Rodney, Standardising Islamic Financial Products, International Organisation of Securities Commissions, IOSCO Task Force on Islamic Capital Market Meeting, February 16, 2003, available at http://www.sc.com.my/eng/html/iaffairs/ioscoislamicpdf/Standardising.pdf.

Wilson, Rodney, Exchange Rate Issues for Muslim Economies, Conference paper, presented at the Gulf University for Science and Technology, Kuwait, 12 February 2005, available at http://www.gust.edu.kw/Workshop/docs/ExchangeratesWilsonGUSTKuwait.doc.

Zaher, Tarek S., and Hassan, M. Kabir, A Comparative Literature Survey of Islamic Finance and Banking, *Financial Markets, Institutions & Instruments*, 10(4), November 2001, Oxford: Blackwell.

Zanina, Putri, Bank Islam Card for Tourists, The New Straits Times Press: *Travel Times*, December 8, 2005, available at http://www.nst.com.my/Weekly/Travel/article/TravelNews/20051108110158/Article/index_html.

Iqba, Zubair, and Mirakhor, Abbas Islamic Banking, International Monetary Fund, Occasional Paper 49, Washington DC: International Monetary Fund, 1987.

Articles and Press Releases

Can a Credit Card Ever be Halal?, *Banker Middle East*, **33**, March, 2003, available at http://www.bankerme.com/bme/2003/mar/islamic_banking.asp.

Drawing a Roadmap for Islamic Banking, *Banker Middle East*, December, 2003, http://www.bankerme.com/bme/2003/dec/islamic_banking.asp.

Gulf Cooperation Council Steps Closer to Single Currency, *Gulf Business*, Dubai: Motivate Publishing, November, 2002.

High Street Bank Offers Islamic Mortgage, BBC News, 1 July, 2003, available at http://news.bbc.co.uk/1/hi/business/3035292.stm.

HSBC Offers Islamic Mortgage, Current Accounts, *IslamOnline*, July 8, 2003, available at http://www.islamonline.net/English/News/2003-07/08/article05.shtml.

Islamic Banks: A Novelty No Longer, International Finance, *BusinessWeek Online*, August 8, 2005, available at http://www.businessweek.com/magazine/content/05_32/b3946141_mz035.htm.

QNB Postpones Loans Instalments for October as *Ramadan* Gesture, Doha: Qatar National Bank, October 17, 2005, available at http://www.qnb.com.qa/news/news_101705.jsp.

Strategy document: To enhance the contribution of an efficient and competitive small and medium size enterprise sector to industrial and economic development in the Islamic Republic of Iran, United Nations Industrial Development Organization (UNIDO), February 2003.

The Best of Both Worlds, *Banker Middle East*, (40), October, 2003, available at http://www.bankerme.com/bme/2003/oct/islamic_banking.asp.

Wanted: More Sharia Banks, *The Banker*, October 10, 2005, http://www.thebanker.com/news/fullstory.php/aid/3480/Wanted:_more_sharia_bankers.htm.

What is Islamic Banking? State Bank of Pakistan, December, 2005, available at http://www.sbp.org.pk/ibd/faqs.asp.

Zeidan Consultancy has become the first PR firm to accept payment by the new e-dinar system, January 16, 2002, available at http://www.ameinfo.com/2461.html.

INDEX

Words and Concepts

Names of Banks, Organizations, and Associations Cited in the Text